Padre Pio
A Man of Hope

RENZO ALLEGRI

CHARIS

SERVANT PUBLICATIONS
ANN ARBOR, MICHIGAN

Charis Books is an imprint of Servant Publications especially designed to serve Roman Catholics.

Servant Publications
P.O. Box 8617
Ann Arbor, MI 48107

Cover design: Paul Higdon
Cover photograph: Courtesy of The National Center for Padre Pio, Inc., Barto, PA

00 01 02 03 10 9 8 7 6 5 4 3 2 1

Printed in the United States of America
ISBN 1-56955-138-3

LIBRARY OF CONGRESS CATALOGING-IN-PUBLICATION DATA

Allegri, Renzo.
    [A tu per tu con Padre Pio. English]
    Padre Pio : a man of hope / Renzo Allegri.
       p.   cm.
    ISBN 1-56955-138-3 (alk. paper)
    1. Pio, padre, 1887-1968. 2. Capuchins—Italy—Biography. I. Title.
  BX4705.P49 A84132000
  271'.3602—dc21
  [B]   99-059678

Contents

Introduction

I first met Padre Pio in 1967, the year before his death. He was old and very ill. As a journalist, I went to his home in San Giovanni Rotondo on assignment, and I had the opportunity to speak with him on two occasions. I was extremely impressed, not so much by the stories of miracles that people told about him but by the extraordinary moral strength that emanated from his whole being.

It was hard for me to watch him walking in the sacristy or the corridors of the monastery, bent over, dragging his swollen feet, and holding on to the walls so that he would not fall down. His suffering was tremendous, but he bore it without complaining as he continued to give himself to those who needed him. When he would lift his head and look around, his big eyes looked like they were burning, not from pain but from a goodness that he could not contain.

In 1969, the year after Padre Pio's death, I wrote a long article for a newspaper on his life and his work. Rumors began to circulate that the economic empire that he had created in San Giovanni Rotondo was on the verge of collapsing. Many people prophesied that within a short time no one would remember the Capuchin friar with the stigmata.

A group of "Friends of Padre Pio," represented by Giuseppe Pagnossin from Padua, one of Padre Pio's spiritual sons, handed me a file that was chock-full of some very interesting, unpublished documents. There were thousands and thousands of them, arranged and bound together in volumes. Studying these documents, I discovered something about Padre Pio that few people knew: he had endured incredibly enormous suffering throughout his life, consisting of more persecution, humiliation, accusations, slanders, trials, and condemnations than one can imagine.

From that time on, I have continued to take a deep interest in Padre Pio, gathering together other documents that I have now arranged in this volume. This book does not claim to be a critical biography. Rather, I have sketched a chronicle of Padre Pio's life, based mainly on the direct testimony of people who knew him thoroughly.

In general, when people write about Padre Pio, they tend to dwell on the penitential aspect of his life, thereby giving a somewhat dark and medieval tinge to his personality. But this is not really the case. Padre Pio was and is a man of hope. Throughout his life, in the midst of the most difficult trials, he always looked to the future with a spirit of optimism, faith, and love. He was a man who believed in progress. From the outset his clinic for the sick was on the vanguard of medicine. In his private life he was never a slave to rules or regulations that made no sense. He undertook colossal endeavors with a faith that bore miracles.

Padre Pio loved people. He wept and suffered with those who were afflicted, yet he laughed with those who were happy. Although he was a tender and affectionate man, he was often brusque with people, even with sick little children. One of his fellow friars, Fr. Pellegrino, once complained to him about this. In reply Padre Pio said: "I act like that so that I don't let myself be overcome with emotion. Seeing people suffer is enough to bring me to tears, and then I would no longer be able to continue my ministry."

From a spiritual perspective, there is no dispute regarding Padre Pio's stature. Cardinal Siri once made the following remarks in an interview with me: "With the stigmata which he bore throughout his life and with the other physical and moral sufferings he endured, Padre Pio calls our attention to the body of Christ as a means of salvation. Jesus died on the cross for us, and the entire theology of redemption rests on this truth, one of the principal tenets of our faith. This truth is so important that, throughout history whenever men have forgotten it or have sought to find it, God has always intervened with events, deeds, and miracles. In our time the temptation to forget about the reality of the body of Christ is enormous. And God has sent us this man with the task of calling us back to the truth."

The life of this man was characterized by some of the phenomena typically associated with the paranormal world: bilocation, levitation, mind reading, premonitions, and clairvoyance. When his friend Angelo Battisti once questioned him about these things, Padre Pio told him: "Angelo, they are a mystery for me too."

Since his death, Padre Pio's renown has continued to grow. Some two hundred monuments are dedicated to him. There are thousands of prayer groups around the world that draw their inspiration from him. He has faithful admirers and followers, even among Protestants, Buddhists, and Hindus. He is a man who will always be loved by people.

ONE

Pietrelcina,
May 25, 1887

When people talk about Padre Pio, foremost in their thoughts is San Giovanni Rotondo, the small town in the Gargano Mountains where the Capuchin friar with the stigmata lived for some fifty years. However, he was really born in Pietrelcina, a village in the province of Benevento.

His real name was Francesco Forgione but, following the custom of the Capuchin friars, he became Padre Pio of Pietrelcina upon entering the order. Pietrelcina is a little country town situated 1,150 feet above sea level. Its origins are quite old, and historians have traced its history back to the time of the Romans. However, the current layout of the town follows a model that was developed in the Middle Ages: it is built around a baronial castle which is standing to this day, rising another three hundred feet from an enormous cliff overlooking the Pantaniello River.

The old part of town is built around the castle, and the houses there are attached to the cliff. Their entrances open out to narrow, winding streets paved with cobblestones. The houses are constructed of limestone. Their walls are unplastered, and cracks can be observed in the stone.

Francesco Forgione was born in one of the oldest of these houses, number 27 on the narrow lane called Storto Valle, on Wednesday, May 25, 1887, at five o'clock in the afternoon.

The house in which the future Padre Pio first saw the light of day consisted of a single room that was about thirty square feet in size. It had a dirt floor and a ceiling constructed of wooden planks. Light flowed in from one small window about sixteen inches square.

Francesco's father, Grazio, was twenty-six years old; his mother, Maria Giuseppa Di Nunzio, was twenty-eight. They were married on June 8, 1881, and already had three children when Francesco was born: Michele, born in 1882, Francesco, born in 1884, who lived for only nineteen days, and Amalia, who was born in 1885 and who died a month after Padre Pio was born. Three children were born afterward: Felicita in 1889, Pellegrina in 1892, and Grazia, who later became Sister Pia, a Brigittine sister, in 1894.

Grazio Forgione, a native of Pietrelcina, was a peasant man who owned a little land but was forced to emigrate twice to America in order to support his family. Those who knew him described him as a man of medium height, with bright eyes, a lean physique, happy, strong, clever, active, straightforward, quick to reply, rough-mannered, hurried, and cordial. He was illiterate.

Maria Giuseppa Di Nunzio, who was also a native of Pietrelcina, was a member of the working class but had the bearing of a woman from a "good family." People in Pietrelcina remember her as having a slender figure, an elegant stride, and in spite of her great poverty, as always being well-dressed with a fresh, clean, white scarf on her head, as was the custom of peasant women of the time.

Mamma Peppa, as Maria Giuseppa was called, later recalled what the midwife said to her when she lifted up her newborn baby son: "Peppa, the child was born wrapped in a white veil, and that's a good sign: he will be great and fortunate."

Francesco was baptized at St. Anne's Church at six o'clock on May 26, 1887, the day after his birth. Fr. Nicolantonio Orlando, the priest who was in charge of parish finances, officiated at the ceremony. The newborn child was called Francesco, at his mother's explicit request, since she had great devotion to St. Francis of Assisi.

We know from what his mother and father remember that Francesco was a healthy and lively baby. However, he had a shrill cry and often screamed during the night, disturbing poor Grazio's sleep after he had worked hard all day long.

One night his father lost his patience. He took the child and shook him so hard that he fell to the ground. "Was a devil born in my house instead of a Christian?" he cried. The angry wife scolded her husband and picked up the child. "You killed my son," she said. But nothing happened to the baby, and from that night on he did not disturb Grazio's sleep again.

"I never goofed off in my life," Padre Pio once said when recalling his childhood. "I was an unsalted piece of macaroni," he observed, referring to his submissiveness and reserve.

"As he was growing," Mamma Peppa reminisced, "he never did anything bad. He never did anything on a whim. He always obeyed me and his father. Every morning and night he would go off to the church to visit Jesus and Mary. During the day, he never went out to play with his playmates. Many times I said to him, 'Franci, go out and play a while.' He would refuse, saying, 'I don't want to because they swear.'"

According to several of his contemporaries, Francesco was a quiet and reserved boy. Although he seemed aloof from the other children and their games, he was not unsociable. He was reserved without being sulky. He often prayed.

Biographies of Padre Pio are full of edifying stories from his childhood. Since these stories were gathered so many years afterward, it is difficult to ascertain how true they are. Some of them, however, have been confirmed by Padre Pio himself. Usually very reluctant to speak about himself, he often refused to share what was going on in him spiritually. But his superiors, knowing that one day it would be useful to know the truth about some of his experiences, asked him to answer out of obedience some questions about his life. Faced with such an appeal to his vow of obedience, Padre Pio could not refuse. Consequently, many of these episodes have been clarified or confirmed. Padre Pio confided some recollections to his spiritual directors, who, in turn, wrote them down; others he jotted down in his own handwriting.

From the *Diary* of Fr. Agostino of San Marco in Lamis, who was one of Padre Pio's first spiritual directors, we have learned that the future servant of God had his first charismatic experiences in 1892 when he was only five years old. Ecstasies and apparitions were so frequent in his life that the young boy thought they were completely normal.

The *Diary* of Fr. Agostino of San Marco in Lamis was edited by Fr. Gerardo Di Flumeri and published in 1971. There he wrote: "The ecstasies and the apparitions began when he was five years old, when Francesco had some thoughts and a desire to consecrate himself forever to the Lord, and they continued throughout his life. When asked why he had concealed them for so long, he answered very candidly that he never revealed them because he thought they were ordinary things that happened to everyone. In fact, one day he asked me rather naively: 'You don't see the Virgin Mary?' When I told him I didn't, he added: 'You're saying that out of humility.'"

The visions were not only of angels and saints, but also of demons. Fr. Benedict of San Marco in Lamis recorded the following episode in his writings: "The devil began to torment him when he was about four years old. The devil appeared under horrible and often threatening and frightening guises. He was such a pest in the middle of the night that he didn't let Francesco sleep." Padre Pio himself recounted once: "My mother would turn off the lights, and so many monsters would close in on me that I would cry. She would turn the lights on and I would quiet down because the monsters vanished. Once she turned them off again, I would begin to cry again because of the monsters."

Don Nicola Caruso, one of the priests in Pietrelcina, wrote: "More than once Francesco told me that when he would return home from school, he would find a man on the doorstep who was dressed like a priest who didn't want him to enter. Then Francesco would pray; a barefooted boy would appear and make the sign of the cross and the priest would disappear. Francesco would peacefully enter the house."

In order to overcome his fear of the monsters and the menacing apparitions, Francesco would subject himself to some rather unusual penitential practices for someone his age. One of his friends who was his age and who lived nearby has shared that when Francesco was nine years old, he would seldom go out and play. Instead he would read devotional books, attend Mass, and with the help of the sacristan, lock himself up in the church, exhorting his friend not to tell anyone. Then he would arrange a time with the sacristan to let him out of the church.

Padre Pio's mother once told how she surprised Francesco one day when he was about nine years old as he was scourging himself next to his bed with an iron chain. She begged him to stop, but he just continued. She asked him, "Son, why are you hitting yourself like that?" Francesco answered, "I have to beat myself like the Roman soldiers beat Jesus and made his shoulders bleed."

Don Giuseppe Orlando, a priest in Pietrelcina, would reprimand Francesco because "instead of sleeping in the bed that his mother so lovingly prepared for him, he would lie down on the ground, using a rock as a pillow."

One day in 1896, Grazio Forgione decided to take Francesco on a pilgrimage to the shrine of St. Pellegrino, near Altavilla Irpina, which was about sixteen miles from Pietrelcina. They left early in the morning, riding on a donkey. The shrine was very crowded because of a fair that was being held in the town. They tied their donkey up in front of a small restaurant and went to the shrine. When they had finished praying, Grazio Forgione told his son that it was time to go, but the boy wanted to stay a while longer.

Next to Francesco a poor woman was holding a deformed child in her arms, praying, weeping, and asking for God's mercy. Francesco was deeply moved as he watched her, and prayed and wept with her. At one point the woman, tired and exasperated of praying perhaps, flung the child on the altar, crying, "Why don't you want to heal him for me?" There was a moment of silence in the church, and then a cry of joy: the child stood up, completely healed.

This event made a strong impression on little Francesco.

Whenever he recalled it as an adult, tears would well up in his eyes.

In spite of these undoubtedly charismatic episodes, Francesco Forgione was also like all the other boys. Eyewitnesses have recounted other episodes in his life that show him to be completely normal and even rather carefree. When Francesco was about nine, it was his job to take some sheep to the pasture each day. There he would meet another young shepherd, Luigi Orlando, who was a little younger than he. The two friends would often wrestle for fun. "Francesco would almost always pin me down," Orlando later recalled. "Once I fell down and he pinned my shoulders to the ground. Then, in an effort to get him off of me, I said a dirty word. Francesco's reaction was immediate: he let go and ran away. He never said bad words and never wanted to hear them."

When he was about ten, Francesco played a prank that deeply upset his mother. For about a month he had been sick in bed, and nothing seemed to cure him. One day his mother had to go to the fields to help with the harvest. Before leaving, she prepared an enormous plate of fried red peppers: half of it was for the workers in the field, and the other half was stored in the cupboard for the following day's meal. As she was leaving, she told little Francesco to stay in bed and to take his medicine.

When he was alone, Francesco could not resist the sweet smell of the fried peppers. As he himself recounted, he got up and staggered to the kitchen, took them from the cupboard, and ate almost all of them. Then he went back to bed and fell asleep. When his mother returned home, she found him in a pool of sweat and redder than the peppers he had eaten. Not realizing what had happened, she was frightened and immediately called the doctor. Fortunately, the peppers, instead of making him sicker, must have purified his intestines. By the following day his fever had disappeared.

One day when talking about smoking and people who smoke, Padre Pio told the following story: "When I was about ten, Uncle Pellegrino sent me to buy a cigar and a box of matches for him. When I was coming back, I stopped at the Pantaniello River.

'Let's see if he knows what smoking is like,' a voice said within me. I took a match and lit the cigar. But the first puff turned my stomach. It seemed like the ground was shaking underneath me. When I felt better, I went back to the farm and told my uncle what had happened. Instead of scolding me, he burst out laughing. Since then there's been a barrier between me and smoking."

TWO

Pio's Early Years

On September 27, 1899, Francesco Forgione was confirmed in Pietrelcina by Bishop Donato Maria dell'Olio of Benevento. He was twelve years old. We do not know if he made his first Holy Communion on that same day, but he certainly made it sometime during the year, since no child was allowed to make his or her first Holy Communion before twelve years of age. More than once, Francesco had gone with his grandfather to ask the pastor of the parish to let him receive the Eucharist. However, his pastor did not want to break what was the tradition at the time, even though he was fully aware that the boy was well prepared to make his first Holy Communion.

Francesco's father, Grazio Forgione, was unable to read or write but did not want his children to be illiterate like him. He had tried to send his oldest son, Michele, to school with no success. When he decided to send Francesco to school, he repeatedly promised: "If you do well in your studies, you can become a monk."

At that time the sons and daughters of poor people living in the country or in the mountains could pursue further studies only if they intended to be a priest or religious. Francesco was prepared to follow such a course. Since he had to be useful to his family by working until that point in his life, he was not able to go to school on a regular basis. He had studied at different times with various self-styled "teachers." His first teacher was Cosimo Scocca, a farmer who had a fifth-grade education. They were related, and Francesco called him "Uncle Cosimo." His second teacher was Mandato Saginario, a tradesman who was able to teach him the letters of the alphabet. His third teacher was Fr. Domenico Tizzani, a priest with whom Francesco finished his elementary school program.

In 1901, when he was fourteen, the future Padre Pio set to work on a high school program under the direction of Angelo Caccavo. Caccavo was an open-minded and honest man who was dedicated to his vocation, but he had been heavily influenced by the Freemasons and his ideas were quite liberal. People who knew Francesco at the time all agree that he loved to study and did very well in his studies.

During the two years that he studied with Caccavo, young Francesco worked on developing thirty different themes that are preserved in a notebook to this very day. The paper in the notebook has grown yellow with time, but it is easy to read, except for a few pages where the ink has faded. From these themes, we are able to learn some interesting details about both student and teacher. Some of the titles of his themes are as follows: *The Hovel of a Beggar; The Mad Dog; Autumn; Rain; The Appropriateness of Self-Control; Rewarding Good; The Wars for Italian Independence; Our King; The Shame of Dishonor.* In developing these themes, Francesco showed himself to be a keen observer of the natural phenomena and the customs of his surroundings. Moreover, he displayed a marked love for history.

On September 22, 1902, Angelo Caccavo assigned him to write a paper entitled "If I Were King." Here is what Francesco Forgione wrote:

> O, if I were king! How many wonderful things I would wish to do. First of all, I would always want to be a religious king, as I am now and as I always hope to be. I would fight, first of all, against divorce, which so many wicked men desire, and make people respect as much as possible the sacrament of matrimony.
>
> What happened to Julian the Apostate, who was brave, self-controlled, and studious, but who made the big mistake of denying Christianity, in which he was educated, because he decided to revive Paganism? His life was wasted because he did not attain

anything but the despicable name of apostate.

Also, I would try to make a name for myself by always fighting for the path of true Christianity. Woe to the person who does not wish to follow it! I would punish him immediately, either by putting him in prison, exiling him, or even by putting him to death. My motto would be the same as Alessandro Severo's: "Don't do unto others that which you would not want them to do to you." During my reign I would spend all my time visiting the provinces in order to improve the government there, and by building everywhere some distinguished monuments as memorials, such as city gates, roads, circuses, libraries, statues, theaters, etc. I would be gracious, humane, and observe the laws; I would travel as a simple citizen, giving audiences to everyone and dressing simply by wearing clothing made by the women back home. I would gather in my court the greatest writers. I would pay teachers of rhetoric well. I would be a patron of the arts. My motto would be that of Vespasiano: "Only a friend of mankind is worthy to lead."

Three days later, he was given the following assignment: "Describe a rainfall after a long drought." His report reads as follows:

Yesterday, on the horizon, the sun was shining in full splendor and was warming the earth with its burning rays. The sky was serene and tranquil when barely, but barely, a breath of wind began to blow softly from the west. But the tranquillity did not last long, because in the afternoon the sky grew dark, the sun was hidden. Creation no longer shone with a multitude of colors, and the melody of the birds could no longer be heard. Everything had changed.

It began to thunder and lightning unceasingly, and everyone was frightened. After a while, rain began to fall sharply and noisily, flooding the streets and trickling off the roofs. I went to the window to watch the drenching rain so that I wouldn't be bored. Many raindrops fell straight down and flowed right into the middle of the street; many others quietly trickled down the sides of the walls of the houses. There were others that were more daring and they clung to the windowpanes, perhaps out of curiosity. I even observed a few that were held back by the raised edges of the sills of the windows, that seemed to creep up to the top of the edge—perhaps to measure how far the fall was. After hesitating a bit, they mustered up the courage to fall to the ground and join the thousands of other raindrops that were falling from the sky.

I saw people who were hurrying by under their soaking umbrellas, and I also saw innumerable puddles of water that were rippling from the raindrops, forming little bubbles that would disappear almost as quickly as they would appear.

At the same time, all of the water was forming little streams and rivulets that skipped around the bumps on the ground, searching for a torrent of water that would lead them out to the sea.

Reflecting on the many benefits that this water would bring to the countryside, I felt happy and content. For a long time not a single drop of rain had fallen, and the rain came just in time to refresh the air and to replenish wells and cisterns. Furthermore, it would revive the grass and the plants that had been scorched by the drought.

Francesco was happy studying with Angelo Caccavo. On July 5, 1901, he wrote to his father, who had emigrated to America: "Now that I have a new teacher, I am noticing how much progress I am making from one day to the next, for which both Mother and I are extremely happy."

Francesco always had a strong affection for Caccavo. When he would write home after entering the monastery, he never failed to send his "greetings," a "big hug," or his "fondest wishes" to his teacher. On May 11, 1919, after he had received the stigmata and was famous, he wrote this letter to his former teacher: "I'm healthy, but extremely busy all day and all night because of the hundreds, even thousands, of confessions that I hear in carrying out my ministry.

"I always remember you in my humble prayers when I'm in the Lord's presence, and only God knows how much I have implored him for your complete conversion.

"I would be so happy if I could see you again and hug you one last time, which is totally impossible since I will never see my hometown again. I send greetings to everybody, and I send you a big hug, asking God's grace to be with you and to sustain you."

Caccavo responded to his disciple's wishes by going to see him several times in San Giovanni Rotondo. He died in 1944 at the age of seventy-five.

Francesco first thought about becoming a monk when he was a child. His mother, his pastor, and his teacher, Caccavo, were all aware of his desire. He chose the Capuchins because of his acquaintance with Brother Camillo, a young mendicant monk from the monastery in Morcone. Brother Camillo periodically visited Pietrelcina and endeared himself to everybody because of his humble and simple demeanor.

In the spring of 1902, Francesco's Uncle Pellegrino asked the pastor of the parish, Fr. Panullo, to write to the provincial superior of the Capuchins and to inform him about Francesco's desire. The provincial superior wrote back saying that there was no place at that moment for him in the Capuchin novitiate in Morcone.

Uncle Pellegrino advised his nephew to consider another religious order. He could choose between the monks at the Marian shrine in Montevergine with their white habits, the Redemptorists at Sant Angelo a Cupolo, or the Franciscans at Benevento. Francesco asked whether they had beards, and when he learned that they did not, he told his uncle, "No, I want to wear a beard like Brother Camillo."

In the autumn of 1902, a second letter arrived. The provincial superior of the Capuchins informed him that there was now a place for him at the novitiate in Morcone, and immediately set the date for entering the order: January 6, 1903. Fr. Pannullo started to prepare the documents he needed, but suddenly stopped the whole process when he received an anonymous letter telling him that Francesco was courting the stationmaster's daughter in Pietrelcina.

Fr. Pannullo was furious. He informed his fellow priests about the situation, and immediately took some drastic steps. Without giving any explanation to Francesco, he barred him from serving at all religious events. When the people of Pietrelcina no longer saw the boy serving at Mass, even though he was the most diligent altar boy, they began to gossip. A scandal erupted, and Francesco suffered tremendously. In the meantime, Fr. Pannullo and the other priests at the parish were trying to find out if the accusation was true, and finally discovered the author of the anonymous letter. One of Francesco's friends, who was also an altar server, confessed that he had invented the whole story because he was envious of the attention he felt the priests were paying to Francesco.

Fr. Pannullo asked Francesco to forgive him and admitted him once again to the ranks of altar servers. He also resumed preparation of the documents so he could enter the monastery.

Francesco's vocation had some dramatic turns. He heard God's call, but he also encountered some difficulties trying to respond to it. He was also attracted by the simple and easy life that the world offered.

Seeking to overcome these difficulties, he had some supernatural and mystical experiences which are difficult for others to evaluate. At the end of December 1902, while he was meditating on his vocation, Francesco had a vision. Several years later he wrote a description of this vision for his confessor. He used the third person to describe it, as if he were an outsider to it:

Francesco beheld a majestic man of rare beauty at his side, resplendent as the sun. This man took him by the hand and encouraged him by saying: "Come with me, for you must fight like a valiant warrior." He was led to a vast field where there was a multitude of men divided into two groups. On one side he saw men of most beautiful countenance, dressed in snow-white garments; on the other side he saw men of horrendous aspect, dressed in black garments and looking like dark shadows.

The young man, who stood in the middle of these two groups of men, saw a man coming up to him with a horrible face. He was so tall that he seemed to touch the clouds.

The resplendent man by his side exhorted him to fight the monstrous-looking man. Francesco begged to be rescued from the furor of that eerie man, but the shining man at his side would not agree to it. "Your every resistance is in vain. You must fight him. Take heart. Enter confidently into the battle. Go forth with courage. I will be at your side. I will help you and I won't let him kill you."

The battle was fierce. With the help of the resplendent man who always stood at his side, Francesco overcame his adversary. The eerie creature crawled into the multitude of horrible-looking men, who fled with shrieks, curses, and deafening cries. The group of men of beautiful countenance broke into cheers and applause for the man who had helped poor Francesco in the fierce battle.

The man who was brighter and shinier than the sun put a crown of rarest, most indescribable beauty on the head of the victorious Francesco. But the good man immediately took the crown off, explaining: "I have an even more beautiful one set aside for you. Know that you are able to fight the good fight with the being whom you have just fought. He will come back to attack you.... Fight valiantly and don't doubt my help.... Don't be afraid of him, don't be frightened by his formidable might.... I'll be with you. I'll always help you, so that you will always succeed in conquering him."

This testimony enables us to understand that there were always "forces" at work in the life of this extraordinary person, forces that cannot be explained in any rational way. In the course of this account, I will register only the facts that I have gleaned from reputable documents, without attempting to evaluate them or draw any conclusions.

On January 3, 1903, the mayor of Pietrelcina gave Francesco Forgione a certificate of "good moral and political behavior," and on January 5 the chancery office in Benevento gave him a "letter of reference" for entering the novitiate.

As the days passed, Francesco experienced tremendous sorrow whenever he thought about leaving his family, to whom he was deeply attached. Years later, he recalled this time in his life in a letter he wrote to his spiritual director, Fr. Benedetto of San Marco in Lamis: "Don't ever think that this soul never had to suffer in its innermost being when he had to leave his beloved ones, with whom he felt such strong ties. He felt as though his bones were being crushed, and his sorrow was so real that he felt he was on the verge of passing out. As the day of departure drew near, his anguish grew more and more."

On the night of January 5–6, Francesco had another vision. He saw and heard Jesus and Mary, who encouraged him and assured him of their protection.

On January 6, the feast of the Epiphany, he attended Mass at the parish church and returned home, where his relatives and friends bid him farewell. He gave everyone a hug, kneeled before his mother, and asked her to give him her blessing. Then, accompanied by Mr. Caccavo and Fr. Nicola Caruso, he left for the Capuchin monastery in Morcone. Later, he was deeply moved and wept whenever he recalled leaving home: "I knew how much my mother suffered. I remember that on the morning of my departure my mother told me, 'Son, I can feel my heart breaking within me, but St. Francis is calling you and you must go.'"

THREE

A Year of Trial

Morcone is located about ten miles from Pietrelcina. The friary, built in 1603, is situated in a distant valley that is far away from everything else. To get to it, Francesco and his companions had to travel by mule down a rough road full of stones. When they finally crossed the threshold of the austere building at around noon, Francesco had a surprise waiting for him: Brother Camillo, the young mendicant friar he had met in Pietrelcina who had been the inspiration for his vocation, awaited him when he opened the door.

The Capuchins have always been known for their hospitality, and the superior of the monastery made sure that Francesco and his companions were fed and refreshed. Francesco was then given permission to walk around the monastery so he could get to know his new home. He was impressed by the deep silence that reigned in the corridors with low, vaulted ceilings.

That afternoon Francesco was given an examination. Before being formally admitted into the friary, the Capuchins wanted to determine how intellectually prepared he was. Upon completion of the novitiate, he would have to continue his high school studies, and they needed to know whether his prior preparation was adequate. The exam went well. The superior himself informed Caccavo about his student's results, and Caccavo was very pleased that Francesco had been accepted. There were some final farewells and hugs before Caccavo and the others started out on their cold journey home and Francesco began his life as a friar.

We do not have any documents to tell us how Francesco spent his first night far away from home, but knowing how sensitive he was and how attached he was to his family, he must have been rather sad. During his first week at the monastery, he had permission to do what he wanted within the community, following the community's schedule as he pleased. Then he began a series of spiritual exercises that were to prepare him for his life as a Franciscan and that served as an initiation into the normal lifestyle of the monastery. For six days Francesco was obliged to maintain absolute silence. The entire time was dedicated to prayer, meditation, and listening to one of the elder members of the community preach four times during the day.

On the morning of January 22, in the presence of the entire community assembled in the church for a long ceremony full of symbolism, Francesco, together with about twelve other candidates, was "stripped" of his secular clothing, which represented his past life, and was "clothed" with the Capuchin habit, a symbol of his new life.

According to a very ancient custom, each candidate received a new name so that his detachment from the world would seem even more concrete. From that moment on, Francesco Forgione became Brother Pio of Pietrelcina.

Why was he given the name of Pio? No one knows the exact reason. One author has speculated that the young man chose this name because he admired Pope Pius X. But this certainly was not the case. Novices did not choose their names; they were given them by the superior of the monastery. He was probably called Pio because the relics of St. Pius, or San Pio in Italian, an early martyr, are venerated at the parish church in Pietrelcina.

In every religious order, the novitiate is a trial period during which the candidate tries to ascertain whether he is capable of living the lifestyle of the monastery and observing its rule. At the same time, his superiors are observing him in an effort to establish whether he is suitable for the community. Generally the novitiate year is comprised of penance and sacrifices that surpass even what is required in the course of normal community life. Moreover, when

Padre Pio entered the Capuchin friary at the turn of the century, their novitiate year was not simply severe; it was downright harsh. Back then the Capuchins wanted to distinguish themselves from other religious orders by adhering to a strict lifestyle, and the friars proudly lived out their ambition.

Padre Pio's surroundings during his novitiate were characterized by extreme poverty. In the narrow and tiny cells of the friary, there was barely enough space for a bed, a little table, and a wash-stand with a pitcher. There was no heat. In winter it was difficult to wash one's face because the water in the pitcher often formed a block of ice.

Padre Pio occupied cell number 28. His bed consisted of a wood frame with a mattress full of corn husks. The novice was expected to go to bed fully clothed. He would take off only his sandals, and he would carefully arrange the fabric of his habit on top of him so that it would not become wrinkled. He was required to sleep flat on his back without moving, with his arms in the form of a cross over his chest and with a large crucifix stuck in his belt.

At midnight his sleep was suddenly interrupted by the sound of a bell. All the monks rose quickly and gathered together in the church to recite matins and lauds. Waking up in the middle of the night, when the body was just beginning to savor sleep's restorative benefits, was an extremely harsh penance. These prayers lasted more than an hour, and when the monks went back to bed they often could not fall asleep. In winter, though, this practice was truly torture. The damp cold of the corridors and of the church penetrated the bones of the monks and made them shiver. No Capuchin friar ever grew accustomed to this penitential practice, so one can imagine how difficult it was for a sixteen-year-old boy.

The monks then awoke at five o'clock in the morning to begin the day's activities. The novice was expected to make his bed, put a wooden crucifix on top of the mattress, and hurry to the church once again. The friars moved from one place to another as a community: the novices had to observe complete silence as they walked in a straight line with their eyes looking down. They were punished for even the slightest failure to do so.

The day was divided between prayer, work, and study. At about eight o'clock, the novices went to the church for meditation, Mass, and thanksgiving. Then they gathered together in the refectory for breakfast. Afterward they gathered in another meeting room, where they were instructed in the rules of the order. At eleven o'clock, they set about cleaning the various rooms in the monastery and other tasks of a similar nature. They ate dinner at noon, followed by a half-hour walk in the orchard during which they prayed aloud. At half past two the novices gathered together for study until five o'clock. This study period was followed by two hours of work, which they always carried out in silence. At seven o'clock they met in church for the rosary. At eight o'clock they ate supper. This was followed by a half-hour of recreation during which they were allowed to talk to each other. They went to bed at nine o'clock.

Three times during the week—on Monday, Wednesday, and Friday—all the monks practiced what was called the "discipline." After supper they met in the church, where, with the lights out, they scourged their bare backs with a chain that had a cluster of iron balls at the end.

The clothing that the Capuchin friars wore at that time consisted of the bare minimum. Under their habits they were allowed to wear only a coarse, wool undershirt. On their feet they could wear only sandals. In winter they would shiver from the cold; in the summer they would sweat from the heat.

Food was sparse. At home these young men had been used to food that was simple but abundant. In the novitiate it was the custom to leave the table with a desire for more food, so that hunger would continue to torment them.

Besides practicing moderation at all times, the Capuchins scrupulously observed various fasts. They fasted every Friday during the year. They also observed the "Blessed Virgin's Fast," a fast that St. Francis initiated in honor of the Virgin Mary. It lasted from

June 30 to August 15. They also fasted from November 2 to December 25 in preparation for Christmas, and during Lent in preparation for Easter. Moreover, in addition to fasting, the friars ate while kneeling down on the eve of any feast in honor of the Virgin Mary, on the eve of the feast day of any major saint, and on Fridays during Lent.

Eating while kneeling was a frequently enforced penance, a punishment for those who failed to observe the little rules. Often it was simply used as a means to mortify a young monk's pride.

Every day in the refectory, before being seated, the novices had to kneel down on the ground, and one of them would say to the superior, "Father, bless us." If the superior answered, "I bless you," the novices rose and began to eat. But if he was silent, they had to remain on their knees until the superior decided otherwise. Occasionally he would finish his meal and go off with the other monks, leaving the novices on their knees.

The novitiate was a year of difficult studies, and Brother Pio dedicated himself to his studies with enthusiasm. Even though he was a simple country boy, he was fully aware that some things were exaggerated. Later he criticized some of these things in a rather benevolent way whenever he recalled those times. He often related this episode: "One day the task of asking for a blessing before being seated at the table was assigned to a twenty-year-old friend of mine from Naples. He had been assigned this task many times before, so he asked in a very precise way, 'Bless us, Father.' But Father Superior didn't answer, and we had to remain on our knees without eating. After a while my friend, who was rather exasperated by then, said in a loud voice: 'Back home in Naples we have to pay a dime to see madmen. Here, though, we see them for free.'"

Brother Pio, who made great efforts to study, did not like the fact that he was not even allowed to read books during his novitiate. "At the end of that year," he would later say, "I had to begin from nothing. I had forgotten everything. And it's no wonder when you consider the system of education that was in effect at that time. We didn't have one single book, either religious or secular. The novices were allowed—even obliged—to read only fifteen pages that were given to them, after which they had to read them again. Imagine how this was for a whole year."

He also criticized the irrational way in which clothing was distributed: "How much clothing was ruined when we got dressed. Everything was in common. When we were given undershirts to put on, it was done army-style. Some were too long or too short, some were too wide or too narrow. Often the clasps were torn off, and we wore them like that."

These difficult conditions did not affect his spiritual life, which was already quite rich and intense. A friend from the novitiate, Brother Gugliemo of San Giovanni Rotondo, has left us this testimony: "After the meditation reading, which was always on the passion of our Lord Jesus Christ, Brother Pio would spend a long time on his knees, weeping copiously. Often he would ask to be excused from recreation, from his walk, and even from dinner so that he could continue praying beyond the time that was set aside for prayer."

According to another fellow friar, Brother Placido of San Marco in Lamis, Brother Pio "wept so many tears once while praying that they left a large spot on the wooden floor. A friend teased him about it. Later Brother Pio put a handkerchief on the floor to catch the tears so the others wouldn't tease him."

During the novitiate year, the novice's contact with his family was extremely limited, to the point of being almost nonexistent. Brother Pio wrote home only once or twice. Recalling this, he often said, "I almost forgot how to hold a pen in my hand."

Toward the end of his novitiate year, his mother decided to visit him. She prepared some candies that Francesco was particularly fond of, and made the trip by herself on foot. When she arrived at the monastery, she was escorted to the guest room, where Brother Pio came down in the company of another friar, as was the custom at the time.

Since she had not seen her son for so long, Mamma Peppa approached him to give him a hug, but he drew away from her. He stood there seriously, almost aloof, with his hands up his sleeves and his eyes lowered. His mother tried to give him the candies that she had so lovingly prepared with her own hands, but Brother Pio did not take them. He thanked her, but showed no warmth and did not look her in the eyes.

Mamma Peppa was upset by her son's behavior. She cried all the way home. When she arrived home, she told her husband what had happened. Grazio, who had returned a few days before from America, thought that Francesco was not feeling well and had lost his love for his family, so he went immediately to Morcone, intending to take his son home. When he saw his son so pale, emaciated, and undernourished, he was frightened and asked the superior, "What have you done to my son? I don't recognize him anymore." The superior went to great lengths to convince Grazio that Brother Pio's health was fine, and that his cold and distant behavior was only in keeping with the order's rules.

Later, Padre Pio recalled those meetings with his parents: "I was forbidden to speak or to look at my family without permission, and I was only obeying. My family, though, thought that I had lost my mind.... I wanted so much to throw my arms around them and hug them."

On January 22, 1904, the novitiate year came to an end. During a solemn ceremony, at which Mamma Peppa, Brother Pio's oldest brother Michele, and Uncle Angelantonio were present, Brother Pio made his simple profession of vows together with the other novices. Three days later, the newly professed monks left the monastery in Morcone for the monastery of Sant'Elia in Pianisi, where they would take up their studies once again.

FOUR

Strange Illnesses

Padre Pio's stay at the monastery in Sant'Elia in Pianisi near the town of Campobasso marked the beginning of a long period during which he was plagued by strange illnesses. These illnesses were never really diagnosed because doctors could not find an explanation for them, yet he never really recovered from them. As a result of these illnesses, the young student was forced to lead a life that was different from that of his fellow students.

In every men's religious order, the period between the novitiate and ordination to the priesthood is considered as a time of formation. Under the guidance of their professors, spiritual directors, and confessors, the young seminarians try to put into practice everything they have learned during their novitiate year so that they might grow in maturity and eventually become masters of the spiritual life. The rules at that time prohibited any seminarian from spending more than a few days outside the seminary without a very good reason.

These rules had little bearing on Padre Pio's life at this time. He started to live outside the monastery at the end of 1905. In 1907 he began to return to his birthplace for long periods of time, where he lived almost uninterruptedly from 1910 to 1916. In reality, Brother Pio ended up living outside the monastery for almost a decade, although the constitution of the Capuchin Order stipulated that if a seminarian ever became sick to the point where he was no longer able to observe the rule, he was to be sent home permanently. Due to a series of unusual circumstances, which we will examine more closely, these rules were not applied to Brother Pio's situation.

Due to the passing of time and a lack of reliable documents for the period of his life that extends from 1904 to 1920, it is difficult to ascertain the exact nature of the illnesses that afflicted Brother Pio. Some type of severe physical breakdown was most likely the origin of his health problems. As we have seen, life in the novitiate was hard, and Brother Pio faced this challenge wholeheartedly, without making any allowances for himself in any way. Although he was required to wake up in the middle of the night only three times a week to recite matins and lauds, this measure did little to improve his health. From the reports of his fellow students, we know that Brother Pio ate very little, imposed severe penances on himself, slept little, and prayed a lot. These ascetical excesses probably weakened his physical condition during a point in his life when he was still growing physically, thereby provoking some hormonal imbalances. Yet, in Brother Pio's case, we cannot overlook some mysterious factors that might have affected his health. These factors are difficult to analyze since they are paranormal and spiritual in nature.

In June of 1905, Brother Pio's health was so poor that his superiors decided to send him to the convent of Santa Maria del Monte for a change of air. For six months the young seminarian had been suffering intensely from intestinal irritability and had been tormented by terrible headaches. He often vomited and could hold down only milk. In order to make the uphill journey from the center of town to the convent of Santa Maria del Monte, he was forced to stop and rest every hundred feet or so. Rumors began to circulate among those who came to pray at the little church in the monastery that the young man was suffering from tuberculosis. Consequently, no one wanted to sit near him.

After a few months at Santa Maria del Monte, Brother Pio returned to be with his fellow students. Then, at the end of 1905, he was sent to the monastery of San Marco la Catola to begin his studies in philosophy. The monastery is situated in an isolated area amid some forests, and Padre Pio was happy there. The solitude and the silence was conducive to prayer and meditation.

The following year Brother Pio returned to Sant'Elia in Pianisi. At this time some strange things began to occur in his life. Occasionally he would fall into ecstacy while praying. Often he was persecuted by the devil. One summer night he was unable to fall asleep because it was so hot, humid, and stuffy. He heard footsteps in the neighboring room, like a man pacing back and forth. "Poor Anastasio is just like me. He can't fall asleep," he thought. "I'll call him and we can at least chat for a while." He went to the window to call to his friend, but was unable to utter a word: an enormous black dog with a huge head and raging eyes was standing on the sill of the neighboring window. Before he could scream, the horrible dog leapt onto the roof in front of him and disappeared. The next day Brother Pio learned that no one had lived in the cell next to his for more than a month.

The devil did not always limit himself to gruesome appearances. He even beat him to the point where he was bleeding. Once Brother Pio recorded the following note in his diary: "Last night it seemed like the demons wanted to finish me off. I didn't know what saint to turn to. I called out to my guardian angel, and after having to wait a little, he finally came to my aid."

In spite of these strange occurrences, Brother Pio proceeded along regularly through the various stages of religious life, and he professed his solemn vows as a Capuchin friar in 1907. Yet his health still grew worse, and he suffered from fevers, coughs, chest pains, fainting spells, and cold sweats. The doctors could not figure out what was happening. His superiors were worried and did not know what to do. Hoping that some fresh air would do him good, they sent him home again. But even the loving care of his mother and his aunts brought little improvement to his health.

From 1907 on, Brother Pio's visits home became more and more frequent. Some of his fellow friars disapproved of these visits home, claiming that he was simply acting on a whim. But the fact of the matter is that many of the problems that the young monk would complain about disappeared the moment he stepped foot in the house, and reappeared upon returning to the monastery.

On April 16, 1907, Brother Pio was ordered to report to the draft office for the military district of Benevento. The authorities declared that he was physically fit and sent him home until further notice.

At the end of the year, after completing his studies in philosophy at home by himself, he joined his fellow seminarians at Serracapriola to begin his first course in theology. But he stayed only a couple of months. His unusual health problems forced him to return to Pietrelcina, where he continued his studies in theology with the help of some priests in town. In December of 1908, he received minor orders at Benevento. Shortly thereafter he was ordained a subdeacon. His health improved in the meantime, and he joined his fellow seminarians at Montefusco.

An incident occurred during this period in his life that some biographers refer to as Padre Pio's first miracle. The monastery at Montefusco was located in a large forest of chestnut trees. One afternoon Brother Pio decided to fill a bag with some chestnuts and send them to his beloved Aunt Daria in Pietrelcina. When she received the chestnuts, she ate them and saved the bag as a remembrance.

Some time afterward, Aunt Daria went rummaging through a shed, using an oil lamp for light. Her husband had stored some gunpowder there, and a spark from the lamp caused an explosion, knocking Daria to the ground. Badly burned and shrieking from pain, Daria ran home and took the bag in which Brother Pio had sent her the chestnuts and put it over her face, hoping to relieve the pain. Immediately the pain disappeared, and no trace of a burn was left on her face.

The fresh air of Montefusco did little to improve Brother Pio's health. In May of 1909, he returned to Pietrelcina. He described his state of health in a letter to his spiritual director: "My stomach can only hold down a little water.... The fever never leaves me, returning every day in the evening, followed by a copious sweat.

The cough and the pains in my chest and my back are a greater source of martyrdom than any other misery. For the past few days a new pain at the bottom of my left lung has begun to torment me. Perhaps Jesus is serious this time. This new pain is more severe than all the others, and renders me powerless to do anything, even, at times, to utter a word...."

To be ordained a deacon, Brother Pio had to take an examination in theology for which he was not prepared. His spiritual director, Fr. Agostino of San Marco in Lamis, wanted things to work out for him. He tried to obtain a dispensation from the examination but was unable to do so. The idea occurred to him of arranging a special examination for Brother Pio in Pietrelcina, but the archbishop expressed a desire to examine the young monk himself when his health was better. Finally, Brother Pio took his exam in Benevento, passed it, and was ordained a deacon immediately afterward in Morcone.

Now Brother Pio needed to prepare for the priesthood. The provincial superior stipulated that he had to return to the monastery, but allowed the young deacon to choose whichever monastery he wanted. However, to everyone's amazement and displeasure, Brother Pio expressed a desire to remain in Pietrelcina. After a time of reflection, the provincial superior decided to send him to the monastery in Campobasso, a peaceful place in the mountains that seemed ideal for someone who was sick. Furthermore, it was next to a hospital where care could be provided immediately if needed.

Brother Pio obeyed. He was in Campobasso for only a few weeks before he became ill again and returned to Pietrelcina.

The young seminarian no longer entertained any hopes of getting well. He even welcomed death so that he might be "freed from the bonds of this miserable body." He had only one remaining desire: to be ordained a priest before he died.

According to canon law at that time, a candidate to the priesthood could be ordained only when he was twenty-four years old.

Brother Pio was only twenty-three. His spiritual director told him that he could request a special dispensation for health reasons, so he wrote to his bishop and his request was granted.

At the beginning of July, the provincial superior told him to report to Morcone so that he might learn the ritual for saying Mass. But after only a day at the monastery in Morcone, he was confined to bed because he was vomiting so much. The provincial superior was frightened, and sent him back to Pietrelcina. Before leaving, Brother Pio wrote a letter to the provincial superior: "I am forced to return home so that I don't get worse. As regards the ritual I need to learn, I can learn it from the pastor of my parish back home, who volunteered to teach me. As for the examination, I'll try to take it as soon as possible. Give me your blessing. Your poor Brother Pio."

The examination was set for July 30, 1910, and Brother Pio passed it without any difficulty. On August 10, Brother Pio was ordained a priest in the cathedral of Benevento. He was twenty-three years and two months old. The ceremony took place in the Canons' Choir. His mother was present, along with Fr. Salvatore Pannullo, the pastor of the parish in Pietrelcina. Grazio Forgione was unable to attend since he had emigrated to America for a second time.

That same evening, Padre Pio returned to Pietrelcina. Four days later, on August 14, he celebrated his first solemn Mass in the town where he was born.

FIVE

Mysterious Events

From 1910 to 1916, Padre Pio spent almost all his time in Pietrelcina. He celebrated Mass in the parish church and helped the priest at the parish, but ate and slept at home, where his mother cared for him.

From all appearances, this period in Padre Pio's life seemed like a vacation or a long convalescence. In reality, it was of fundamental importance for his formation.

San Giovanni Rotondo is known as the place where Padre Pio manifested the charismatic gifts that God gave him. But his stay in Pietrelcina prepared him for his extraordinary mission. It was in Pietrelcina, the place where he was born, that he experienced the mystery of the stigmata that characterized his later life.

The houses where Padre Pio lived during those years are located in Borgo Castello, the old part of the town. They are humble, tiny abodes that are still maintained as he left them. The house called *Torretta* is rather impressive because it is built over other houses. From its one window, one can enjoy an enchanting view of the countryside. This is one of the most important places in Padre Pio's life. Here he locked himself up for hours on end, praying and writing letters to his spiritual director. Here he experienced dozens of visions of Jesus and Mary and fought raging battles with the devil.

Several people who live in Pietrelcina knew Padre Pio when he lived there. I have spoken with them in an effort to record their simple yet valuable stories. They remember him as an extremely thin man. Whenever he would pass by, people would stop and stare at him. He walked upright, but with his eyes cast down. He protected himself from the sun with a grey umbrella. Everyone said he was a saint.

His best friend was Mercurio Scocca. Their families both owned land in Piana Romana, about a half-hour walk from Pietrelcina. In their youth they tended their sheep together. Mercurio was lively and spontaneous. Padre Pio, on the other hand, was reserved but felt completely at ease with his friend.

Every day after celebrating Mass at the parish church in Pietrelcina, Padre Pio would go to Piana Romana, where his brother Michele had built a cabin for him next to a huge elm tree. There he could pray and meditate while enjoying the fresh air that was so helpful for his sick lungs. Now and again Padre Pio would go and chat with his friend, Mercurio, who worked in the fields nearby. In the afternoons, they would nap together on some sacks of grain. Once Mercurio decided to pull a trick on Padre Pio. Seeing that Padre Pio was fast asleep, he built a "tomb" around him with the sacks of grain, covering him on the sides and from above. Padre Pio woke up in a sweat. Finding himself completely in the dark, he began to cry out for help.

Mercurio knew that his friend would repay him for his prank, and he was careful not to take a nap on the sacks of grain during the following days. At nap time he would disappear. A couple of days later, Padre Pio discovered that his friend was hiding in a wagon. He waited until Mercurio was fast asleep. Then, little by little, he dragged the wagon up a hill and let go. Mercurio woke up while the wagon was racing downhill and became very frightened. The prank might have turned into a disaster if a large pear tree had not interrupted the wagon's wild race downhill.

On another occasion Padre Pio confided to his friend that he was concerned about his poor health. Mercurio listened to him for a long time in silence. When Padre Pio finished speaking, Mercurio said to him: "I know a sure remedy to make you well." Anxiously Padre Pio asked him, "What should I do?" "If you want to get well, then get married." His friend had overstepped his bounds. Padre Pio grabbed a pitchfork and began to chase Mercurio, who took off running. Padre Pio often recalled this episode many years afterward.

When Mercurio later visited him at San Giovanni Rotondo, Padre Pio recounted this story and, turning to his friend, said, "Dear Mercurio, I still should stick that pitchfork in your rear end."

Padre Pio enjoyed being with his people. Numerous testimonies attest to this. Giuseppe Fuci, a friend from Padre Pio's childhood who was of the same age, recalled: "After having celebrated Mass in town, Padre Pio would go to Piana Romana around ten or eleven o'clock, taking the road through Quadrielli, where I lived. He would stop and sit on a chair in the shade of a fig tree. He would drink some water, and we would always have a nice chat together.

"One time the conversation turned to the Jewish people, some of whom I had met when I lived in America. I was telling him how they prayed and what they did. Padre Pio told me, 'Each person clings to his own religion, and we have to respect those who don't profess our faith.'"

Lucia Iadanza recorded the following story: "When Padre Pio would return from Piana Romana for evening services, he always stopped at my house, covered with sweat. My grandmother would always tell me, 'Go to the well and bring some water for Padre Pio.' He would sit down and catch his breath. He would ask about my father, who had emigrated to America. The water would be used to cool some white wine in which Padre Pio would dip some biscuits that we had offered him and that he gratefully accepted."

In the evening, Padre Pio would often sit outside people's houses to chat. Every day he would stop at the postman's house to read the newspaper. He also liked to visit with another friend, Filippo Gagliardi, and on cold and rainy days he would go to Gagliardi's house and they would sit together next to the fireplace. Filippo would cook some potatoes on the open fire, which Padre Pio enjoyed immensely. Padre Pio also bought a lottery game so that he could spend Sunday afternoons with the young people in town. During Lent he taught a boys' choir the songs for Holy Week.

Every evening he would take a walk with the parish pastor, Fr.

Salvatore Pannullo. At that time a large bell would ring throughout the area to mark the main hours of the day: at sunrise, noontime, three o'clock, six o'clock, and seven o'clock. One evening, while Padre Pio was out walking with Fr. Pannullo and some other people, the bell rang at seven o'clock. Its echo could be heard coming from one particular spot in the countryside. Padre Pio said, "Where the echo of the bell is heard, a large monastery of Capuchins will be built, along with a church." Although his words seemed rather absurd at the time, his prophecy was eventually fulfilled.

By that time Padre Pio had a reputation among the people in Pietrelcina for being a very holy man. Many people would ask him for prayers.

In April 1913, lice infested the bean crops after they had bloomed. Every plant was covered with lice. This meant that the beans would not grow and the crops would be ruined. One man suddenly had the idea of asking Padre Pio to pray in his fields so that the lice would go away. Padre Pio walked through his fields, praying over them and blessing them. All the while the lice fell from the beans with a popping noise. Then other people asked him to pray over their fields, and through Padre Pio's prayers the insects were destroyed everywhere. Within a week all the beans were free from infestation, and the harvest was particularly abundant that year.

Padre Pio's Mass usually lasted about three hours. Many people complained about it, but they understood that only a "saint" was capable of celebrating such a lengthy Mass.

Throughout the area people were aware of the battles that Padre Pio waged every night against Satan. Often the noise from the fight that was going on in his room was so great, people could even hear it over a great distance. In the middle of the night, neighbors would run from their homes, scared by what was happening. In the morning, Padre Pio's mother would find his room in complete disorder: everything—the mattress, the chairs, the bed—would be overturned. Padre Pio's body would be covered with bruises from the devil's blows.

Satan continued to infest Padre Pio's room even after he had left for good. For months people continued to hear noises and blows on the walls. Earthenware pots and wooden chairs would break apart without anyone touching them. Padre Pio's oldest brother, Michele, was finally forced to summon a priest to bless the house. After the exorcism, the noises disappeared.

Strange things also happened to Padre Pio when he was in church. After saying Mass, he would spend a long time in thanksgiving, and he often fell down unconscious. The first few times it happened, Michele Pilla, the sacristan, was frightened. He then grew accustomed to it. He would go home but leave his keys in the door so that Padre Pio, once he came to, could lock up the church. Once when the sacristan returned to the church to ring the bell at noontime, he discovered that Padre Pio was still unconscious. Thinking he was dead, he ran to Fr. Pannullo, shouting, "The monk has died." Fr. Pannullo, who understood what was happening, assured him, "Don't worry. He'll come to."

All these things aroused people's curiosity, but no one knew why they were happening. This was God's precise plan for Padre Pio's life. Several times he had offered himself to God for the salvation of men, and God had accepted his offer.

These events are difficult to explain because they are closely related to the mystery of the passion and death of Jesus Christ. According to the teachings of the Catholic Church, God in his infinite love wanted to save men through the sacrifice of his only Son. The Church also teaches that a Christian, through his own suffering, can "participate" in this sacrifice, thereby "continuing" this work of salvation. Reflecting on this mystery, some particularly holy souls offer themselves up as victims so that they might be like Christ, and God has accepted their sacrifice by allowing them to experience in their bodies the physical suffering that Christ endured on the cross. This explains why the stigmata have appeared on the bodies of some great mystics, such as St. Francis of Assisi and St. Catherine of Siena. Padre Pio also experienced this great mystery, and it happened when he was living in Pietrelcina.

The years that Padre Pio spent in his hometown helped him to grow spiritually, and this process was also guided by God's direct intervention. All the qualities that people later came to admire in Padre Pio during the fifty years that he lived in San Giovanni Rotondo were developed in Pietrelcina. And according to Fr. Salvatore Pannullo, the pastor of the parish in Pietrelcina, this included the stigmata which Padre Pio received when he was living in Pietrelcina, although the wounds were invisible to others at the time. When Fr. Pannullo was told in 1918 that the stigmata had appeared on Padre Pio's hands, he said: "You see them now. I saw them in 1910." He then described how this mysterious phenomenon took place on the afternoon of September 7, 1910.

Padre Pio was praying in Piana Romana when Jesus and Mary appeared to him and gave him the wounds. Returning home, he told Fr. Pannullo what had happened. Then he added, "Father, do me a favor. Ask Jesus to take them away. I want to suffer, to die from suffering, but in secret." They prayed together, and God answered their prayer. The visible signs of the stigmata disappeared, but the suffering continued.

Padre Pio himself has also left us an account of this event in the form of a letter to his spiritual director, Fr. Benedetto of San Marco in Lamis, dated September 8, 1911: "Yesterday evening something happened to me that I don't know how to explain or understand. In the middle of the palms of my hands red spots appeared, almost the size of a penny, accompanied by sharp, strong pains. This pain was especially sharp in the middle of the left hand, so much so that it continues even now. I also experience some pain in my feet. This phenomenon dates from about a year ago, and continues even now."

Needless to say, such a special, mystical privilege roused Satan's anger, and his attacks on the poor monk intensified. From the letters that Padre Pio wrote during this time to his spiritual director, we know that he waged violent battles with the devil every night:

"That wicked thing beat me continuously from about ten o'clock at night when I went to bed, until five o'clock in the morning. I thought it was going to be the last night of my life.... Those evil things fling themselves on me like hungry tigers, cursing me and threatening to make me pay. Father, they've kept their word: since then they have beaten me daily.... At this point Jesus has permitted them to vent their anger upon me for twenty-two continuous days. My body is bruised all over from their many blows...."

Moreover, in an effort to spite him, Satan outrightly destroyed the comforting letters Padre Pio's spiritual director wrote to him. In one of Padre Pio's letters he noted: "Your last letter was opened in the presence of the pastor of the parish and we found a blank sheet. Satan had erased everything."

At times his spiritual director would write in French or Greek, naively hoping that Satan would not be able to read them. One day a letter arrived written in French. Fr. Pannullo opened it in Padre Pio's presence and found ink blots all over the letter. Believing it was one of Satan's nasty tricks, he blessed it with holy water. Immediately the ink blots faded away and they were able to read the letter.

On another occasion Padre Pio's spiritual director wrote him a letter in Greek, a language which the young monk did not know. Nonetheless, Padre Pio read the letter. Fr. Pannullo marveled at this and asked him how he learned the language. "My guardian angel explained everything to me," Padre Pio replied. Fr. Pannullo has confirmed these two incidents in writing.

After 1918, Padre Pio never again returned to his hometown. Yet he always felt close ties to it. Whenever people talked about Pietrelcina, tears would well up in his eyes. One day someone was showing him some pictures of familiar places in Pietrelcina. He looked at them for a long time and said, "You've given me back some forty years of life."

Padre Pio was always anxious that the places where he had lived be well maintained. He made such a recommendation to his niece,

Pia: "Keep the house in Castello in order. Jesus appeared there and everything happened there."

One day, while talking with Silvio Scocca, the son of his childhood friend Mercurio, he asked him about the farm at Piana Romana. "I'm keeping everything as it was back then," Silvio assured him. Padre Pio nostalgically remembered two particular items. He told Silvio: "At one end of the farm there are two stones: one is big and cannot be moved, and the other is smaller. They were my chairs. From them I could watch the sunrise and sunset."

When he returned to Pietrelcina, Silvio went to see the stones and thought about bringing the smaller one home as a memento. He tied it to a tractor and tried to pull it out of the ground, but two times the chains broke. Examining the stone closely, Silvio saw that a cross had appeared where Padre Pio used to sit, so he decided to leave the stone there. Three months later, he returned to San Giovanni Rotondo. When Padre Pio saw him, he exclaimed: "You, thief! Is that how you take care of my things? You wanted to take my chair away! Leave that stone where it is."

Repeatedly he made the following exhortation in his letters to his spiritual daughter, Lucia Iadanza: "My daughter, remember Pietrelcina stone by stone."

SIX

Six Years Outside the Monastery

As we have already noted, Padre Pio received a special dispensation to be ordained a priest even though he had not reached the minimum age established by canon law. He received this dispensation because his superiors feared that his death was imminent. It is for this same reason that he was allowed to live in his hometown away from the monastery. Yet as time passed, Padre Pio's health did not grow worse even though it was always rather precarious. Consequently, some of his fellow friars began to criticize his special living arrangements. They also began to criticize their superiors because they felt they were giving in to his whims.

By 1911 this discontent appears to have been rather widespread because the provincial superior of the Capuchins felt obliged to resolve the matter by taking some rather harsh and decisive measures.

At that time Fr. Benedetto of San Marco in Lamis, a very learned monk who was an expert in spiritual direction, was the provincial superior of the Capuchins in Foggia. He met Padre Pio in 1905, when they were both at the monastery of Sant'Elia in Pianisi, and he became Padre Pio's first spiritual director. Because of the unusual events that were taking place in Padre Pio's life, Fr. Benedetto suspected that Padre Pio's mysterious illnesses might also have some unnatural origins, even though he was not completely sure this was the case. Moreover, since people outside the province were now familiar with Padre Pio and what was happening in his life, he felt he needed to make some decisions about the future of his disciple.

Being a wise and prudent man, Fr. Benedetto wrote a long letter to the superior general of the Capuchin Order, asking him for advice. In the first part of his letter, he described Padre Pio. He wrote about his virtues, but he also wrote about the rather sensational mystical events that were happening to him. He devoted the second part of his letter to the delicate question of the young monk living outside of the monastery. The letter is dated September 11, 1911:

Now I have some good news for you, as well as a request for some advice. A young priest, whose moral life is of angelic character, and who has, from my intimate knowledge of him, preserved his innocence since the moment of his baptism, has been growing in the ways of the Lord since he received his habit as a friar. He spent nine months in this monastery when he was studying philosophy and, as was the custom at the time, came to me for spiritual direction. Since that time he has wanted me, either in person or by letter, to continue to provide him with such direction. In order that you might know something about his fervor, I can tell you that the passion of our Lord caused him to weep so much and so long, we feared that he would lose his vision at a certain moment of his mystical ascent. He also asked that he might participate in the pains of our Savior, and his prayers have been answered in an ineffable way. Migraine headaches that are resistant to any remedy, and an illness that no doctor can explain, even those who are renowned in the healing art, come to torment him along with great spiritual suffering. The doctors suspected that he might be suffering from tuberculosis and they ordered him to breathe the fresh air of his hometown, especially when for days and days an uncontrollable vomiting prevented him from holding down even a spoonful of broth.

I have always urged him to clearly reveal to me everything happening in his soul. (I already have a sizeable collection of letters.) Lately he has been telling me, "to his incredible embarrassment," that the Lord has favored him with the gift of his wounds, so that this young priest feels acute pain in the middle of certain red marks that have visibly appeared on his hands and his feet.

This is the good news. Now for the advice. After having been sent back to his hometown to enjoy the fresh air there as I mentioned above, he was called back to one of our monasteries on three different occasions and has had to leave them for an equal number of times against his will because of the doctors' orders. He is presently living outside the monastery and it grieves my soul that this should be the case. Well aware that until now this has been the expressed will of God, I want to summon him at this time to return to the cloister, but I hesitate to do so because I do not want to offend God. What do you think?

The reply to Fr. Benedetto's letter has not been preserved, but we can deduce from what happened afterward that Fr. Benedetto must have been told to thoroughly investigate such an unusual situation.

This was the beginning of a difficult period in Padre Pio's life. He found himself caught in the crossfire between his superiors, who wanted him to return to the monastery, and some "mysterious forces" that seemed bent on keeping him in Pietrelcina.

But why did Padre Pio "have" to stay in Pietrelcina? We can never know for certain. From his *Diary*, we know that Fr. Agostino of San Marco in Lamis, Padre Pio's confessor, tried to determine his reasoning for staying. But Padre Pio's answer did not shed any light on the question: "I can't say why the Lord has wanted me in Pietrelcina, or I would be lacking in love...."

After having consulted with the superior general, Fr. Benedetto seemed not to have any doubts as to what he should do: bring Padre Pio back to the monastery at any cost. He wrote him: "If the Lord wishes to call you to glory, it's better that you move back to the monastery where he has called you."

Padre Pio answered him in a very unusual way: "I don't believe that you really would want me to die. It's true that at home I have suffered and am suffering, but I've never been unable to fulfill my duties, which has not been the case in the monastery. If I must suffer alone, very well. But to be a cause of pain and anxiety without any result other than my death, to that I wouldn't know how to respond. Moreover, it seems to me that I have the right and duty of not depriving myself of life at twenty-four years of age! It seems to me that God does not want this to happen. Consider the fact that I am more dead than alive, and that I am prepared to make any sacrifice if it is a matter of obedience."

Fr. Benedetto was not swayed and wrote back to his disciple: "Staying with your family troubles me very much. If your illness is truly the expressed will of God's desire and not some natural phenomenon, it is better that you return to the shadow of community life. The fresh air of a person's hometown cannot cure a creature visited by the Most High, and that creature cannot fear death only because he has been forced back to the cloister. Whether at home or in the monastery, your health will always be what God wills.

"Before undertaking this long experiment on account of your health, I would have had scruples about forcing you to return to us. But now that I've seen that things are just the same even when you're at home, I would have scruples about not insisting on your return.

"Fr. Giustino, Fr. Agostino, and our Father General, to whom I have written in this regard, share my thoughts. Resolve, then, to obey, and God will bless you for doing so."

Given his superiors' position on the matter, Padre Pio had no choice but to obey. But he still gave some resistance and asked that a medical specialist examine him. He pointed out, though, that his family's limited financial resources did not permit him to pay for an examination by a specialist.

Fr. Benedetto acceded to Padre Pio's request, feeling that an examination by a specialist might clarify once and for all his unusual situation. He decided to seek out the leading medical doctor of that time, Antonio Cardarelli, a professor of medical pathology at the University of Naples. Dr. Cardarelli was an expert in circulatory diseases and the author of numerous scientific publications. He was named a lifetime senator by the Italian parliament in 1906, on account of his fame. It was no easy task to get an appointment with this doctor, but Fr. Benedetto made every effort possible and was successful in doing so. He himself accompanied Padre Pio to Naples. The appointment took place toward the end of October, and the response of the illustrious doctor was shattering. Dr. Cardarelli said that Padre Pio would be dead within a month. He advised Fr. Benedetto to take the sick monk to the nearest friary so that he might die in peace.

Fr. Benedetto was frightened. He immediately thought of the monastery in Venafro, which was closest to Naples.

Padre Pio arrived at the monastery in Venafro on the evening of October 28. He was assigned a cell on the second floor, three cells down from the church. The first few days were rather peaceful, but then his health grew worse. He ate hardly anything, and he immediately vomited anything he ate.

In the middle of November, Fr. Evangelista, the superior of the monastery, was alarmed. He decided to take Padre Pio to Naples for another examination, but the doctor found no change in his condition.

Upon returning to Venafro, Padre Pio's health grew steadily worse. He was forced to stay in bed night and day, and even had to give up celebrating Mass. It was at this point that some sensational occurrences began to take place that were visible to everyone: ecstasies and apparitions of demons.

Fr. Agostino of San Marco in Lamis, Padre Pio's confessor, was curious and witnessed these phenomena with his notebook in hand, writing down everything Padre Pio said while talking with these mysterious, invisible people. In his *Diary*, Fr. Agostino noted: "Fr. Evangelista and I first became aware of these supernatural phenomena in November of 1911 in Venafro. I was present for a considerable number of ecstasies, and many instances of demonic oppression."

Ecstasies alternated with demonic apparitions. Fr. Agostino wrote in his *Diary:* "One night before supper, I was advised that Padre Pio was not well and was delirious. No one had yet noticed the supernatural phenomena, not even me. Indeed, I thought he was very ill. I ran to his room where there were some other friars already, and I saw him in bed, looking agitated and saying, 'Get that cat who wants to pounce on me away from here.' I could not endure such a scene, and I ran away to the church to pray."

Fr. Agostino tells us that Satan appeared under various forms to the young priest: "as a nude woman dancing lewdly, as a crucifix, as a young man who was a friend of the monks, as his spiritual father, the provincial superior, Pope Pius X, his guardian angel, St. Francis, the Virgin Mary, but also as his horrible self with an army of demonic spirits. At times there was no apparition, but the poor priest was beaten until he bled, tormented with deafening noises, covered with spit, etc. He was able to free himself from the torments by calling on the name of Jesus."

The ecstasies occurred two or three times a day. While the diabolical apparitions lasted about fifteen minutes, the ecstasies lasted from one to two and a half hours. His eyes were open the entire time, fixed on one point in the room. He spoke in a different tone of voice, and from his words it was clear that he was speaking with Jesus, Mary, or his guardian angel.

Some doctors also were present for these ecstasies. Once Fr. Agostino wanted to compare his heartbeat with his pulse. He noted in his *Diary,* "There was no correspondence between his heartbeat and his pulse: the former would be super fast and super strong, while the latter would be just strong and accelerated. It was as if his heart wanted to explode."

Besides the visions, the monks at Venafro also witnessed some other things that they could not explain. In spite of his extremely poor state of health, Padre Pio demonstrated an ability to read people's thoughts. One day Fr. Agostino went to see him. "This morning, please pray especially for me," Padre Pio asked. On his way up the stairs into the church, Fr. Agostino decided to remember his fellow monk in a special way during Mass, but then forgot to do so. When he returned to Padre Pio's side, Padre Pio asked him, "Did you pray for me?" Fr. Agostino admitted that he had forgotten to do so. "That's all right. The Lord accepted the intention you made while going up the stairs."

On another occasion, Fr. Agostino found Padre Pio very sick and delirious. Fearing that he was dying, he went to the church to pray for him. After about fifteen minutes, he went back to Padre Pio's room and found that he was well again. "You did well to go and pray for me," Padre Pio said. "You were thinking about the eulogy at my funeral. But there's still time, there's still time."

Fr. Agostino noted another curious fact in his *Diary:* "During one ecstasy, Padre Pio was praying in ecstasy for a soul whom I knew as intimately as myself. That person was troubled for more than a year by some terrible temptations, that only God, and I, as his confessor, were aware of. Padre Pio couldn't have known anything about them. Nonetheless, he prayed for this soul, asking God to free him from such dreadful temptations."

When receiving Holy Communion in bed, Padre Pio always wanted to wear a clean, white shirt on top of his habit, which a benefactor delivered every morning to the monastery at an appointed time, freshly washed and ironed. One morning, when the doorkeeper of the monastery went to pick up the shirt at the regular time, Padre Pio said to him, "Don't go. She'll be coming about an hour late." And so it was. An hour and a half later, Padre Pio told the doorkeeper, "Go now because she is coming." The doorkeeper went, opened the door, and saw the woman approaching the monastery at that very moment.

These incidents convinced the monks at Venafro that a man whom God had blessed in a special way was living in their midst. They began to protest against the decision of the provincial superior to make Padre Pio live at the monastery. They wrote to him, trying to convince him to send him back to Pietrelcina. When they received a negative response to their request, they decided to go directly to the superior general of the Capuchin Order. On December 3, 1911, Fr. Evangelista, the superior of the monastery in Venafro, sent the following letter to the superior general in Rome, in the name of all his fellow monks:

"I appeal to your goodness to simply state some facts and to make a request.

"I and my friars here, and almost all the friars in the province, can sincerely attest to the fact that Padre Pio of Pietrelcina, who has been sick for three years now, cannot retain any food in his stomach except when he is at home. For nearly two years he breathed the air of his hometown, and he never suffered from vomiting there. During the month and a half that he has been here, I can attest that he has never held his food for more than fifteen minutes. For sixteen days now, he has been confined to bed and can retain not even a teaspoon of water.

"Hardly did he arrive in this friary than he began to vomit. Yet as soon as he sets foot on his native soil, his stomach recovers. Might it be, therefore, the will of God that this poor priest always remains at home?

"We can all attest to the fact that he is an excellent priest. Therefore he does not have the slightest wish to stay at home, nor do we, his fellow monks, wish to be deprived of his presence which is so dear to us. Therefore, you can deduce that what we are saying is not at all subjective, but clearly reflects reality.

"The provincial superior has been informed of the situation with a similar letter, but he has not replied. I am not turning to you for advice out of any desire to go against my immediate superior, but my conscience impels me to do so because it seems to me that God would not want a brother to remain in the monastery and to live without any kind of food."

The superior general intervened this time in Padre Pio's favor. In fact, Fr. Benedetto was forced to give in against his will. He complained to the monks at Venafro that they went over his head to the superior general, but he gave Padre Pio permission to return home.

On December 7 Padre Pio arrived in Pietrelcina with Fr. Agostino of San Marco in Lamis. There, as if by magic, his illnesses immediately disappeared. The following day, December 8, the feast of the Immaculate Conception, he was almost strong enough to sing a Solemn High Mass. "It's almost as if he had never been sick," Fr. Agostino wrote in his *Diary*.

According to canon law, Padre Pio could not live at home. As a friar, he was required to live in a monastery. Unable to do so, he needed to request "secularization," a dispensation whereby a monk is released from his religious order. The provincial superior, Fr. Benedetto, decided that Padre Pio should put some order into his situation. Furthermore, he felt obliged to do so in light of the fact that other monks who were under his direction and who were needed in their families were not allowed to go home to be with them.

Once again Fr. Benedetto turned to the superior general. The superior general was in favor of secularization. Padre Pio was very alarmed. He wept. He wrote to the provincial superior: "The many tears that I have shed have affected my health to the point that I was forced to remain in bed where I am even to this moment."

The whole matter moved along slowly in the bureaucracy, handled, it seems, by powers from on high. Three years went by before Rome replied, and the answer was not what anyone expected. Instead of secularization, a "letter of exclaustration" was sent. Padre Pio was granted permission to live outside of the monastery for the time he needed to get well, while still continuing to be a monk. It was clearly a compromise in Padre Pio's favor.

SEVEN

Serial Number 2094/25

Padre Pio received permission from the Vatican to live outside the monastery on February 25, 1915, after much controversy and many struggles. It was the beginning of a truce in his relationship with the provincial superior, who, nonetheless, never abandoned his struggle to persuade Padre Pio to live in the cloister like his fellow friars. Fr. Benedetto kept silence for a few months before making a fresh attempt at the beginning of 1916. This time his efforts were successful after resorting to some trickery.

Padre Pio was a good friend of Raffaellina Cerase, a noblewoman from Foggia, whom people considered a saint. Although they did not know each other personally, they had been regularly corresponding for several years, sharing with each other their rather unusual spiritual experiences.

One day Raffaellina Cerase gave Fr. Agostino the following advice: "Have Padre Pio return to the monastery and grant him permission to hear confessions. It will do him a lot of good." Even though he had been a priest for five years, Padre Pio had never been granted permission to hear confessions, mainly because some doctors suspected that he might be sick with tuberculosis. His superiors tried to keep him away from other people, fearing that he might be contagious.

Fr. Agostino felt that Raffaellina's words were prophetic. When he told Fr. Benedetto what Raffaellina had said, the two men decided to act upon them and have Padre Pio return to the monastery.

Raffaellina was very sick at the time. She had just had an operation and was given only a short time to live. Fr. Agostino and Fr. Benedetto took advantage of this opportunity and wrote Padre Pio that Raffaellina was dying and had expressed a desire to meet him and talk with him in person at least once before dying. Padre Pio was easily swayed. Raffaellina Cerase's sister paid for his trip. Padre Pio left Pietrelcina first thing in the morning on February 17, 1916.

No one was to know about this trip, since the people of Pietrelcina would be opposed to it. By now they were very devoted to their "little saint" and were afraid that he might be removed from their midst. In order not to arouse suspicion, Fr. Agostino, who decided to accompany Padre Pio on the trip because of his poor health, waited for his fellow monk at the train station in Benevento.

The two monks arrived at St. Anne's Monastery in Foggia at around noon. Padre Pio was planning on staying one or two days at the most. However, upon arriving in Foggia, he discovered that his provincial superior, Fr. Benedetto, had peremptorily ordered him to "stay forever in Foggia, whether dead or alive."

When confronted with such a strong order, Padre Pio could only obey. He wrote home, asking that his family send him his personal effects. He also informed Fr. Salvatore Pannullo, the pastor of the parish in Pietrelcina. Both his discouragement and his will to obey were obvious in his letter:

"Dearest Uncle, my provincial superior is determined to make me stay here to experience the climate. Moreover, he feels that, because of my spiritual condition, I am in great need of a good and assiduous spiritual director. Truly I cannot disagree with him on this point. I believe that even you, whom the Lord has put in a position to know what is going on in my life, would fully agree with him.

"Thus, I have to undergo this old yet always new test, so that *maiora premunt*. You alone can understand how much strength is required of me in order to perform this latest sacrificial act to him who has given me everything. For this reason, pray for me so that God will deign me a worthy victim and that I will be pleasing to our Divine Father."

Padre Pio went to Foggia to visit a dying woman, and he did not forget his duties in this regard. The day after his arrival at St. Anne's

Monastery, he went with Fr. Agostino to visit Raffaellina, whose elegant home was located near the monastery.

"The meeting," Fr. Agostino wrote in his diary, "was a meeting of two souls who had known each other in the Lord for a long period of time. They exchanged few words, but their angelic looks were more eloquent than words can tell."

Padre Pio visited the sick woman every morning. He would celebrate Mass in her private chapel, and then would visit with her until noon. Raffaellina died on March 25. Padre Pio sadly informed his confessor, Fr. Agostino, about her death:

"Raffaellina fell asleep in the Lord, with a smile of disdain for this world. Blessed is she!... I am envious that she has been chosen and may it please God, through the intercession of this elect soul, to also grant me the repose of the just. I am tired ... of life: I loathe this world."

In the meantime, word about Padre Pio's "holiness" was spreading throughout Foggia. Every day people came to the monastery to tell him about their problems. Padre Pio even wrote to his spiritual director, "If you don't hear very often from me, don't blame me. I don't have a moment of free time. Crowds of souls thirsting for Jesus are flocking to me so that I would lay hands on them."

St. Anne's Monastery was located at that time on the edge of Foggia, in a very poor section of town. It did not seem to be the best place for Padre Pio. In fact, his health immediately grew worse. The superior of the monastery, Fr. Nazareno d'Apaise, noted in his diary that "the young priest was always subject to extremely high fevers." Dr. Del Prete, the monastery's doctor, was summoned and noted that the "right apex of his lung was a hotbed of infection, and the left one contained light murmurs." He ordered total seclusion for his patient. Given the seriousness of the situation, Dr. Tarallo, a more renowned doctor, was called in and made the same diagnosis.

At the same time, the strange phenomena that had characterized Padre Pio's life for years were very evident during the time he was at the monastery in Foggia.

Because of his fever, Padre Pio seldom ate dinner with his fellow monks. He would stay in his room, which was located just above the refectory of the monastery. Every evening while the monks were eating, they would hear deafening noises coming from Padre Pio's room, that would always culminate with a loud bang. The monks were always extremely frightened. They would run to Padre Pio's room and find him in bed, all pale, surrounded by signs of a violent brawl, and unable to speak. Moreover, he was dripping with sweat. His shirt seemed like it had been dipped in a bucket of water.

Fr. Nazareno d'Ariase, the superior of the monastery, noted all these details in his diary. Among other things he wrote: "One evening Bishop D'Agostino, the bishop of Ariano Irpino, was passing through and I felt it would be good to tell him about what was happening in the monastery. He told me, 'Father, the Middle Ages are over. Do you still believe in this nonsense?' I said to myself, 'He's like the apostle Thomas. If he doesn't see, he won't believe.... You'll see.'

"At a certain point during dinner, I heard the characteristic pattering of feet that generally preceded the infamous bang. I told the monks to be quiet. Suddenly we heard the loud bang.

"The bishop's servant, who was eating in the pantry, ran into the refectory, scared to death. The bishop was so terrified that he didn't want to sleep alone that night. He left first thing in the morning and never returned."

Fr. Paolino of Casacalenda, a fellow friar who was the superior of the Capuchin monastery at San Giovanni Rotondo, described how he wanted to stop at the monastery in Foggia when he was passing through one time so that he might personally experience the strange phenomena that everyone was talking about. Instead of going to the refectory with the other monks at dinner time, he went to Padre Pio's room. "I'll stay here because I want to see if the devil will have the courage to come even when I'm present," he said. Padre Pio, smiling, tried to dissuade him, adding that he hoped nothing would happen that evening.

As it turned out, nothing did happen. Fr. Paolino was convinced that the devil did not want any witnesses. Since it was well past the time when the din normally occurred, he left the room and headed toward the stairway to join the other monks in the refectory. "I had hardly gone down more than a step," he wrote in his memoirs, "when I heard a deafening explosion. It was the first time I had experienced it and I was shaking from head to toe. I ran into Padre Pio's room as fast as a shooting star and found him all pale and immersed in a pool of sweat."

These events lasted a long time. At one point the provincial superior intervened and implored Padre Pio to stop what was happening because the monks were terrified. From that moment on, the noises ended but the demonic oppression continued.

During the summer of 1916, Fr. Paolino of Casacalenda was passing through Foggia and visited Padre Pio. Seeing that he was suffering tremendously from the heat, he invited Padre Pio to accompany him to San Giovanni Rotondo, situated in the Gargano Mountains, where it was relatively cool. Padre Pio asked his superior for permission to do so, and it was granted. On July 28, 1916, Padre Pio set foot in San Giovanni Rotondo for the first time, the place where he would eventually live for half a century.

At that time the region where the Gargano Mountains were located was uncharted territory. Francesco Morcaldi, who subsequently was mayor of San Giovanni Rotondo for several years, described the town at that time: "Then, San Giovanni Rotondo was a little town of a couple thousand inhabitants that was almost entirely isolated from other towns because of a lack of good roads and rapid transportation.

"The inhabitants, who were mainly farmers, were forced for the most part to look for work in the plains of Tavoliere, which were marshlands infected by malaria.

"The mountains had some good pastures for herds and flocks, and the fertile valleys were good for growing potatoes and vegetables, producing products of high quality that were in demand at markets in the region. But these areas were accessible only by steep and difficult mule trails that were often washed out by floods. In winter, they were buried under heavy snow.

"Whoever was forced to earn their living in the mountains had to reside in miserable shacks covered with branches and straw. They also had to watch out for armed bandits, who would hide in the treacherous terrain and who would form gangs that did not spare anyone's property—nor the life of the inhabitants in many cases.

"Unfortunately, cattle-stealing was widely prevalent. Robberies and bloody crimes caused terror and untold anguish for the local population. Living conditions in town were downright primitive. There was no running water and no electricity. The sewage system was rudimentary. Many families were forced to live side by side in inhumane conditions with their livestock, in dark hovels, located below street level without sunlight and fresh air. Infectious diseases claimed numerous lives. The few doctors who lived in the area, in spite of their high level of personal sacrifice, often had to undergo trials that challenged their professional skills. Given these circumstances, they often had to perform delicate surgery in makeshift operating rooms in their patients' houses."

The Capuchin monastery was about a mile from the town and was accessible by a mule-track. The building appeared rather desolate, and the rocky countryside that surrounded it appeared even more desolate. The monastery was the poorest and most isolated Capuchin monastery in the province, and no monk went there voluntarily. Founded in 1540, it was considered a place of punishment for those monks who needed discipline, so that they could meditate and do penance.

Yet, Padre Pio liked San Giovanni Rotondo even though it was so isolated and so poor. His first stay there lasted a week. Upon returning to Foggia, he wrote to his provincial superior asking him if he could return to San Giovanni Rotondo. "Jesus is calling me to do so," Padre Pio wrote. "He told me that I need to strengthen my body so that I will be ready for the other tests he wants me to undergo. There are other reasons that impel me to ask for this favor, and on these points silence is golden."

Fr. Benedetto granted Padre Pio his request. He left for San Giovanni Rotondo on September 4. He remained there until he died, except for a period of time when he served in the army.

Padre Pio was drafted on November 6, 1915, while he was still living in Pietrelcina. He reported to military headquarters in Benevento, and was assigned to the Tenth Company of the Italian Medical Corps in Naples. His assigned serial number was 2094/25. However, he continued to suffer from fevers, so he was granted a year's leave of absence for convalescence on December 10.

By December 8, 1916, when his leave was over, Padre Pio had been living for the past three months in San Giovanni Rotondo once again. He traveled to Naples, where he duly reported to military headquarters. Once again he had to undergo several long medical exams, and after two weeks he was sent home on leave for another six months. A notation was made in his military file that the leave of absence was extended for health reasons and "until further orders."

Since Padre Pio was accustomed to strict obedience, when the six months were over he quietly remained at the monastery, awaiting "new orders," which never arrived. Because of his scrupulosity, he was almost court-martialed on charges of desertion.

As it turned out, military authorities were waiting for Padre Pio to report back to headquarters in Naples. When he failed to show up, they declared him a deserter and a warrant for his arrest was issued. Since he was known as Francesco Forgione by the civil authorities, it never occurred to anyone at San Giovanni Rotondo that the skinny monk they knew as Padre Pio was a deserter. They discovered what had happened when a warrant officer suddenly showed up at the monastery to arrest Padre Pio. "My file says to wait for further orders, and I'm still waiting," Padre Pio protested. When he arrived in Naples, he repeated his story to the captain, who believed him and acquitted him on the spot.

This time, even though his health was still precarious, he was considered fit for duty and assigned to the barracks at Sales. He resigned himself to his fate, and for a few months he was, to all intents and purposes, a soldier.

Padre Pio often recalled this episode in his life and spoke about it good-naturedly. The friends from his army days later described him as a comrade-in-arms who was full of wit and good humor.

The first uniform that he wore was too large for him, mainly because he was so skinny. Feeling rather ridiculous in it, he often joked, "My mother made me a man; St. Francis a woman (alluding to his monk's habit); and the government a clown."

In Naples Padre Pio lived together with the other young recruits, who usually collaborated on different pranks. Fearing that the men would steal his clothes, Padre Pio would wear all of them at the same time: two shirts, two jackets, two coats, and so on. One day a nurse called him out of the blue: "Francesco Forgione, report for a medical exam." Padre Pio reported to the doctor, who told him to undress. He obeyed and peacefully began to take off his clothing. The doctor was both amazed and amused when he saw this strange soldier take off one coat and then another, one jacket and then another, one undershirt and then another. Finally he exclaimed, "Forgione, you're wearing enough clothing to stock a department store!"

While Padre Pio was a soldier in Naples, his father, Grazio Forgione, went to visit him. His wife prepared a bag of food for her son, filled with fresh eggs, olive oil, cheese, and some grapes plucked from the vines in Piana Romana. When Grazio arrived in Naples, he immediately went to Carolina del Mastro's *pensione*. Carolina del Mastro was from Pietrelcina, and all the people from the town stayed there when they went to Naples. Padre Pio joined his father there. Grazio was amazed to see his son arrive in a carriage. "What do you have left from the seventy-five cents you get for saying Mass if you spent fifty cents for a carriage and if you gave twenty-five cents to the sacristan?" he asked. Padre Pio reassured his father that he could allow himself the luxury of a carriage because he also celebrated Mass in a private chapel for which he received fifteen cents.

After lunch, the two men took a walk together so that they could pick up a pair of army boots that Padre Pio had dropped off for repair. Apparently some nails were bothering him whenever he walked in them. Grazio wanted to pay the cobbler for the repairs, but Padre Pio would not let him. "No," he said. "He kept the nails. They're worth five lire and that's already enough."

As Christmas approached, Padre Pio was granted a leave. He decided to return to San Giovanni Rotondo by way of Pietrelcina, so that he might spend a few days at home. He would often remember this trip, and would describe it in vivid detail. On one occasion, his story was recorded on tape and then transcribed. Although it is quite long, I would like to retell it in its entirety. It is a good example of how Padre Pio would describe events in his life.

In December of 1916, I was at the military hospital in Naples for observation. I was given a health leave. I was summoned to the captain's office at the hospital, where I was handed my papers and a free ticket from Naples to Benevento. I was also given one lira as a traveling allowance.

Leaving the hospital, I slowly made my way to the train station, passing through a *piazza* where there was a market. You've never seen anything if you haven't seen the markets in Naples, packed with happy people who are whistling and singing, who come and go in a never-ending state of chaos.

Out of curiosity, but also for a little distraction, I stopped for a while to see what people were selling. Then, as I was heading down the street to the train station, a man approached me who was selling paper umbrellas. He wanted one lira for them, but said he would take fifty cents. Immediately I thought: "Since I'm going home, I'd really like to take something for my little nieces and nephews. Each of them would like something." I decided to buy them some souvenirs, but I knew that I only had one lira. "If I spend it," I said to myself, "what will I do to get to Pietrelcina?"

I continued walking and arrived at the Piazza Garibaldi. There, more vendors were selling everything under the sun. I arrived at the station and went to the ticket window so that they could endorse my ticket. While I was walking to the tracks where the train would be departing, another man who was selling umbrellas approached me, saying, "Get your umbrellas now. See how beautiful they are? Hurry so you can get something for your children!"

I didn't pay attention to him, but he continued walking at my side, treating me first like I was a corporal and then like I was a captain, when, in fact, I was only a simple soldier. Seeing how excited the man was as he followed me, I turned to him and said, "I don't want anything. I have no use for them. Anyway, you're asking for a lira and a half while at the other market they were offering them for half a lira!" Since he was as stubborn as all the other street vendors, he said, "I have children. Help me out and buy some umbrellas." Handing me one, he said, "Out of love, take one as a souvenir for your loved ones." Still confronted with his banter, I asked, "You'll give it to me, then, for fifty cents?"

At that moment the whistle blew for the train to depart. I ran on board and looked out the window at that poor man who had wasted so much time and effort trying to sell me an umbrella so that he could take some bread home to his kids. I took fifty cents from my pocket and cried out: "Here, take this. May the Lord bless you." He was all excited and waved good-bye as the train left.

I was tired and burning up with a fever. I felt cold and wrapped my cape around me. The train got into Benevento rather late. As soon as I got off, I ran outside the station to catch a bus, but the bus to Pietrelcina had already left. So I had to spend the night in Benevento. I decided I'd stay in the train station so as not to bother my friends in Benevento.

I went back into the station and looked for a seat in the waiting room, but it was packed with people. At the same time, my fever was going up and I could hardly stand up anymore. When I got tired of sitting, I would walk around the station, both inside and out. The cold and the dampness penetrated my bones. I put up with these conditions for several hours. Often I was tempted to go into the coffee shop in the station since it was heated, but I was disappointed when I saw that it was filled with other soldiers and officers who were waiting for trains, and everyone was spending something for drinks.

I thought to myself: "I only have fifty cents on me and if I go in, what will I do?" I was feeling colder and colder all the time. I was still burning up with a fever. It was two o'clock in the morning and there still wasn't an inch of space in the waiting room where I could lie down on the ground. I offered up the whole thing to the Lord and to my heavenly Mother. Finally I couldn't stand it anymore and went into the coffee shop. All the tables were taken. But I waited for someone to leave so that I could sit down for a while. But no one got up. Around half past three, they announced that the train for Foggia and Naples was leaving. Finally a couple of tables were free, but because of my timidity, I didn't make it in time to get a seat. I thought, "Even if I sit down, I don't have enough money to spend on a coffee. And if I don't buy anything, what will the poor owner earn after sacrificing his whole night here?" Finally, when it was four o'clock, more trains arrived and, thanks be to God, two tables were free in a corner of the coffee shop.

I sat down in the corner, hoping that the waiter wouldn't notice me. I had only sat down for a few minutes when three officers sat at the table next to me. Right away the waiter came and took their order. Then he asked me what I wanted.

I, too, felt obliged to order a coffee. He served all four of us at the same time. The officers paid right away and left. I kept thinking: "If I drink it right away, I'll have to pay and go." But that coffee had to last me until the bus arrived. Every time the waiter wasn't looking, I would sit still. When he would look at me, I'd take my spoon and pretend that I was stirring some sugar in my coffee.

Finally, the time came for the bus to arrive. I got up. I also got up the courage to pay. In a kind voice the waiter told me, "Thank you, soldier, but everything's been paid for." Since the waiter was quite elderly, I thought, "Maybe he knows me and wants to be nice to me." Also the thought crossed my mind that maybe the officers paid for me.

In any case, I thanked the waiter and went outside the station. I found the place where the bus to Pietrelcina would be leaving. I looked around for someone I knew who might lend me the money for the ticket from Benevento to Pietrelcina, but in vain. The ticket cost a lira and eighty cents. "How will I pay with only fifty cents?" I asked myself.

Trusting in God, I got into the bus and sat down in the back so that I could talk with the ticket man and arrange to pay for the ticket when we arrived in Pietrelcina. At that moment, some other people got on. A very tall and handsome man sat down next to me. He had a new suitcase with him and set it on his knees. The bus was full, but I didn't see anyone I knew. I was afraid of embarrassing myself but I thought to myself, "Perhaps a lot of soldiers find themselves in my situation or worse. At least I have fifty cents." The bus left and the ticket man was taking the tickets of those people in the front of the bus. Slowly he made his way to me. The man next to me took a thermos and a cup out of his suitcase, and poured himself some hot coffee. Then he refilled the cup and offered me some coffee. I thanked him and tried to refuse it, but he insisted that I use the cup while he drank out of the thermos. At that moment the ticket man came up and asked us where we were going.

I didn't even have a chance to open my mouth when he said

to me, "Soldier, your ticket to Pietrelcina has been paid for." He handed me a ticket. On one hand, I was thrilled. But on the other hand I was mortified. "Who paid for it?" I asked myself. I wanted to know so that I could thank that person at least. I asked God to bless that person for his good deed. Finally we got to Pietrelcina. A few people got off. The man who sat next to me got off before me. I followed him off the bus and turned around to say farewell and to thank him. But I didn't see him again. He disappeared as if by magic. I looked around in every direction as I walked home, but I never saw him again.

Padre Pio returned to army headquarters in Naples on March 6. The doctors carefully examined him and found that his state of health was even worse. He was suffering from double pneumonia. On March 17 he was permanently discharged from the army and sent home.

EIGHT

September 20, 1918

W hen Padre Pio's army days came to an end, he was sent permanently to San Giovanni Rotondo. There he was assigned to be the spiritual director of the minor seminary that was annexed to the monastery. This seminary received boys from the region who were thinking of joining the religious life. At that time there were about fifteen boys at the seminary. Padre Pio was enthusiastic about his new assignment, and was very committed to it.

Even though he was living in such an isolated place, people managed to make it there so that they might seek his advice. They even came from far away. Other people wrote to him for advice. Padre Pio's days were always full, so the only time he could reply to the letters was at night. He noted in his letters that he would work about seventeen hours a day.

It was up there, in a monastery on that barren and deserted mountain in a poor and insignificant town, that one of the greatest mystical events of our time occurred: Jesus' wounds were imprinted on the hands and feet of the poor Capuchin friar known as Padre Pio.

In Christianity the stigmata are phenomena whereby the five wounds of Christ are imprinted either in whole or in part on some holy person. So far about three hundred cases are recorded in history where people received the stigmata. The first recorded case was that of St. Francis of Assisi, who received the stigmata in 1224. Among more recent cases, those of Anne Catherine Emmerich, St. Gemma Galgani, and Theresa Neumann are most widely known. To the present, Padre Pio is the only priest to receive the stigmata.

Professor Michele Capuano has written a description of the stigmata: "Anatomically the stigmata are genuine lacerations of the soft tissue that are not produced by external agents or by disease, and that manifest themselves in an unforeseen way in predetermined places on the body. They appear suddenly and unexpectedly, and are preceded and accompanied by hemorrhaging and by acute physical and moral pain.

"They are not subject to infection or decomposition, do not result in the death of any living tissue, do not emit any foul odors, do not change, do not form any scar tissue, and remain unchanged for years and years, against all biological laws of nature."

As we have already noted, Padre Pio first experienced this mystical phenomenon in September of 1910, after he was ordained to the priesthood. At that time he begged God to "take away these confusing things." The Lord answered his prayer. The visible signs of Jesus' passion were removed from his body, but the suffering continued. Padre Pio had already been living with this suffering for more than eight years. Now, in this isolated spot whose peace and tranquility were conducive to meditation, something else was about to happen.

On August 5, 1918, while he was hearing the confessions of his seminary students, Padre Pio had a mystical experience that he described in the following terms to his spiritual director: "I was filled with extreme terror at the sight of a heavenly Being who presented himself to the eye of my intellect. In his hand he held some kind of weapon, like a long, sharp-pointed steel blade, which seemed to spew out fire. This Being hurled this weapon into my soul with all his might. It was only with difficulty that I did not cry out. I thought I was dying. I told the boy whose confession I was hearing to leave because I wasn't feeling good and I didn't have enough strength to continue. This agony lasted uninterruptedly until the morning of August 7. I can't describe how much I suffered during this period of anguish. Even my internal organs were torn and ruptured by that weapon. Since that day I have been mortally wounded. I always feel in the depths of my soul a wound that is always open and that causes me continual agony."

The pain that resulted from this mystical experience was very intense. At times it was so intense that Padre Pio begged God to let him die. During that time he wrote to his spiritual director: "The wound is so painful that it is enough to cause one thousand and one deaths. Oh my God, why don't I die? Are you without any mercy? Do you turn a deaf ear to the cries of those who suffer and are not comforted? Please forgive me, Father, I am beside myself and I don't know what I am saying. So much pain causes me to be frantic, much against my will."

But was it a "mystical" wound or a real one? In a letter dated September 5 to his confessor, Padre Pio speaks about a "bleeding wound." He wrote: "The wound that opened up once again is bleeding and continues to bleed.... The intense pain that the open wound causes leaves me feeling frantic and like I'm losing my mind, to the point of delirium." Most likely Padre Pio is describing a wound on his side, which he managed to hide from his fellow monks until September 20, when wounds also appeared on his feet and his hands.

On that morning, the monastery was more deserted than usual. The superior had gone to San Marco in Lamis. Brother Nicola, who was a mendicant monk, was out making his rounds. The students were playing in the courtyard. Padre Pio was alone in church for his thanksgiving after Mass. He was kneeling in the choir, which was on an elevated platform in front of the main altar. He was sitting in the seat in the middle of the last row. In front of him, hoisted up on the balustrade of the choir, was a large crucifix made out of cypress by an unknown sculptor from the seventh century. This cross is still visible in the Capuchin church in San Giovanni Rotondo. The dying Christ has a very sorrowful expression. His eyes are open and his mouth is drawn with pain. Blood is flowing abundantly from his head and from the wounds in the hands, feet, and side.

In those days people all over Europe were grieving from the loss of so many victims to World War I, which was waging on various fronts, and to the Spanish influenza epidemic that was decimating Europe's population. Perhaps Padre Pio, who was very sensitive to suffering, was praying for all these dead or dying people. At a certain moment, something very mysterious occurred. Since there was no one else in the church, there are no witnesses to what happened. But this is how Padre Pio described it a month later to his spiritual director.

"I was sitting in the choir, after celebrating Holy Mass, when I was overtaken by a repose, similar to a deep sleep. All of my senses, both internal and external, as well as the faculties of my soul were steeped in an indescribable peace. As I was in this state, I saw before my very eyes a mysterious Being similar to the one that I saw on the evening of August 5, with the main difference being that this one had blood dripping from his hands, feet, and side. His look frightened me. I experienced something that I don't know how to describe. I felt like I was dying, and I would have died if the Lord had not intervened to strengthen my heart, which was ready to burst out of my chest.

"When the mysterious creature left, I found that my hands, feet, and side had been pierced and were bleeding. Imagine the anguish that I experienced at that moment and that I have been experiencing continually since then. The wound in my heart bleeds continuously, especially from Thursday evening until Saturday. I'm afraid that I will bleed to death if the Lord doesn't hear my groans and take these wounds away from me. He can even leave the anguish and the pain, but let him take away these visible signs that are a source of embarrassment for me and an indescribable and unbearable humiliation."

This letter is dated October 22, 1918. Padre Pio waited thirty-two days before deciding to tell his spiritual director what had happened to him. He even tried hiding the wounds from the monks of the monastery. But it was not an easy thing to do.

From the testimony of the monks that were living at San Giovanni Rotondo at that time, we know that after receiving the stigmata Padre Pio would drag himself laboriously from the church to his cell, leaving spots of blood in the corridor. He tried to stop the hemorrhaging by wrapping his hands and feet with bandages, and covering the wound in his side with handkerchiefs. But his fellow monks could not help but notice the bandages, and the superior of the convent, Fr. Paolino, wanted to know what had happened. Padre Pio was forced to show him the wounds. Fr. Paolino immediately informed the provincial superior, who ordered him to keep what had happened a secret until he arrived. He, too, examined the mysterious wounds, and not knowing what to do, wrote to the superior general, telling him among other things: "They are not stains or marks, but true wounds perforating his hands and feet. The one in his side is truly a deep gash, and it bleeds continually."

The superior general also gave orders that the monks keep what had happened a secret, and to follow the course of these events with utmost prudence.

NINE

The Doctors and the Stigmatic

Even though Padre Pio and his superiors were careful not to speak about his stigmata, news about the "monk with the stigmata" slowly spread. Padre Pio's wounds tended to bleed when he was celebrating Mass and were clearly visible to those present. Beginning in 1919, people began to arrive from the surrounding countryside. Then news about the stigmata spread throughout Italy and abroad, resulting in an influx of pilgrims wishing to see Padre Pio.

Renato Trevisiani was the first journalist to arrive in San Giovanni Rotondo, sent by a newspaper in Naples called *Mattino*. He wrote a lengthy article on Padre Pio, in which he proclaimed him the "saint" of San Giovanni Rotondo and described how he had performed a miracle on a local government official.

It was as though a bomb exploded. Other journalists began to arrive. At first, some rather amazing conversions and "miracles" were attributed to the "saint with the stigmata." Then, skeptics began to challenge these reports. At this point, Padre Pio's Capuchin superiors felt that a medical examination of his unusual wounds was needed in order to respond to these growing attacks against Padre Pio and the entire monastic community at San Giovanni Rotondo.

Dr. Luigi Romanelli, physician-in-chief at the hospital in Barletta, first examined Padre Pio's stigmata on May 15 and 16, 1919, at the request of Padre Pio's provincial superior. He described the wounds in his report:

> The lesions on his hands are covered with a membrane that is reddish-brown in color, without any bleeding, swelling, or

inflammation of the surrounding tissue. I am convinced without a doubt that the wounds are not just superficial. When I press together my thumb on the palm of his hand and my index finger on the back of his hand, I clearly perceive that a vacuum exists between them.

The lesions on his feet have the same characteristics as those on his hands. I have also noticed a visible cut in his side that is parallel to the ribs and that is three inches long, penetrating the soft tissue. As in any wound to the thorax, it is impossible to ascertain how deep the wound penetrates and what direction it takes in the chest cavity. The wound is bleeding profusely, and the blood is arterial blood.

Two months later, on July 26, Dr. Amico Bignami, a professor of pathology at the University of Rome, was sent to San Giovanni Rotondo by Church authorities to study the wounds. Dr. Bignami conducted his examination over a period of one week. His observations matched those of Dr. Romanelli, and he expressed his own profound admiration for Padre Pio. Since he was a proclaimed atheist, his conclusions were consistent with his own beliefs. In his opinion, he felt the stigmata were a product of a "morbid state," and involved "multiple neurotic necrosis of the skin, perhaps unconsciously caused by a phenomenon of suggestion, artificially maintained by some chemical means, such as iodine."

Dr. Romanelli rejected Dr. Bignami's statements, repeated his examination of Padre Pio, and formulated a new report that repudiated Dr.Bignami's theories point by point. Dr. Romanelli observed:

After almost sixteen months, I have observed some changes in the lesions, of varying degrees of significance. These changes do not affect either their importance or their nature....

The lesions on Padre Pio's hands, which are now covered with scabs and which are bleeding in some places, were covered by a swollen membrane that was reddish-brown in color when I examined him in June and July of 1919. There was no bleeding, swelling, or inflammation of the surrounding tissue.

Scientifically wounds heal if they are treated in the right way, or present complications if they are treated badly. Now, how can a person scientifically explain why Padre Pio's wounds, which have not been treated using any scientific norms, do not present any complications? In my own presence I have seen him wash his wounds, especially those on his hands, in water that is anything but sterile. He covers them with ordinary wool gloves or with unsterile bandages from the cupboard. They are washed with soap of the poorest quality. Yet, they do not fester, do not present any complications, nor do they heal. I have examined Padre Pio some five times in fifteen months. I have not found any significant changes, and I have not found any clinical report that would enable me to classify these wounds....

Together with Dr. Romanelli, Dr. Giorgio Festa also made a long and in-depth study, which he published shortly thereafter in a lengthy volume entitled *Mysteries of Science and the Light of Faith*. Dr. Festa challenged Dr. Bignami's hypotheses: "The lesions, once they were produced and in whatever way they were produced, should have followed the laws of nature and formed scar tissue. If not, some type of necrosis would certainly have occurred given the fact that they would inevitably be infected by germs."

Dr. Bignami's argument was contradicted by a test that he himself ordered. The illustrious scientist maintained that if Padre Pio were not allowed to use iodine on his wounds for a week as a disinfectant, the wounds would heal up. Padre Pio's provincial superior chose three monks and made them promise under oath to inspect Padre Pio's wounds each day, and wrap them with new bandages which they would seal in such a way that no one else could touch them. The experiment was carried out with the utmost diligence. At the end of the week, instead of being closed, the wounds were bleeding more than ever. Fr. Paolino of Casacalenda, one of the three witnesses, wrote: "The last day, when Padre Pio's bandages were taken off for good, so much blood was dripping from his hands when he was celebrating Mass that we had to send for some rags to wipe up the blood."

After Dr. Bignami's visit, Fr. Agostino Gemelli, the distinguished founder of the Catholic University in Rome, arrived in San Giovanni Rotondo to visit Padre Pio. Afterward, Fr. Gemelli expressed his doubts whether Padre Pio's stigmata were genuine. His evaluation had a negative influence on people's opinions, both in Catholic and secular circles, for many years to follow. Fr. Gemelli was often quoted in articles, books, and radio and television interviews on Padre Pio.

In 1920, Fr. Agostino Gemelli was thirty-two years old. He was a convert to Catholicism. With a degree in medicine and psychology, he was held in high esteem. Being a physician, psychologist, and theologian, he was very qualified to make a judgment. However, his visit with Padre Pio has been challenged historically.

Fr. Gemelli did indeed go to San Giovanni Rotondo on April 18, 1920. In fact, his signature appears in the guest book of the monastery. He was accompanied by Armida Barelli. Fr. Benedetto of San Marco in Lamis was an eyewitness to his visit and knew how it turned out:

> Everything that I write, I write with absolute certainly as if it happened yesterday, and I can confirm it under oath if need be.
>
> Fr. Gemelli wrote to the provincial superior, Fr. Pietro, asking him for permission to visit San Giovanni. Fr. Pietro replied that if he intended to observe Padre Pio as a scientist, then he had to ask Rome for permission to do so. Gemelli answered that he was only going there for private, spiritual purposes.
>
> I happened to be in Foggia myself on that very day while I was en route to San Giovanni Rotondo, and Fr. Pietro read me Gemelli's response on a postcard, and asked me to wait until the next day to continue my trip so I might accompany the illustrious priest to San Giovanni Rotondo.

Gemelli arrived in the evening and did not express any desire to visit Padre Pio in his capacity as a doctor. The next day, together with the vicar general, Fr. Gerardo, the secretary of the province of Foggia, and the superior of the Friars Minor, we accompanied Fr. Gemelli and Armida Barelli to San Giovanni Rotondo. Armida Barelli asked to speak with Padre Pio. In my presence, she asked him whether the Lord had blessed future plans for the Catholic university. Padre Pio answered with a single word: "Yes."

The next day, Miss Barelli began to press me to let Gemelli examine Padre Pio's wounds. I told her that I could not authorize him to do so because I had been clearly ordered not to subject Padre Pio to such a mortifying experience. Moreover, Gemelli did not have permission from Rome to do so and had already stated that he did not come with such a purpose in mind. Miss Barelli insisted over and over again, but I simply repeated that I could not allow him to do so.

Having given up on the idea of examining Padre Pio, Gemelli asked to speak to him. The conversation took place in the sacristy and lasted a few minutes. I stood in the corner and I had the impression that Padre Pio was trying to get rid of him because Gemelli was annoying him.

From Fr. Benedetto's detailed testimony, it is clear that Gemelli did not examine nor did he see Padre Pio's wounds. Nonetheless, several months later rumors were circulating that he had written a "terrible report" afterward. There is no trace of this report, even though many people have cited it.

Nonetheless, this report has been the source of controversy over the years. This controversy has also been fueled by some strange statements that Gemelli himself later made. At one point he made the following claim: "Church authorities, who shall remain unnamed, entrusted me with the responsibility to conduct an investigation. I have sent my reports to these Church authorities." On another occasion he also affirmed: "I accurately examined Padre Pio and his stigmata. The provincial superior was present during this examination." From a historical point of view, there is no documentation to verify Fr. Gemelli's claims. Neither does he say when, where, or how he examined Padre Pio's stigmata. And we know that he went only one time to San Giovanni Rotondo. Ultimately those authorities who are responsible for Padre Pio's beatification will have to verify these claims.

Fr. Gemelli was ambivalent about his claims in following years. He met Dr. Festa in Rome in 1921, and the two men discussed Padre Pio's stigmata. Gemelli seemed interested in pursuing the discussion and set up an appointment with Dr. Festa, but it never took place. Later Dr. Festa recalled his meeting with Fr. Gemelli:

A particular priest and doctor, Fr. Gemelli of the Order of Friars Minor, came to San Giovanni Rotondo some time before my second examination of Padre Pio's stigmata, intending to examine Padre Pio. Since he did not have necessary authorization from Padre Pio's superiors to do so, he was not allowed to examine the wounds. He only had a short conversation with Padre Pio. In fact, Padre Pio himself cut off his conversation with him after a few minutes. His demeanor was in stark contrast with his usual gentlemanly, humble, and sweet demeanor, even though he was still humble and meek. Some time later, in September of 1921 to be exact, on the occasion of the celebration of the centennial of the Third Order Franciscans in Ara Coeli, the superior of the tertiaries there introduced me to Fr. Gemelli, who was also present. He told Fr. Gemelli that I had been entrusted by the General Curia of the Order to examine and study Padre Pio on two different occasions. This seemed to pique his interest, and the next day we had a long and exhaustive conversation on this topic. From our conversation I could see why Padre Pio behaved toward him like he did. Undoubtedly he sensed that Fr. Gemelli visited him with the preconceived idea that he would be meeting a neuropathic individual face to face, and with the presumption that he would be able to cure him with his knowledge of psychology....

I could clearly perceive this in Fr. Gemelli's thoughts. He ventured to express an *a priori* opinion without having any knowledge of the anatomical and pathological nature and conditions of Padre Pio's wounds that we observed in our study, and without having had the opportunity of performing even the most basic tests on him. I informed him about the real condition of Padre Pio's lesions. I argued through clear scientific deductions that these lesions were not characteristic of any disease, psychopathic condition, or auto-suggestion. I also had him read some documents that at least demonstrated the superiority of this soul. He was so impressed and so moved that he said the following words to me: "Dear doctor, I have to leave for Milan this evening, but I will return in a few days. Please allow me to stay at your house with you when I return, so no one will disturb us and we can continue our discussion. From everything you have told me and shown me, this is without a doubt a topic of great interest for me too."

In the following days and following months, I waited for Fr. Gemelli to return, but he never came. I can understand and justify his failure to do so. I never asked to see him again. He requested such a meeting on his own. I can also justify his failure to do so given the many duties he had to attend to. From everything that I have written, however, it is clear how superficially he related to such an important matter. Nonetheless, he still wants to make a verdict on it without having ever examined Padre Pio.

In 1924, on the occasion of the seventh centennial of the stigmata of St. Francis of Assisi, Fr. Gemelli published a lengthy article in *Vita e Pensiero* in which he maintained that the only true stigmatic in the Church was St. Francis of Assisi. With some reservations he also mentioned St. Catherine of Siena. All of the others "were only the products of hysteria." His article clearly was an attack on Padre Pio. The article was supposed to be the first in a long series. Fr. Gervasio Celi, a Jesuit priest, immediately replied to this attack by publishing a commentary in his magazine, *La Civilta Cattolica,* saying that Gemelli's statements were "inexact and imprudent." He reminded readers that the Church canonized some sixty other stigmatics after St. Francis, and announced that some articles critical of Gemelli's theses were forthcoming. The founder of the Catholic University probably feared such criticism, and took advantage of his friendship with Pope Pius XI to stop these articles from being published. Even though Fr. Celi announced that they would be published, the articles were never printed.

On December 15, 1924, Dr. Giorgio Festa asked Church authorities for permission to conduct a new clinical examination of Padre Pio as part of an updated study, but did not obtain permission to do so. However, he was able to examine Padre Pio's wounds once again on October 5, 1925. This occurred during an operation on Padre Pio for an inguinal hernia.

In his book *Mysteries of Science and Light of Faith,* Dr. Festa wrote:

I waited for Padre Pio to return from the Mass that he was celebrating on the morning of October 5 in the little church in the monastery.

When we saw him, he was walking slowly. He was pale from the fatigue he was suffering, as well as the physical pain that his wounds and his hernia were causing him. When he saw me, he said: "Dear doctor, I place myself in your hands, but please don't use chloroform on me." My strong opposition to his request was all in vain, as were my thoughts of a more technical nature. He remained steadfast in his wishes, assuring me that he would not budge from the position that we put him in. Then he added: "After giving me the chloroform, are you prepared not to examine my wounds that others have studied?" With all honesty I answered: "No, Father. This has truly been my desire for a long time and it seems as if I should have the satisfaction of fulfilling it after so long." Padre Pio answered me with these words: "See why I'm right in refusing anesthesia. No one has prohibited me personally from being examined by you or by others. I know, however, that this order was given to my superiors and it's my duty to do whatever I can to see that it is respected. It is for this reason that I intend to remain in control of my acts and my will during the operation."

As one might expect, in spite of his strong will during the operation that lasted almost two hours, Padre Pio went into a state of intense shock, during which he was unconscious at various times. During one of those moments, I reexamined without his knowledge the five wounds that I had been able to study some five years earlier. Even then they had the identical characteristics that I described in my first reports.

After this operation, no doctor officially examined Padre Pio's stigmata again. However, the wounds were seen by thousands of people because Padre Pio celebrated Mass for years without wearing gloves. Moreover, his fellow monks were able to observe them every day.

TEN

A Yes and a No From the Vatican

Padre Pio's stigmata were a source of fame and they were also his heaviest cross. His stigmata drew crowds of curious visitors from around the world. His stigmata also piqued the interest of scientists, doctors, theologians, bishops, cardinals, and pontiffs. They were the subject of much controversy. They divided people into followers or foes of Padre Pio.

Because of his stigmata, Padre Pio was suspected of being a swindler, a hoax, a neurotic, and a victim of obsession. Not only nonbelievers and atheists harbored such suspicions. Some of his fellow monks, superiors, and certain Church officials felt the same way. At one point Padre Pio was condemned by the Holy Office (now known as the Congregation of the Doctrine of the Faith, the Vatican office responsible for overseeing questions of faith and morals). He also had restrictions placed on his freedom to carry out his ministry. This suspicion and doubt persisted until his death, and for years afterward. Today his stigmata remain an enigma for many people.

There were some people who looked forward to examining him after his death, since an autopsy would be able to establish whether the wound on his side was deep enough to touch the heart, as some people maintained, or was only a superficial skin wound. However, his death shed no light on the matter. The mysterious wounds disappeared completely when he died. The skin on his hands, feet, and side, where the wounds that bled for fifty years were located, healed without leaving any scars.

But let us return to Padre Pio's story, and the events in his life in the years following September 20, 1918. We have already observed the reaction of his fellow monks to his mysterious wounds and the opinions of those doctors who were responsible for making a scientific evaluation. But how did the Church react?

It is important to remember that the Church, while generally recognizing the supernatural origins of the stigmata, has always been very prudent when evaluating an individual case, and has never made a judgment while the stigmatic was still alive.

Since Padre Pio's stigmata were so well known, it was only natural that the Church would be interested in them and would want to determine the nature of this phenomenon. In 1920 Pope Benedict XV sent his personal physician, Dr. Giuseppe Bastianelli, to examine Padre Pio and his stigmata. He was accompanied by Fr. Luigi Besi, the attorney general for the Passionist Fathers. Upon their return to Rome, the two men expressed their high esteem and great admiration for Padre Pio to the pope.

Shortly thereafter, the pope sent Archbishop Anselm Edward John Kenealy of Simla (India), Archbishop Giovanni Antonio Zucchetto of Smyrna, and Fr. Antonio of Tesson to San Giovanni Rotondo. They, too, interviewed Padre Pio at length and examined the stigmata. Upon returning, they also made enthusiastic reports to the pope.

Before returning to his diocese, Archbishop Kenealy wrote down a rather extraordinary testimony giving his impressions of Padre Pio:

I wanted to see Padre Pio's stigmata at any cost, not because I doubted the word of the many people who had seen them, but simply because, except for dogmas of the faith, I am rather slow in believing extraordinary things without seeing them with my own eyes.

I went to San Giovanni Rotondo on March 24, 1920, accompanied by Archbishop Zuchetto, who is now in Trebisonda but who was in Smyrna then, and by Fr. Antonio of Tesson and Fr. Pietro, the provincial superior. *Veni, vidi, victus sum!* I examined the stigmata at length. I returned from San Giovanni Rotondo and from Foggia deeply convinced that, from what I saw and experienced, we have a true saint there. He has been singularly blessed by the Lord with the five wounds of his passion, along with some other gifts that he has been freely given that we normally read about in the lives of the great saints. I did not observe the slightest affectation either in Padre Pio's manner or in his speech. He is an observant and industrious man. The Lord has given him great gifts, but he is, nonetheless, completely at ease. If he knows how to suffer, he also knows how to laugh. I am persuaded that within a short time the Holy See will have the fortunate gift of examining Padre Pio's life, gifts, and work for the purpose of writing his dear name among those of the most privileged saints of God's Church, and that the humble Capuchin Order will have the glory of counting among its members this humble Franciscan priest with the stigmata, the first one after St. Francis. Foggia, March 27, 1920—Most Reverend Anselm Edward J. Kenealy, Archbishop of Simla.

The pope was not satisfied, so he sent to San Giovanni Rotondo Archbishop Bonaventura Cerretti of Corinth, the Secretary of Extraordinary Ecclesiastical Affairs at the Vatican. Archbishop Cerretti spent a few days at the monastery in San Giovanni Rotondo, where he spoke at length with Padre Pio and examined his wounds. He, too, was deeply impressed and gave the pope a very positive evalutation.

Reassured by such authorities, Pope Benedict XV spoke favorably about Padre Pio on several occasions. On December 27, 1921, he told Cesare Festa, a lawyer whom Padre Pio had been instrumental in converting from the Freemasons: "Padre Pio is truly a man of God. Some people have doubted this, but you help make him known." During a private audience in 1921, he told Msgr. Ferdinando Damiani, the vicar general of the Diocese of Salto in Uruguay, "Padre Pio is truly an extraordinary man, the like of whom God sends to earth from time to time for the purpose of converting men." From 1919 to 1921, Cardinal Augusto Silj visited San Giovanni Rotondo on several occasions, accompanied by various priests. Each time he would return to Rome more enthusiastic than the time before, and expressed his favorable opinion of Padre Pio to other cardinals, bishops, and even the pope himself.

The first impressions of many important Church figures were very positive. But trouble began when Pope Benedict XV died and Cardinal Achille Ratti, who assumed the name of Pope Pius XI, was elected as pope.

Although Pope Pius XI was not prejudiced at first, he had received some false information which led him to form some negatives opinions regarding Padre Pio's charisms. Padre Pio's critics began to send anonymous letters to the Holy See, accusing Padre Pio of being a "dangerous hoax" and a "corrupter of morals." The Archbishop of Manfredonia, Pasquale Gagliardi, visited the pope to inform him that he had seen Padre Pio's stigmata and, in his opinion, they were caused by a combination of iodine and nitric acid. "With my own eyes I saw Padre Pio," he affirmed, "put makeup on his face and perfume himself as he prepared to face the people. I swear this is true on my pectoral cross."

After the death of Pope Benedict XV, the Holy Office began to believe such accusations. In fact, on June 2, 1922, four months after Pope Pius XI's reign began, the Holy Office sent a stern letter to the superior general of the Capuchins regarding Padre Pio, imposing the first severe restrictions: "We find it necessary to put Padre Pio under observation to avoid rumors about him. He should not celebrate Mass at any set time but at random times, preferably *summa mane* and in private. He should not give people a blessing. He should not show people his alleged stigmata, speak about them, or let people kiss them. He should openly declare in word and in deed, both to his fellow monks and to strangers, his firm desire to be left alone and to tend to his own sanctification.

"Furthermore, we consider it wise that Padre Pio have a spiritual director other than Fr. Benedetto of San Marco in Lamis, and that he discontinue any contact with him, including all correspondence.

"In order to carry out these orders, Padre Pio should be moved from San Giovanni Rotondo and relocated to a place outside his religious province, in a monastery in Northern Italy, for example. This move should take place immediately. However, since some difficulties of a local nature might prevent such an immediate move, steps should be taken to prepare the move so that it might take place as soon as it is convenient to do so.

"Also, Fr. Benedetto must abstain from speaking or writing about Padre Pio, and from maintaining any communication with him, even through correspondence."

Thus, the first large-scale persecution of Padre Pio, the Capuchin friar with the stigmata, started. It ended, as we will see, in an astonishing way in 1933.

ELEVEN

The First Persecution

M uch has been written and said about Padre Pio's enemies and the persecutions that he had to endure. Some people claim that these persecutions never existed, except in the minds of his somewhat fanatical followers. Padre Pio himself signed a document on December 16, 1964, which stated that he had never been subjected to any kind of persecution in his entire life. However, Padre Pio was compelled out of "holy obedience" to copy and sign the letter in question when authorities both in the Church and the Capuchin Order sought to save face.

There is no doubt that Padre Pio suffered persecution during his entire life. He was defamed by vulgar accusations and accused of being a vile swindler. He was punished and imprisoned. He died without having ever been officially rehabilitated. When he died, his name was still on the list of people condemned by the Holy Office. Any attempt to deny these facts would amount to censorship, and would do Padre Pio one more wrong. His love, his goodness, his heroic virtue, and above all, his holiness stand out precisely because he never complained and never criticized anyone even though he was persecuted by his "family"—some representatives of the Church and some of his fellow monks.

Cardinal Giacomo Lecaro, commemorating Padre Pio after he had died, said:

> Indeed, the world around him was small and restricted. Now and then, in times of intense persecution, it was like the world of a prisoner,... the world of the poorest of the poor,... the world of those who never breathe fresh air, who never enjoy the birds and the flowers.... Padre Pio's resemblance to Christ shines out

mainly in his suffering.... His life was a passion and the similarities to the suffering of our Savior are all too evident, beginning with the unbelief and persecution of those who could have and should have been able to understand.

In his passion, Padre Pio experienced moments of particular intensity. The first one occurred when his name began to be more widely known—when the austerity of his humble life, the zeal of his words and his hidden ministry disturbed some unworthy pastors and provoked a crisis in the Church of Manfredonia.

Unfortunately, these poor souls, who felt threatened by such a pure and holy man, found a ready audience when they denounced the humble monk as a hypocritical exhibitionist, and denounced the charismatic gifts that evoked so much faith from his followers as deceptive and fraudulent.

His condemnation by higher authorities, and the judgment that followed (which was never defended by an objective investigation) made him all the more ready to obey, as would future decisions by the authorities....

Cardinal Giuseppe Siri, commemorating Padre Pio in St. Catherine's Church in Genoa on the fourth anniversary of his death on September 13, 1972, noted: "The ones who should have first recognized Jesus Christ are those who sentenced him to be crucified. The same thing happened also to Padre Pio.... He was made an outcast, stripped of his duties, and isolated to the point where he was forbidden to communicate with other people...."

In the letter that the Holy Office sent to the superior general of the Capuchins on June 2, 1922, it was suggested that Padre Pio be transferred from San Giovanni Rotondo. This was not the first time that such a move was contemplated. Padre Pio's superiors considered moving him at the end of 1919 in an attempt to contain the enthusiasm of the crowds, but it was difficult to implement the idea at the time. The people of San Giovanni Rotondo considered Padre Pio to be a precious commodity in their community, and were prepared to defend him by whatever means possible.

One of the main protagonists in the struggle to keep Padre Pio in San Giovanni Rotondo during those years was Francesco Morcaldi, a friend of Padre Pio and a longtime mayor of the town. I met him in 1969, when he was eighty years old. His mind was still very lucid, and he remembered in detail the events of so long ago, partly because he had also written a series of reports on them. Morcaldi told me that in 1919, when rumors were first heard about transferring Padre Pio, the people of the town went *en masse* to the monastery so that Padre Pio himself could assure them that he would never leave.

In the summer of 1920, these rumors surfaced again and were circulating among the people. Their reaction was instant. This time the crowd was even more angry and threatening because people were beginning to perceive the injustices that Padre Pio had to suffer.

The district police inspector was dispatched with the head of the local police force and some policemen to stem the angry crowd. But when the crowd threatened him, he begged Padre Pio to come out and reassure the crowd with his presence. The archbishop of Manfredonia also came to San Giovanni Rotondo to reassure the people that Padre Pio would never leave, and went to the monastery to pay him his respects. No one suspected at the time that the archbishop himself was the main person who was making accusations against Padre Pio.

In 1922, some new restrictions were placed on Padre Pio, and once again there was a popular uprising.

One morning, when Padre Pio finished celebrating Mass, a group of young people flocked to the sacristy afterward. One of them held a revolver to Padre Pio's back and said: "I would rather have him be dead here in San Giovanni Rotondo than leave us." Undoubtedly, it was a rather foolish display of loyalty, but it demonstrated how angry the people were.

In the summer of 1923, rumors about Padre Pio's transfer surfaced again. On the morning of June 25, Padre Pio did not show up at the church. He had received the order to celebrate Mass behind closed doors in an inner chapel within the monastery, without anyone in attendance. The faithful, who saw the sacristan arrive at the church alone, his eyes filled with tears, heard about this new order. News traveled through the countryside. Within a short time all the inhabitants of San Giovanni Rotondo, led by the town officials and the local band, were making their way to the monastery.

It was an explosive demonstration of love. The streets, the piazza, and the church were swarming with people. The entire town was there, including women and children. The superior of the monastery capitulated to their demands and promised that Padre Pio would return the following day. However, the people refused to believe him. They constructed barricades so that no one could enter the monastery. Armed guards took turns watching the monastery night and day.

Finally, a committee was elected to go to Rome and negotiate with Church authorities. On July 1, 1923, the committee members left for Rome. They included the town's political secretary, the head of the voluntary national police corps, the president of the Congregation of Charity, a representative of the town's businessmen, and the mayor, Francesco Morcaldi. The committee also included representatives from the towns of Monte Sant'Angelo, San Marco in Lamis, and Apricena.

"Cardinal Gasparri, the Secretary of State, Cardinal Lega of the Holy Office, and Cardinal Sbarretti, Prefect of the Congregation of the Council, received us very cordially," Morcaldi recalled.

However, we did not see Cardinal Merry del Val, Secretary of the Holy Office. Our mission did not obtain any positive results.

Returning home, some very confidential information was waiting for me. I learned that Padre Pio's move was now very imminent. I went to the prefecture in Foggia where the news was confirmed. With a heavy heart, I went immediately to the monastery at San Giovanni Rotondo. I found Padre Pio alone in the sacristy, leaning on a window that glowed with the light from the setting sun. He was very pale. I realized that he was suffering even more than me. "Are you leaving your people for good, Padre Pio?" I asked. He opened his arms, and embracing each other, we cried together. "Locked up, tormented, and who knows where? And will you leave in the night with the police?" I asked. "If those are the orders," Padre Pio answered, "I can only obey the decision of my superiors. I am committed to being an obedient son."

Two days later Padre Pio sent me the following letter: "The events that have unfolded in these recent days have profoundly troubled me because they give reason to fear that I might be the unwilling cause of some grievous events in this my beloved town. I pray to God that he might prevent such a catastrophe by pouring upon me some kind of mortification. As you know, the decision has been made to transfer me. I beg you to find the proper means to bring it about, since the will of my superiors, which is the will of God, must be carried out, and I will blindly obey. I will always remember you, such generous people, in my poor but earnest prayers, interceding for your peace and prosperity, as a token of my love for you, which is all that I have. I hereby express my desire, if my superiors do not oppose it, that my mortal remains will be buried in this tranquil corner of the earth. Respectfully yours in the Lord, Padre Pio of Pietrelcina."

Accusations against Padre Pio continued to flow into the Vatican, some of which must have come from very influential people because officials there believed them. Since Fr. Agostino Gemelli was a consultant to the Holy Office, his evaluations of Padre Pio contributed a great deal to the negative decisions that this supreme tribunal of the Church often made.

On May 31, 1923, the Holy Office issued its first decree against Padre Pio: "The Supreme Congregation of the Holy Office, responsible for upholding the faith and defending morals, held an inquiry on the phenomena attributed to Padre Pio of Pietrelcina, a member of the Friars Minor of the Capuchins at the Monastery of San Giovanni Rotondo in the Diocese of Foggia, and declares that it cannot confirm from this inquiry any basis for the supernatural character of these phenomena, and exhorts the faithful to conform their practices to this declaration."

The decree was published in *L'Osservatore Romano* of July 5, 1923, and reprinted in newspapers around the world. By issuing this document, the Church unambiguously decreed that Padre Pio's stigmata were unrelated to the wounds of Christ, thereby giving credence to the story that Padre Pio was a poor, sick man or a hoax.

The superior of the monastery of San Giovanni Rotondo did not have the courage to inform Padre Pio about this decree. He hid the issue of *L'Osservatore Romano* in which it was published. But a few days later, when the latest issue of the Capuchin magazine *Analecta Cappucinorum* arrived, the text of the decree in Latin was reprinted there. As usual, the magazine was placed on the table in the room where the monks gathered together for recreation. When the superior noticed that Padre Pio was not there yet and heard him coming, he shoved the magazine to a corner of the table. But when Padre Pio entered the room, he took the magazine and opened it to the page where the decree was reprinted and read it carefully. His face did not show the slightest emotion. Having finished reading it, he put the magazine back where he found it and began to speak to his fellow monks as if nothing had happened.

When recreation was over, his superior walked with him to his cell. Padre Pio went straight to the window of his room to close the blinds, but remained there without moving, looking at the plains below. Then he turned around abruptly and broke down in tears.

The Holy Office's decree caused quite a stir, since it incriminated not only Padre Pio but the whole Capuchin Order. Secular priests and other religious congregations joked with glee over the misfortune of the "friars with beards." Then the highest authorities of the

Capuchin Order met together and decided to find a way to remove Padre Pio from the scene so that people would stop talking about him over time. They decided to send him to Spain. However, they realized they needed to act tactfully and prudently to avoid any confrontation with his followers.

A rather robust and courageous monk, Fr. Luigi Festa d'Avellino, was chosen to carry out their plan. He himself later described the plan to remove Padre Pio from San Giovanni Rotondo:

In the middle of July 1923, in my capacity as provincial vicar, I was summoned to Rome where I accompanied our superior general, Fr. Giuseppantonio of Persiceto, to the Holy Office. I waited for him in the waiting room, ready to provide him with any necessary information.

On our way back to our motherhouse on Via Boncompagni, Father General told me: "The roof is going to cave in on you. You have to carry out the order of the top authorities." I answered: "I'm ready to do whatever Reverend Father orders me to do."

Back at the motherhouse, Father General told me about the order to transfer Padre Pio from San Giovanni Rotondo to Ancona. He handed me the order, dated July 30, 1923, and said: "Padre Pio is in your hands. Take him away from San Giovanni Rotondo and take him to the provincial superior of Ancona who is to wait for further instructions. I'll make arrangements with General De Bono, who is in charge of public safety, while you make arrangements with the prefect in Foggia, in order to avoid any trouble from those people who are opposed to Rome's order. Go and tell Padre Pio to obey, and when the time is right, carry out the order."

I left for Foggia, and during the first half of August I went to San Giovanni Rotondo. Late one evening, I called Padre Pio to my room, and read the order to him, commanding him to place himself in my care as Father General had requested. Padre Pio bowed his head, folded his arms across his chest, and said: "I'm at your disposal. Let's depart at once. When I am with my superior, I am with God."

At that point I asked, "You mean you want to come with me right away? Why, it's the middle of the night! Where would we go?" Padre Pio responded: "I don't know. But I'll go with you, when and where you wish." Since it was midnight, I calmly told him: "I was only told to give you the order of obedience. It will be carried out only when Rome sends further instructions."

I told Father General about the talk I had with Padre Pio, and a few days later he sent me a reply: *Ordo suspendatur* (The order is suspended).

Then I received a letter from General De Bono, assuring me that he was prepared to use the police force to carry out the order, but asking me who would assume responsibility if there was a massacre. Later General De Bono informed me: "We'll escort Padre Pio away in safety, but it will be amid bloodshed. The prefect of Foggia said he would carry out the order, but it would mean walking over dead bodies."

In the meantime, I had already laid out my plans for the move to Father General. I told him about the steps we needed to take, and the help we procured. I assured him of my willingness to help and my steadfast desire to obey, in spite of the fact that the people of San Giovanni Rotondo had already made three violent attempts to intervene. People were saying: "Fr. Luigi was a soldier and is brave. He'll try to carry out the whole ordeal. If we don't break all his bones, he won't give up."

On August 23, Padre Pio wrote me: "I don't think it is necessary for me to tell you how ready I am, thanks be to God, to obey whatever my superiors order me to do. For me, their voice is God's voice. I want to serve him faithfully until I die. With his help, I will obey whatever command I am given, even if it adds to all my suffering."

Padre Pio was prepared to submit willingly to these drastic measures from the Holy Office. But since no one had ever come to question him and explain the reasons for such measures, he tried to find out what was wrong. He asked his dear friend and neighbor, Giuseppe Orlando, a former priest, a nobleman, and a doctor, to help him. In Orlando's unpublished diary, he left the following testimony "I was a very intimate friend of Padre Pio, so when the famous decree was issued by the Holy Office, Padre Pio wanted me to go to Rome to find out precisely what the situation wasI went to Rome to confer with Fr. Lottini, a Dominican who was a member of the staff at the Holy Office. I went to Rome to confer with Fr. Lottini, a Dominican who was a member of the staff at the Holy Office.

Fr. Lottini didn't want to see me at first because he said that staff members at the Holy Office were bound by orders of strict secrecy. But at my insistence, he granted me an appointment that lasted more than an hour.

He told me that a detailed report was on file with the Holy Office from the Archbishop of Manfredonia, the Most Reverend Pasquale Gagliardi, who depicted Padre Pio in the darkest of terms and attributed his stigmata to fakery and fanaticism, which was detrimental to the serious nature of our faith. He ended the report with a dilemma: "Either Padre Pio goes, or I go."

My arguments against the accusations fell on deaf ears, as did the oaths I made as a priest. Fr. Lottini ended our conversation saying, "We sent him the order, calling him under obedience to be transferred to some unknown destination. Instead of obeying, he has, by means of some fanatical women who surround him, staged some demonstrations of a magnitude as to throw not only the town but even the civil and military authorities into confusion."

I told Fr. Lottini that it simply was not true: "If Padre Pio had received the order you are referring to, he would have obeyed without any discussion. Give me a mandate to investigate and I swear to you that I will accurately report the results to you."

Fr. Lottini answered me: "Swear upon this missal and go." I knelt down, put my right hand on the missal, and swore. The next day I was in Padre Pio's cell. "They are accusing you of all kinds of things," I told him, "but, most of all, they say you are disobeying the orders of your superiors. They say they ordered you to leave this place, and that you don't want to obey."

Padre Pio fell to his knees, opened his arms, and answered: "Peppino, I swear to you on this crucifix of Jesus here on the table that I never received such an order. If my superiors ordered me to jump out of the window, I wouldn't argue. I would jump."

On July 24, 1924, the Holy Office made a fresh attempt to deal with Padre Pio by issuing another condemnation that was even more severe:

By means of a declaration dated May 31 of last year that was published in the *Acts of the Apostolic See,* this Supreme Tribunal of the Holy Office, which aims to defend faith and morals, wished to admonish the faithful that an investigation into the phenomena surrounding Padre Pio of Pietrelcina failed to find anything of a supernatural character. The faithful were exhorted to conform their practices to this declaration. Now, based on other information from various reliable sources, this Supreme Congregation believes it to be its duty to exhort the faithful once again to abstain from maintaining any kind of contact, even by letter, with the above-named priest.

Until that time, Padre Pio had maintained extensive correspondence with people. Being able to write letters was the only way in which he still felt useful. He corresponded regularly with his spiritual sons and daughters. These letters, when they were eventually collected, filled several large volumes. Experts say they constitute a valuable document in mystical literature, comparable to the letters of St. Catherine of Siena. After the decree of July 24, 1924, Padre Pio, out of obedience, stopped writing letters completely. He even interrupted his correspondence with his confessor.

Giuseppe Orlando wrote in his diary:

Because of the two decrees from the Holy Office, the superior of the Capuchin monastery was forced to keep Padre Pio strictly secluded within the walls of the monastery of San Giovanni Rotondo, forbidding him to go down to the parlor, to write letters, and to look out the window. He had to be completely isolated from the human race. He couldn't even celebrate Mass in public. The monastery truly became a prison for Padre Pio. Only Dr. Mario De Giacomo had free access to him because of his poor health. But this wasn't always the case. Being with Padre Pio when he was in such a prison and hearing him talk about his physical and spiritual suffering was truly like dying. "It is only now that I understand," he would say, "how much greater is the punishment of innocent people who are put in jail, compared to the suffering of guilty prisoners. Blessed are they! At least they know, after they are sentenced, how many days, how many months, and how many years they will still be locked up. They can tell how much time has gone by and how much time still has to go by. But me?"

There was a tremendous contrast between the monks, who were carrying out the order from the Holy Office to keep people away from Padre Pio, and the crowds of people who were flocking to the monastery, threatening to see and speak with him at any cost.

Padre Pio shared his most intimate thoughts with me and with Dr. De Giacomo, but even then he was always resigned to his fate in a most holy way. Often he entertained us and made us laugh at his jokes.

Dr. De Giacomo told me that one night he and Padre Pio

began to talk about that famous Italian dish, spaghetti alla napoletana. The doctor described the dish in vivid terms, noodles covered with tomato sauce and veal, and then said to Padre Pio: "Would you gladly eat a big dish of it?" Padre Pio answered: "I wish it were so! Many years have gone by since I tasted it."

Seeking to satisfy Padre Pio's desire, even though it was late at night, he got into his car and went to Foggia to buy the meat. The next day he had someone prepare a delicious meal, and hurried over to the monastery with it at dinner time. He took the spaghetti to Padre Pio's cell, and then went to look for him. He found him in the corridor, went up to him and whispered in his ear: "Father, the spaghetti alla napoletana is steaming hot and ready to be eaten in your cell." He turned to me and said: "Bravo! Now I know you are truly a friend." He went to his cell and was jubilant when he saw the table prepared for such a feast. He blessed the food, sat down, and picked up his fork. He didn't say anything for a little while, but then turned to me: "Mario, why don't we do a good deed for the Virgin Mary? Take this dinner to the poor, and she will bless you."

The Holy Office condemned Padre Pio in 1926 as well. At that time, a book was published called *Padre Pio da Pietrelcina*. The Holy Office condemned it on April 23, recalling all the points made in its preceding decrees. Three months later, on July 11, the Holy Office confirmed its condemnation of Padre Pio, hoping that the faithful, who continued to flock to San Giovanni Rotondo, would not be deceived.

The Supreme Tribunal of the Church remained silent for several years. Then in 1931, Alberto Del Fante was converted. Del Fante was an atheist and a member of the Freemasons. He was from Bologna, and he was renowned for his vicious attacks on Padre Pio in the press. He accused him of being a "fake who was capable of duping people who were naive, enthusiastic, and easy to sway." Del Fante had a grandson, Enrico, whom he loved dearly. The child was seriously ill with tuberculosis of the bones and of the lungs, and had abscesses in his kidneys. The doctors said that he was a terminal case.

Del Fante's family members interceded with Padre Pio and did not have to wait long for a miracle. Alberto Del Fante's life was completely changed by the miracle that occurred before his very eyes. He went straight to San Giovanni Rotondo, where he was converted. As a sign of thanksgiving and gratitude for the faith he had regained, he wrote a book called *Padre Pio of Pietrelcina, Herald of the Lord*. The Holy Office promptly intervened and condemned the book, declaring that it should not be "either printed, read, kept, or sold, nor translated into other languages." On May 23 of the same year, new and more severe measures were taken against Padre Pio. He was deprived of all his ministerial functions, except for saying Mass. But even then the Mass "could not be celebrated publicly in church, but privately in a chapel inside the monastery without anyone attending."

Padre Pio was virtually isolated from everyone. News about these measures provoked angry discontent once again in San Giovanni Rotondo. Yet Padre Pio made no public statement. In complete submission, he began to live as a cloistered monk. In the morning he would celebrate Mass, which normally lasted about two hours, except on feast days and special occasions, when it lasted four. He then spent an hour in thanksgiving, before joining the other monks in the church for an hour of prayer. Then he would go to the library, where he would spend time reading and studying. He did the same thing in the afternoon. His day was divided between prayer and study. He never dined in the evening, and would retire very late at night. "Often I would go looking for him in the library," Padre Alberto D'Apolito, one of his disciples, later told me. "He was grateful that he had a little company, but was upset if I criticized how the Holy Office treated him. He would stop the conversation immediately. If I tried to continue, he would get up and leave."

Padre Pio lived as a recluse uninterruptedly for three years.

TWELVE

A Deep Sorrow

While Padre Pio was being investigated by the Holy Office, the pain inflicted by the various condemnations and restrictive measures was compounded by the death of his mother.

Even though Mamma Peppa was kept busy by the work in the fields and the work that comes from being mother of a large family, she was always aware of what was happening with her son in spite of the distance that separated them. She had always felt that something mysterious was taking place, and had followed the strange phenomena that occurred around him in humility and love. She had cared for him during the years when he was sick at home in Pietrelcina. She was always concerned that he would feel that she, his mother, was available for him.

When Padre Pio received the stigmata, he took great pains so his mother would not know about it. Around that time (September 25, 1918), a telegram arrived with news about the death of his sister, Felicita, who was only twenty-nine years old. He immediately wrote home to tell everyone that he would not be able to join them, without specifying the reason:

> Dear family, it is with a heart full of sorrow that I am writing you this letter. What can I say? I choke on every word because of the bitterness of my sorrow.
>
> My dear ones, in the harshness and affliction of my sorrow, the only strength that I have left is the strength to exclaim: "Your ways are just, O Lord, and your judgments are righteous." God gave me my poor sister, and God has taken her away. Blessed be his holy name!

This exclamation and these words of resignation give me the strength not to succumb to the burden of my sorrow. I resign myself to God's will. I exhort you to also seek relief from sorrow.

I'm very sorry and very troubled at not being able to come for a few days to be with you and to share your tears and your sorrow. I'm feeling rather ill and unable to undertake such a difficult journey.

Don't worry about me. I'm not in any danger. You must not be alarmed about my health. It has been exceptionally good and, compared to my fellow monks who are living here, I am doing rather well.

Write to me as soon as you can and let me know some details about my poor sister. Also send me some news about your health and my mother's health. I embrace you all affectionately, and I ask God to be your comfort.

Mamma Peppa first learned about the stigmata in 1919 from the parish priest in Pietrelcina, Fr. Salvatore Pannullo. But she did not understand exactly what it was. Only the words "bloody wounds" remained imprinted in her mind. "If my son is covered with wounds," she thought, "it means that he is sick and that he needs me."

With her husband and her sister-in-law, she left for San Giovanni Rotondo. Upon entering the mule track leading to the monastery, the three travelers met two other women. Mamma Peppa asked them: "Do you know Padre Pio?" They told her that they did and that they had just left the monastery, where they had spoken with him. "Then he's not sick in bed," Mamma Peppa exclaimed.

The two women, Maria Pompilio and Rachelina Russo, Padre Pio's spiritual daughters, accompanied Padre Pio's relatives to the Capuchin monastery. They were deeply moved as they observed Padre Pio's meeting with his relatives in the monastery guest room. "Mamma Peppa," Maria Pompilio wrote in her testimony, "opened a basket and took out some pastries filled with grape jam, inviting everyone to eat. Padre Pio ate heartily, exclaiming with a smile, 'How wonderful homemade cooking is! Eat, Rachelina, eat.' We each had one and everyone was satisfied."

Even on this visit, Mamma Peppa did not comprehend the strange wounds on her son's hands and his feet. In fact, she was so concerned about Padre Pio's health that she asked her oldest son, Michele, to come back from America. He had hardly set foot in Pietrelcina before he left again for San Giovanni Rotondo, "to see my sick brother."

A little while later, Mamma Peppa spent forty days in San Giovanni Rotondo because she could not live in peace so far away from her wounded son. She stayed in the home of Maria Pompilio, who was now her good friend. Every morning she went to the monastery for Mass, and received communion from the hands of her son.

During his childhood, Padre Pio's relationship with his mother was based on intense affection. Yet, Padre Pio later kept any feeling of affection to himself and never displayed it in public. He would never let his mother show him any special attention. People around Padre Pio tried to kiss his hands, and he let them do so. But he would never let his mother kiss his hands. Even Maria Pompilio wrote: "The poor woman approached Padre Pio many times in the sacristy to talk to him, but he never paid much attention to her. When she approached him, he moved away. He never let her kiss his hands. Many times the poor woman was on the verge of doing so, but he would immediately withdraw his hand."

According to Maria Pyle, an American benefactor of the Capuchin Fathers, Mamma Peppa finally managed to kiss Padre Pio's hand on December 5, 1928. Maria Pyle had gone to live for a while in Pietrelcina. When she returned to San Giovanni Rotondo, she brought Mamma Peppa with her so that she could spend Christmas with her son. The two women went to the monastery where they found Padre Pio. "Mamma Peppa," Maria Pyle wrote, hiding her great joy under a veneer of apparent calmness, took her son's hand, and, before he could take it away, said: "Padre Pio, I kiss your hand for Aunt Libera (and kissed his hand), and for Aunt Pellegrina (followed by another kiss), and for Aunt Filomena (a third kiss)." She went on and on, for about ten other aunts and godmothers. Finally she said, "And now, Padre Pio (she always addressed him in this way), this kiss is for me." She tried to do so, but wasn't successful. When she bent down to kiss his hand, Padre Pio quickly took his hand away. He lifted them up and said: "Never! A son should kiss the hand of his mother. A mother shouldn't kiss the hand of her son."

From that day on, Mamma Peppa never tried to kiss his hands. But every day after she received Communion from his hands, she "would get down on her knees and kiss the ground where he stepped with his wounded feet" as soon as he passed by.

During that time, Mamma Peppa and her son would see each other often. In spite of the snow, the freezing cold, and the biting wind, Mamma Peppa would go every morning to the monastery to attend Mass and see Padre Pio. She would wear a very simple dress, which was much too light for winter. Some friends from San Giovanni Rotondo gave her a heavy wool dress as a present, but they never were able to convince her to wear it because she was "afraid of looking like a rich woman."

She spent almost all of Christmas in church. She wanted to attend midnight Mass, and then two other Masses afterward. However, she was not feeling well on the feast of St. Stephen, so she went to bed. Three days later, doctors diagnosed her with double pneumonia.

Padre Pio went to see her on New Year's Day. He remained at her bedside from one o'clock in the afternoon until midnight. Francesco Morcaldi, who was present at the time, remembered: "It was a tender sight to see Padre Pio smiling and praying next to his mother's bed, a tender sight to see him caring for her so she could rest."

Padre Pio went back to see her on January 2 and found her in very serious condition. He remained at her bedside until the very end. In the midst of the commotion, he gave her the last rites. When he saw that she was about to breathe her last breath, he could resist no longer. He kissed her on the forehead, and then broke down in tears. He wept so much that he fell down on the ground semiconscious. Two doctors carried him to a neighboring room and gently laid him down on a bed. Mamma Peppa died at 6:15 in the morning on January 3, 1929. Padre Pio was so overcome with sorrow that he had to remain in the house for two more days, under the care of the same two doctors, who feared for his own life.

THIRTEEN

Padre Pio Is Given His Freedom

The four decrees that the Holy Office issued between 1923 and 1931 caused immense sorrow among Padre Pio's faithful followers. They did not understand why Church authorities waged such a tenacious campaign against such a humble monk who was unable to defend himself.

In San Giovanni Rotondo and in the neighboring areas, committees were formed to defend Padre Pio. People met to discuss what could be done to help him.

One of Padre Pio's most fervent followers was Emanuele Brunatto, a young man who was about thirty years old, who had a rather adventurous and troubled past. At one time or another, he had worked as a sales representative, author, impresario, industrialist, and fashion designer. At times he had been extremely wealthy and at other times he lived in poverty and shame. He led a very dissolute life and had committed many kinds of shameful acts.

One day, out of desperation, he went to San Giovanni Rotondo. Padre Pio brought peace into his life. From that moment on, Emanuele Brunatto never wanted to leave the shadow of his savior.

Emanuele Brunatto held a special place in Padre Pio's life, a place that makes some people uncomfortable. Yet it cannot be ignored. He was a sincere follower, a generous supporter, and a fierce and sometimes violent defender of Padre Pio. He tended to exaggerate at times, most likely out of love.

From the testimonies that have been recorded, Brunatto appears to be a rather complex character. When he arrived in San Giovanni Rotondo in 1919, seeking some kind of conversion experience, he tried to deceive Padre Pio by presenting his lover to him as though she were his sister.

Even after his conversion, he was never a saint. From time to time he would disappear. He would spend a lot of time arranging mysterious business deals that would earn him a great deal of money. Then, suddenly and unexpectedly, he would once again be reduced to poverty.

During World War II, he collaborated with the Vichy Government. Afterward, he was arrested and spent a few weeks in prison. At one point he was condemned to death, but then he was acquitted. During the forties he lived in Paris, where people thought highly of him. He spent his time doing social work and works of charity. At his own expense he opened a "soup kitchen" for the poor people in Paris. He also gave considerable sums of money toward pensions for war veterans who had been decorated for their valor or who had been handicapped during the war. He also organized theological conferences that were highly acclaimed, and corresponded with Archbishop Roncalli, the future Pope John XXIII, who was the papal nuncio in Paris at the time.

During the time when he lived in San Giovanni Rotondo, Emanuele Brunatto was extremely dedicated to defending Padre Pio. He did so using every means, both licit and illicit, thereby creating some extremely embarrassing situations for some Church authorities. Because of his unbiased devotion, many of Padre Pio's biographers ignore him, even resorting to fictitious dates and events in order not to mention him.

Undoubtedly the information he left is exaggerated, one-sided, and at times downright false. But this information is the only information that lifts the veil on the religious underworld where many accusations against Padre Pio originated and matured. During the time of Padre Pio's "martyrdom," Emanuele Brunatto, together with Francesco Morcaldi, was a keen lay observer of what was going on, and their evaluations are often based on solid ground. Because of their activities on Padre Pio's behalf, often made amid threats and blackmail, Padre Pio was finally "rehabilitated" in 1933 after several years of persecution.

Padre Pio knew Brunatto intimately. His numerous letters to Brunatto indicate that he wished the very best for him. At times he would entrust Brunatto with some very delicate assignments, which he carried out in very precise detail. Brunatto often described himself as Padre Pio's "firstborn son, because I was sinner number one." He was among the few people who did not try to take advantage of Padre Pio. He would appear when Padre Pio needed him. Then he would disappear. Despite what people say about Brunatto, they cannot deny his deep love for Padre Pio.

When the persecution of Padre Pio first broke out, Emanuele Brunatto was among the many people who were upset. He had a deep desire in his heart for justice. He started attending meetings of a committee for Padre Pio's defense. This committee would regularly send representatives to the Vatican to protest the slanderous accusations that were being made. But Brunatto also perceived from the start that the generous defense of the townspeople of San Giovanni Rotondo served no purpose. "If the Vatican believes his critics and is completely deaf to our cries of justice," Brunatto told the committee, "it means that his critics are very influential people. If we want to defend Padre Pio, we have to find out who they are and why they are doing it." A group of Padre Pio's friends, with Emanuele Brunatto at their head, began a long and hard battle against Padre Pio's mysterious critics.

Brunatto discovered that Padre Pio's enemies were three secular priests in San Giovanni Rotondo: Canon Domenico Palladino, Canon Giovanni Miscio, and Archpriest Giuseppe Prencipe. These men, who led lives that were anything but edifying, had a hard time with all the people who were flocking to the monastery so that they could go to confession to a "saint." Padre Pio incarnated all the qualities they lacked. In their eyes, he needed to be eliminated at any cost.

Don Domenico Palladino, canon of the church of the Carmine, was Padre Pio's most malicious critic. Brunatto began his investigation with him. He uncovered intrigues, affairs, dirty schemes, and lies. With all the ability of a top-notch spy, he collected many documents proving that Padre Pio's critics were acting in bad faith.

Emanuele Brunatto ended up in a legal battle with one of the three critics, Canon Giovanni Miscio. Miscio was an avid lover of money and tried to make five thousand lire off of Padre Pio. However, he was foiled in his attempt by his own ineptness.

In November 1925 Fr. Miscio told Maria Pompilio, whom he knew was a faithful follower of Padre Pio, that he had written a rather salacious book about Padre Pio, a book that included a chapter in which the Capuchin monk was depicted as a kind of Rasputin—sensual, arrogant, a willing instrument of greedy monks intent on financial gain. Fr. Miscio said that the book was ready to be published and that a contract had been signed with an editor in Milan who was ready to pay Fr. Miscio five thousand lire as an advance on the royalties. If Fr. Miscio did not deliver the manuscript, he, in turn, would have to pay a penalty of five thousand lire. Fr. Miscio explained that his conscience was bothering him now, and he hoped to avoid involving Padre Pio in a scandal. He no longer wanted to publish the book, but he did not have enough money to pay the penalty.

Maria Pompilio believed Fr. Miscio's tale. She was alarmed, and on the advice of the blackmailer himself, she hastened to inform Brunatto about the threat.

"I met Fr. Miscio in Maria Pompilio's house," Brunatto recalled.

I was faced with a dilemma. I needed five thousand lire right away, or the defamatory book would be published. I told Fr Miscio: "Padre Pio's life is like a window. You are risking a lawsuit for defamation of character." Fr. Miscio's reply was, "No Catholic will sue me. Canon law forbids Catholics to sue priests in a civil court." I told him that Padre Pio's relatives were poor. "Where do you want them to find five thousand lire for you?" I asked. Fr. Miscio was undaunted: "There are lots of people who would be happy to lend the money," he answered. I tried to procrastinate.

But Fr. Miscio brought his brother Vincenzo on the scene, and he turned out to be unbending, insistent, and threatening.

I had to let Padre Pio's brother, Michele Forgione, know about the book. Michele, with tears in his eyes, told me: "I don't even have fifty lira, but I'll sell my land. I assure you that I'll find all the money that is needed. But I beg you, Emanuele, do everything that's possible so that Padre Pio doesn't have to suffer."

Fr. Miscio's insistence and threats grew more serious each day. Padre Pio's brother borrowed three thousand lire. But I warned the police. On January 5, 1926, Fr. Miscio withdrew the three thousand lire that had been deposited in his account. He even signed a receipt for the money he had extorted because he was so sure that no one would turn him in. But the police arrested him with the money in his hands. He was sentenced to twenty months in jail.

Even though these three priests were Padre Pio's main foes, they had a powerful leader and protector in their unedifying conduct. In fact, he incited them to slander the Capuchin monk with the stigmata. He was none other than the archbishop of Manfredonia, the Most Reverend Pasquale Gagliardi. Archbishop Gagliardi was mainly responsible for sending reports on Padre Pio to the Vatican, where he had many friends. For this reason, no one doubted his word.

After a pastoral visit to San Giovanni Rotondo in 1920, Archbishop Gagliardi publicly declared that he had seen Padre Pio applying makeup to his face and putting perfume on himself. Moreover, he had discovered a little bottle of nitric acid that the monk used "for making the stigmata."

A few months later, in the presence of several other bishops and archbishops, he claimed that "Padre Pio is possessed, and the monks of San Giovanni Rotondo are a gang of thieves."

Archbishop Gagliardi was also a good friend of Fr. Palladino, who was his advisor.

Emanuele Brunatto, assisted by other faithful friends of Padre Pio, began to investigate the activities of the archbishop of Manfredonia. They discovered some extremely serious and compromising situations.

In June of 1925, Emanuele Brunatto left for Rome. His suitcase was full of documents proving that Padre Pio was being falsely accused by unworthy men who were liars and slanderers. He was convinced that Padre Pio's calvary was coming to an end. No one in Rome would ever believe Padre Pio's critics. He was convinced they would go to San Giovanni Rotondo and see how things really were.

Upon arriving in Rome, Brunatto sought the advice of Fr. Orione, the founder of the Sons of Providence, a man who was highly esteemed for his holiness. He looked over the documents and then advised Brunatto to make some copies and distribute them to various cardinals. By the end of July, the reports were on the desks of Cardinal Gasparri, the secretary of state; Cardinal Merry Del Val, secretary of the Holy Office; Cardinal Basilio Pompilj, the Pope's vicar general; Cardinal Donato Sbarretti, prefect of the Council; Cardinal Gaetano De Lai, prefect of the Consistory; Cardinal Michele Lega, prefect of the Sacraments; Cardinal Guglielmo Van Rossum, prefect of Propaganda Fide; and Cardinal Augusto Silj, prefect of the Tribunal of the Segnatura. All of them showed keen interest in the matter, but none of them were willing to take any concrete steps.

Since Brunatto never received a reply to the dossier he had compiled, he decided in 1926 to publish a book defending Padre Pio, using the pseudonym of Giuseppe De Rossi. The book consisted of the information he had gathered on Archbishop Gagliardi and the other priests from San Giovanni Rotondo. The Vatican quickly bought up all available copies of the book, and the Holy Office promptly put the book on the index of forbidden books.

Brunatto's book shook the Roman congregations out of their apathy. In January of 1927, Msgr. Felice Bevilacqua, of the Vicariate of Rome, was sent to San Giovanni Rotondo with the task of conducting an apostolic visitation on the local clergy. Monsignor Bevilacqua was completely familiar with the documentation that Emanuele Brunatto had presented to the cardinals, and wanted him to accompany him as his "lay assistant."

The visitation was short. The evidence against Padre Pio's critics turned out to be overwhelming. Testimony after testimony confirmed the investigation that Brunatto had carried out. Monsignor Bevilacqua returned to Rome and proposed that Padre Pio's critics be given the maximum penalty. But the Congregation of the Holy Office, which was so hasty to condemn Padre Pio, was very respectful in punishing the priests involved. Only Fr. Palladino was suspended *a divinis* and immediately removed from San Giovanni Rotondo. No measures were taken against the others, even though they were censured.

Fr. Palladino did not waste any time in fretting over his sentence. He went straight to his friend, Archbishop Gagliardi of Manfredonia, and the archbishop permitted him to live in his palace like a prince until two months later, when, using his friendships in the Vatican, he succeeded in obtaining permission for Fr. Palladino to celebrate Mass once again. A little later he appointed him pastor of St. Michael's Church in Manfredonia.

It now appeared that all of the work of Padre Pio's friends, who had struggled for years to collect hundreds of documents proving his innocence and the malice of his accusers, was in vain. It also seemed like Monsignor Bevilacqua's apostolic visitation was also in vain. But when they saw that the true culprit in this rather absurd and incredible situation in the archdiocese of Manfredonia had been set free, they decided to play another trump card before declaring themselves conquered.

On May 5, 1927, Cardinal Sbarretti, prefect of the Council, received the following letter:

The undersigned, Felice Bevilacqua, assumes full responsibility for his actions during the apostolic visitation to San Giovanni Rotondo. He was entrusted with the assignment, with God's help, of unraveling the intricate web entrusted to him, and if the Congregation desires to follow it to its very end and bring it to closure, it should remember that the sorry truth must appear in its full light. The procedure will be as follows: cards on the table without any secrets, and each one assumes civil responsibility for what he says.

Only in this way will the criminal attempt to defraud Church authorities be debunked and dispelled. It is only when they are faced with the prospect of jail that the defamers will come to their senses and be silenced. Otherwise Rome will be deceived *usque ad consumationem saeculi.*

On December 28, 1927, Mgsr. Felice Bevilacqua wrote to Emanuele Brunatto: "Dear Emanuele, the Cardinal Prefect of the Council begged me to deliver to him as soon as possible the report on the archpriest. He would like to use it to obtain permission to proceed before the archbishop's arrival and without having to go through the Consistory, seeing now the need to bypass it.

"If you should read this before leaving, by that time I will already be in a good place. As soon as you arrive, come immediately with the documents and ... don't make me look like a fool!"

Monsignor Bevilacqua wanted to avoid going through the Consistory, because he knew that the prefect of the Consistory was Cardinal De Lai, Gagliardi's close friend. In fact, during the summer of 1927, when serious accusations were made about Gagliardi and an investigation was being conducted, Cardinal De Lai was Gagliardi's guest, and the two friends spent their summer vacation together at the seashore.

Cardinal De Lai knew what Monsignor Bevilacqua was up to, and arranged to have Monsignor Bevilacqua's apostolic visitation declared closed. He also was arranging for a new visitation to take place, which would encompass the whole diocese of Manfredonia, and which would be entrusted to another visitor. Msgr. Giuseppe Bruno was chosen to conduct this second visitation, a person who was acceptable to the defendants because they knew they would be out of danger while Padre Pio's fate would be endangered.

When Monsignor Bevilacqua was ending his mandate, he wrote: "I don't believe that there is another den of such wicked people like this one."

On September 26, 1927, almost all the canons in the archdiocese of Manfredonia sent a statement to the Sacred Congregation of the Council, followed by a second one dated October 18 that was addressed to both the Sacred Congregation of the Council and the Consistory, confirming the accusations that had been made against Archbishop Gagliardi. The priests who signed this statement were suspended *a divinis* by the authorities in Rome and sent to Naples for some spiritual exercises. This letter of punishment was delivered to the priests by none other than Fr. Palladino. One of the priests who was punished was the archpriest Fr. Guerra, an eighty-year-old man who took ill during the spiritual exercises and died, apparently out of grief.

The battle, which was carefully documented so that justice might prevail, was coming to an end. Padre Pio's friends decided to use threats.

Commander Festa of Arenzano wrote the following letter to Vatican authorities in the name of Brunatto and Padre Pio's other friends: "Either you see that justice is done, and only justice, or justice will be done without you, but with irreparable moral damage to you. If the Pope learns the facts (and he should be aware of them after so many written reports), there is no doubt he will have to act. If he is not aware of them because he was prevented from learning about them, then he will hear about them from the public outcry. At that point he will have to act."

This letter made a deep impression on everyone. Promises were made that justice would be carried out, "in the shortest possible time." But even Festa's threats were not enough to assure that these promises would be carried out.

Finally, the book was published in May of 1929 in Leipzig. Five thousand copies of *A Letter to the Church* were printed in Italian, bearing the signature of the mayor of San Giovanni Rotondo, Francesco Morcaldi. Original documents were reprinted in an appendix. When the forthcoming publication of the book was announced, more promises were made. Padre Pio's friends decided to postpone distribution of the books, and they were stored in a warehouse in Munich, together with copies of the proofs. The original proofs were stored in a secret location.

The Vatican was concerned about the book. In September 1929, Archbishop Gagliardi was removed from his post, stripped of his title, and transferred from Manfredonia. But no measures were taken in Padre Pio's favor. Moreover, his situation took a turn for the worse when the Holy Office issued a new decree confirming its four previous condemnations. This decree stipulated that Padre Pio could not have contact with anyone, could not bless religious objects, could not hear confessions, and could not even look out the windows of the monastery. He was allowed to celebrate Mass only in a private chapel on the second floor of the monastery.

In October of 1931, while Emanuele Brunatto was abroad on business, Francesco Morcaldi, the author of *A Letter to the Church,* though he was upset with the ruthless sentence imposed on Padre Pio, reached a reasonable agreement with Cardinal Rossi, who asked him to show himself to be "an obedient and devoted son of the Church." He agreed to deliver the books and documents that were in storage to the Holy See. In exchange, Cardinal Rossi promised that Padre Pio would immediately be set free. On October 10, the books and proofs were delivered to the apostolic nuncio in Bavaria, who sent them to Rome by diplomatic pouch so that they would not be examined by customs officials at the border. Once he had the compromising materials in his hands, Cardinal Rossi immediately forgot the promises he had made to Morcaldi, and Padre Pio's imprisonment continued.

When Brunatto returned to Italy, he was furious. He announced that a new book would be published. Padre Pio, on orders from Church authorities in Rome, asked him to calm down and return to France. Brunatto obeyed but wrote a book called *The Antichrists Within the Church of Christ* while he was in Rome, which he had printed in three languages at the beginning of 1933. He wrote to Cardinal Rossi: "If you do not free Padre Pio by Easter, I will distribute the book." Cardinal Rossi forced Padre Pio to intervene. On March 28, 1933, Padre Pio wrote to Brunatto, begging him not to distribute the book, but Brunatto sadly wrote back: "This time, Father, I must disobey you."

The book was distributed abroad, but not in Italy. Thousands of Catholics read it and were indignant. Hundreds of letters were sent to Rome. At the same time, a book by Dr. Giorgio Festa, the doctor who did a scientific study of Padre Pio's stigmata, was published in Italy. The Most Reverend Cornelio Sebastiano Cuccarollo, a Capuchin bishop, presented Pope Pius XI with a dossier of sworn testimonies from Padre Pio's fellow monks, attesting to the saintly life of the monk with the stigmata. These three events convinced the Pope to "release" Padre Pio from his "prison," allowing him to take up his ministry once again. On July 16, 1933, after eleven years of persecution and twenty-five months of absolute isolation, Padre Pio resumed his priestly ministry. In a conversation with Bishop Cuccarollo, Pope Pius XI said: "This is the first time that the Holy Office is retracting its decrees." But this was not entirely true. The Holy Office never formally issued any decree rescinding its various condemnations of Padre Pio.

FOURTEEN

At the Limits of Reality

Padre Pio's "rehabilitation" did not occur instantaneously, but was spread over time. It was a signal from Vatican authorities that they were not acting out of any deep conviction but wanted only to avoid the threat of any further scandal.

Padre Pio was allowed to publicly celebrate Mass in church once again on July 26, 1933. Eight months later, on March 25, 1934, he was granted permission to hear the confessions of other men. Women had to wait until May 12, 1934, to go to confession with Padre Pio.

May 5, 1934, was Padre Pio's first feast day after his "rehabilitation." His friends and followers were expecting a great celebration, but no special event was held. Nor was there a celebration on August 10, 1935, the silver jubilee of his ordination to the priesthood.

Padre Pio's superiors related to him prudently and cautiously, as they would relate to a person guilty of a crime who had been pardoned. Whenever anything suspicious happened in the monastery, Padre Pio was the first "suspect." One evening some people passing by thought they saw some women walking around the monastery. A scandal ensued. Padre Pio was immediately questioned and had to defend himself against some rather serious and vulgar accusations. In another instance, a benefactor, who wished to remain anonymous, asked Padre Pio to deliver some money to a certain poor family. Padre Pio readily did so, but this act alone was enough for him to be accused of not observing his vow of poverty. He was always the center of accusations, suspicion, gossip, and judgment. But he always remained calm and serene, and never criticized anyone.

Yet, word about his holiness was spreading around the world. Anyone who came to see him and was fortunate enough to speak with him went home convinced that they had met a saint.

Besides the stigmata, Padre Pio had other charisms that generally characterize the lives of the great saints and mystics, such as bilocation, visions, prophecy, and the ability to read people's minds. These charisms were manifested in his life in a particularly strong way.

One of the inexplicable phenomena that captured the attention of the medical doctors who cared for him was that of hyperthermia, a sudden rise in body temperature. In Padre Pio's case, his temperature attained extremely high levels. His case of hyperthermia is unique in the annals of medical history.

This unusual anomaly was discovered while Padre Pio was performing his military service in Naples. The doctors noticed immediately that the young soldier needed more care than their other patients, but they were unable to determine the nature of his illness. In an attempt to do so, they undertook some tests to measure his body temperature in a methodical way. But they soon had to give up their experiment. Every time they tried to record his temperature, the column of mercury shot up so rapidly that it broke the thermometer.

The first doctor to accurately measure Padre Pio's temperature was a doctor from Foggia. While he was on a sick leave, Padre Pio stayed in a monastery in Foggia. After having destroyed several thermometers, the doctor who was caring for Padre Pio found a thermometer that would be able to withstand boiling water. Within seconds, the thermometer registered 118 degrees.

Between 1920 and 1922, Dr. Giorgio Festa, the first doctor to scientifically study Padre Pio's stigmata, observed that on those days when Padre Pio was feeling well, he had a normal temperature of 97 degrees in the morning and 97.7 degrees in the evening. Whenever he complained that he was not feeling well, his temperature registered between 118 and 120 degrees on an extremely accurate thermometer.

In his book *Mysteries of Science and the Light of Faith,* Dr. Festa published the results of his long study on hyperthermia. He noted that in certain illnesses, such as epilepsy, tetanus, and uremia, a fever can reach points between 109 and 111 degrees. These are called "agonal" or "pre-agonal" temperatures, because they always are a prelude to death. Although Padre Pio would be sick in bed and feeling uncomfortable, he was never delirious, nor did he show any of the other symptoms that usually accompany high fevers. After a day or two, he would be feeling normal again. By the third day, he would resume his mission in the confessional.

Another phenomenon that characterized Padre Pio was the fact that his body, his clothing, and any objects that he had touched would give off a sweet fragrance, leaving a trail in those places where he walked. Hundreds of testimonies have been recorded confirming this phenomenon. The most reliable testimony comes from Dr. Festa. According to Dr. Festa, the fragrance did not come from Padre Pio's body but from the blood that flowed from the stigmata. He deduced this from several incidents that occurred while he was conducting his study of the Capuchin friar's mysterious wounds.

One day he took from the wound on Padre Pio's side a dressing that he had put there to stop the flow of blood. He placed it in a container so that he could take it to Rome and analyze it. During his trip to Rome, some people who were riding in the car with him remarked that they could smell the fragrance that usually came from Padre Pio. None of them knew that Dr. Festa had a dressing in his briefcase that was soaked with Padre Pio's blood. Dr. Festa kept this dressing in his studio, and the unusual fragrance impregnated the room for a long time afterward, so much so that the patients who came to see him would ask him what it was.

In his book on Padre Pio's stigmata, Dr. Festa wrote:

Anyone who has any experience with preserving meat from dead animals knows that you have to make sure that you drain the blood very well in order to avoid unpleasant odors. Of all organic tissue, blood is the one that decomposes most rapidly. Consequently, the dressings that were soaked with the blood from Padre Pio's wounds, especially since they were often stored for such a long time, should not have exuded such a sweet fragrance. This phenomenon, in all its simplicity and with all the eloquence that it lends to our study, is, nonetheless, contrary to all laws of nature and science.

There are also numerous testimonies of such phenomena as the multiplication of bread and other similar things. During the war, bread was rationed. Since there were always guests at the monastery of San Giovanni Rotondo, there was even more need of food for the poor people who would come. One day, when the monks gathered together in the dining room, there was only a pound of bread in the bread basket. The community of monks said grace and then sat down to eat some soup. Padre Pio stopped at the chapel. A little later he returned with some loaves of fresh bread. The superior of the monastery asked him, "Where did you get them?" He answered, "A pilgrim at the door gave them to me." No one said anything, but everyone knew that he was the only one who would meet such a "pilgrim" at the door.

One morning the sacristan forgot to make sure that enough hosts were consecrated for Holy Communion, and there were very few consecrated hosts in the ciborium in the tabernacle. Having finished hearing confessions, Padre Pio began to help distribute Communion to the faithful at Mass. There were a large number of people present. He gave Communion to everyone, yet there were still some hosts left over in the ciborium.

Another mysterious phenomenon that often occurred in Padre Pio's life and that was amply documented was his ability to bilocate. According to experts on mysticism, bilocation is the "simultaneous presence of the same person in two different places." It differs from "agility," which is the "ability of the body to move almost instantaneously from one place to another." There was only one recorded instance of "agility" in Padre Pio's life, while there are numerous testimonies of his ability to bilocate.

This phenomenon cannot be rationally explained. It is often believed that the spirit somehow detaches itself from the person's body to move to another place, but no one knows how this can happen. While the person's spirit "travels," the body remains immobile. Often Padre Pio would stop talking in the middle of a conversation and appear to be dozing off. Many people believe that he was bilocating during such moments.

Maria Pompilio, Padre Pio's spiritual daughter, told several stories about this phenomenon. One night while her brother, Nicola, was praying, he began to doze off. Suddenly, someone slapped him on his right cheek. He felt as though the hand that had hit him was covered with half of a glove. Immediately he thought of Padre Pio. The next day he asked Padre Pio whether he was the one who had slapped him. "That's what happens when you doze off while you're praying," Padre Pio replied.

On another occasion, Maria Pompilio was in the sacristy, where Padre Pio was removing his vestments after having celebrated Mass. A man entered, looked at Padre Pio, and said: "Yes, he's the one. I'm not mistaken." He approached him, fell on his knees in tears, and said over and over again, "Father, thank you for saving my life." Later the man told Maria Pompilio his story: "I was a captain in the infantry. One day when I was in the battlefield under heavy fire, I saw a monk a short distance away. He was pale but had very expressive eyes. He wasn't wearing a chaplain's uniform, only the habit of a simple monk. He called out to me and said, 'Captain, get away from there. Come here by me immediately.' I walked toward him and, even before I reached him, a grenade exploded in the place where I had been, leaving a hole in the ground. When I turned back around, he wasn't there anymore."

Fr. Michelangelo Bellini related the following story:

In November of 1921, while I was still a student, I wrote Padre Pio telling him to pray for my dying grandmother, who was over eighty years old. I felt very close to her because she had been praying that I would be a priest. I asked him to pray so that my grandmother would live to see me ordained. A few days later, I went to her bedside and found her in a coma. I thought she would die during the night, but by morning she had made an extraordinary recovery. She told me that she had dreamed that a monk had brought her ten more years of life. My grandmother lived for exactly ten more years.

One day Cardinal Pietro Gasparri and Cardinal Augusto Silj were visiting the home of Countess Virginia Salvicci Silj to bless her new private chapel. A nun came in, holding what she said was a relic of the true cross, enclosed in a reliquary. She said that Padre Pio had appeared in her cell in flesh and blood, and had entrusted the reliquary to her with orders to take it the next day to the home of Countess Silj. Seeing the reliquary, the two cardinals were convinced that the nun had not made up the story. A few days later, the countess traveled to San Giovanni Rotondo to seek some kind of clarification on the incident. Padre Pio confirmed that he had given the reliquary to the nun in Rome in person.

A general in the Air Force, Dr. Bernardo Rosini, told me the following story:

> After the war, I was serving in Bari at the United Air Command, which was responsible for all the new units that were created after Italy's defeat and that operated side by side with the Air Force.
>
> The General Command for the U.S. Air Force was also in Bari. I got to know several officers who told me that Padre Pio had saved them during one of their operations. Even the commanding general played a role in this incident, which was widely discussed. One day he himself wanted to pilot a squadron of bombers on a mission to destroy a German muni-

tions dump that was located near San Giovanni Rotondo. The general said that when he and his pilots were in the vicinity of the target, they saw the figure of a monk with upraised hands appear in the sky. The bombs broke loose from the plane on their own, and fell in the woods, destroying the target without the pilots intervening.

That evening this episode was the main topic of conversation among the pilots and their officers. Everyone wanted to know who the monk was. Someone told the commanding general that there was a monk who worked miracles living in San Giovanni Rotondo. He decided to go to San Giovanni Rotondo as soon as the country was liberated to see if it was the same monk that he had seen in the sky. After the war the general, accompanied by some of the pilots, went to the Capuchin monastery there. As soon as they entered the sacristy, they saw several monks and immediately recognized Padre Pio as the one they had seen in their planes. Padre Pio introduced himself and, putting his hand on the general's shoulder, said, "So you're the one who wanted to destroy everything." Overwhelmed by the monk's look and his words, the general knelt down in front of him. Padre Pio had spoken, as usual, in his own dialect, but the general was convinced that the monk had spoken to him in English. The two became friends. The general, who was Protestant, later converted to Catholicism.

The Most Reverend Alfredo Viola, the bishop of Salto, Uruguay, recorded the following story:

In 1937, Msgr. Ferdinando Damiani, who was the vicar general of the diocese of Salto at the time, was suffering from severe coronary disease. He went to San Giovanni Rotondo so that he might die close to Padre Pio. Padre Pio told him to return to his diocese and to continue his work there. He assured him that he himself would see to it that he was assisted spiritually when the time came for him to die.

In 1941 I organized a congress in my diocese in which the Most Rev. Alberto Levame, the papal nuncio, the Most Rev. Antonio Maria Barbieri, the archbishop of Montevideo, and the Most Rev. Michele Paternain, the bishop of La Florida, took part. During the night, Archbishop Barbieri heard a knock at the door of his room and opened it. A Capuchin monk was standing at the door. He told him to hurry to Bishop Damiani's bedside because he was dying. Archbishop Barbieri went immediately to his room. The bishop was suffering a heart attack. He received Holy Communion and the last rites while he was still conscious. Then he died. While visiting San Giovanni Rotondo on April 13, 1949, Archbishop Barbieri recognized Padre Pio as the Capuchin monk who had knocked at his door eight years before, asking him to go to Bishop Damiani's bedside.

Fr. Alberto D'Apolito, who met Padre Pio in 1917 and who was close to him for fifty years, related these two incidents:

One afternoon, when I was walking in the corridor of the monastery, I saw Padre Pio standing at the window, looking at the mountains. I walked up to him and kissed his hand, but he didn't even realize I was there. His hand was stiff from the cold. At that moment I distinctly heard him say the prayer of absolution in a very clear voice. I was scared and ran to look for the superior. Together we returned to Padre Pio's side, and after a few minutes he woke up from what seemed like a daze. He turned to us and asked, "Are you here? I didn't notice." A few days later a telegram arrived from Turin, thanking the superior for having sent Padre Pio to help a dying person. From the telegram we were able to determine that the dying person was breathing his last breath at the very moment when Padre Pio, who was in San Giovanni Rotondo, was praying those words of absolution.

In 1957 I witnessed the miraculous healing of Fr. Placido Bux. He was a patient at the Hospital of San Severo suffering from a serious form of cirrhosis of the liver. In spite of the medical care he was receiving, his condition was hopeless. One night Fr. Placido saw Padre Pio next to his bed. Padre Pio spoke to him, comforted him, and assured him that he would be healed. Then he went to the window of the room, put his hand on the glass, and disappeared.

In the morning Fr. Placido felt better. Remembering what had happened during the night, he looked at the window and saw the imprint of a hand on it. He went to check and recognized it as Padre Pio's hand. He was convinced from that moment on that Padre Pio's visit during the night wasn't a dream, but was real. He told the sisters and the nurses what had happened, and news about it spread throughout the hospital and throughout the city. Immediately curiosity seekers flocked to the hospital, wanting to see the imprint of Padre Pio's hand on the window. The doctors, who refused to believe the story and were angry so many people were coming and going, complained and ordered that the imprint be cleaned off. An attempt was made to clean the imprint with a rag soaked in detergent, but the imprint kept reappearing.

Since I had a hard time believing what I had seen with my own eyes, I went right away to San Giovanni Rotondo, seeking an explanation from Padre Pio himself. I found him in a corridor in the monastery. Before I could tell him the purpose of my visit, he asked me, "How's Fr. Placido?" I told him that he was getting better. Then I asked: "Is it true that during the night you went to the hospital and left the imprint of your hand on the window?"

Padre Pio looked at me and replied, "Do you doubt it? Yes, I went, but don't say anything to anyone."

I returned to San Severo and told them what Padre Pio had said. Even the doctors didn't say anything more. Fr. Placido was completely healed.

Fr. Alberto D'Apolito told me another story along these lines, involving Padre Pio and Mother Speranza, a Spanish nun who lived in Collevalenza, near Perugia. Like Padre Pio, she had the stigmata. She died in 1980 after living a holy life. His story was as follows:

In 1970, I went to Collevalenza to meet Mother Speranza. I was accompanied by a lawyer, Guglielmo Giordanelli, and by Fr. Gino, who was the superior of the institute to which Mother Speranza belonged. I had a conversation with her which I would categorize as a hallucination if I wasn't convinced that Mother Speranza was a saint. After greeting her, I said: "Mother, I'm a Capuchin monk from San Giovanni Rotondo. I don't want to waste your time, so I only ask you to pray for me and that Padre Pio be glorified." Mother Speranza raised her eyes, looked at me, and said, "I've always prayed for Padre Pio."

"Do you know him?" I asked.

"Yes, I've seen him many times," she answered.

"Where? At San Giovanni Rotondo?" I suggested.

"No, I've never been in San Giovanni Rotondo," she replied.

"Where, then?"

"In Rome," she said.

"Mother, that's not possible. Padre Pio went to Rome only one time in his life, in 1917, to accompany his sister to the Convent of St. Brigid. At that time you were in Spain. Certainly you've mistaken Padre Pio for some other Capuchin friar."

"No, I'm not mistaken," Mother Speranza replied. "It was Padre Pio himself."

"Where in Rome did you see him?" I asked.

"At the Holy Office, every day for a whole year. He wore some half-gloves on his hands to hide the wounds. I would greet him, kiss his hand, and sometimes we exchanged some words. This took place between 1937 and 1939 when I was working at the Holy Office."

"Mother, don't be offended, but I just can't believe what you're telling me," I said boldly.

Without any hint of resentment, Mother Speranza answered in a very sweet voice, "You are free to think what you want. I repeat, I saw Padre Pio every day for a whole year in Rome. I've always prayed for him and now I am praying that he be glorified."

There is another incident of Padre Pio bilocating that has been recorded, that is connected with the life of the Marchioness Giovanna Rizzani Boschi. It is a rather extraordinary story with vivid details. It certainly merits a chapter of its own.

FIFTEEN

"Your Name Will Be Sr. Jacopa"

I first met the Marchioness Giovanna Rizzani Boschi at Trevi Umbro, near Foligno, in the spring of 1984. Fr. Alberto D'Apolito, Padre Pio's longtime friend and biographer, was the first person to tell me about her. He had met Giovanna a couple of years earlier, and was personally involved in the last part of her extraordinary story.

Fr. Alberto explained that the Marchioness Rizzani Boschi had first met Padre Pio in 1923, and immediately became his spiritual daughter. From that moment on, she had always been close to him and had played an active role in his various projects. During the process of his beatification, she was one of the sixty witnesses who testified to his sanctity. Fr. Alberto warned me that the Marchioness Rizzani Boschi was very shy, and that it would be difficult to convince her to talk.

"My story is truly incredible," were her opening words to me when she welcomed me into her beautiful home. "It's full of strange coincidences that have no rational explanation. If it weren't for all the written documentation and the many testimonies of other people that simply cannot be disputed, I myself wouldn't believe it could be true even though I'm the one who experienced it! For this reason, I've always been careful about telling my story. It's easy for people to think you're some kind of fanatic. My family is very well known, and I can't involve my family members in my own private life."

After giving some thought to what she wanted to say, she began to tell her story. Here is her extraordinary account in her own words:

My life was intertwined with Padre Pio's from the moment that I entered this world. Of course, I can't give you a firsthand account since I don't remember that day at all, but a mysterious document exists, written by Padre Pio, which clearly gives the impression that he was present at my birth.

On January 18, 1905, my father, Giovanni Battista Rizzani, was on his deathbed in his mansion in Udine. My mother, Leonilde Serrao, was with him and was caring for him. She was a very strong and holy woman. Even though she was in the last month of her pregnancy, her only concern at that time was the fate of her husband. When darkness had fallen, the dogs began to howl, probably because they sensed that their master was on the verge of dying. My mother went outside to calm them down. While she was outside in the courtyard, she began to have labor pains. With the help of the family servant, she gave birth to me right there. Then she had the strength to take me in her arms, climb the stairs, and return to her husband's side. He died shortly thereafter.

From the time I was little, whenever my mother would tell me about my birth, she also told me that when she was in the courtyard and I was being born, she saw a young Capuchin friar. She never quite knew whether it was a vision, a hallucination, or reality, probably because no one in our family had ever known any Capuchin friars.

Many years later, when I had become Padre Pio's spiritual daughter, I learned some facts that cast some light on this particular episode in my life. Padre Pio's confessor, Fr. Agostino of San Marco in Lamis, gave me a page from a notebook that Padre Pio had given him in 1905. Padre Pio wasn't a priest at that time. He was studying philosophy and was living at the Monastery of Sant'Elia in Pianisi, in the province of Campobasso. He was eighteen years old and had only been with the Capuchins for two years. However, some mysterious things were already happening in his life, which he revealed in long letters that he wrote to his confessor. In February of 1905, among other things, he wrote Fr. Agostino these words, which Fr. Agostino kept along with everything else that he wrote.

The Marchioness Giovanna Rizzani Boschi took a photocopy from a desk and showed it to me. "There's no doubt that this is Padre Pio's handwriting," she said. "I've consulted some experts, and there is no reason for doubt since it comes from Padre Pio's confessor."

Padre Pio had written the following words: "Several days ago, I had an extraordinary experience. While I was in choir with Brother Anastasio, about eleven o'clock at night on the eighteenth of last month, I suddenly found myself far away in a wealthy home, where the father of the family was dying while a child was being born. Then the Virgin Mary appeared to me and said: 'I am entrusting this child to you. Now she is a diamond in the rough, but I want you to work with her, polish her, and make her as shining as possible, because one day I wish to adorn myself with her. Do not doubt. She will seek you out, but first you will meet her in Saint Peter's.' Afterwards, I found myself back in the choir."

"It's hard to explain this experience," the Marchioness Rizzani Boschi said.

Maybe Padre Pio was referring to a dream or a vision, or maybe he bilocated. Yet, it's hard to explain the coincidences with my own life: the date, January 18, 1905, the day on which I was born; the place, a "nobleman's home"; and the entirely unusual circumstances found in the words, "a father was dying while a child was being born."

Since my mother was left a widow, she moved to Rome to be near her parents. I grew up and went to school there. I was educated in Catholic schools, but during high school I was tormented by a lot of doubts about faith. I wanted to find a priest who could help me, but I just couldn't find the right one.

One afternoon in the summer of 1922, I went with a friend

to visit St. Peter's Basilica. While we were walking under the colonnade, I experienced a growing desire to tell a priest about my doubts. I asked a sacristan if this would be possible, but he told me that it was too late and that all the priests had already left. "It's only a half hour until closing," he said.

My friend and I continued on our visit to the basilica. While we were looking at a statue, I saw a Capuchin friar in front of me. I went up to him and asked him if he would hear my confession. He said he would, and we went into the nearest confessional. Right away I told him that I didn't intend to confess, but that I only wanted to ask him to explain some things. We spoke for a long time. He was precise and convincing. Immediately I felt relieved.

As we were leaving, I told my friend: "That priest is a very gifted man. Let's wait for him. I want to ask him where he lives, so that I might speak with him again." At that moment the sacristan arrived and asked us to leave because it was closing time. "We're waiting for the Capuchin priest in that confessional to come out," I said. "He has to leave too or he'll be in there all night," the sacristan said. He walked up to the confessional, raised the curtain, but nobody was there. "He already left," he said. Astonished, I looked at my friend and murmured, "How did he ever manage to get out?"

I continued to have doubts about my faith. But I never met another priest like the Capuchin priest I met in St. Peter's. During the summer of the following year, I heard someone talk about a certain Padre Pio for the first time, a priest with the stigmata who lived in San Giovanni Rotondo. Immediately I had a strong desire to meet him. Together with an aunt and some friends, we arranged a trip there.

There were people from all walks of life in the little monastery of San Giovanni Rotondo. The corridor from the sacristy to the cloister was crowded, but I managed to find a place in front of everyone. When he was passing by, Padre Pio stopped in front of me. He looked into my eyes. Smiling he said to me: "Giovanna, I know you. You were born the day your father died."

I was dumbfounded. How did he know this particular circumstance from my life? The next morning I went to confession to him. When I went up to him and after he blessed me, Padre Pio said: "My daughter, at last you've come to me. I've been waiting for you for so many years!"

"Father, maybe you've mistaken me for someone else," I replied.

"No, I'm not mistaken. I knew you before," he added.

"This is the first time I've been to San Giovanni Rotondo," I rebutted. "Until a few days ago, I never knew you existed."

"Last year," he said, "on a summer afternoon, you went to St. Peter's Basilica with a friend, looking for a priest who could help you understand the doubts you were having about your faith. You met a Capuchin priest and talked with him. I was that Capuchin priest."

After a brief pause, Padre Pio continued: "When you were being born, the Virgin Mary took me to Udine, to your mansion. She wanted me to be present at your father's death, and then she asked me to take care of you. The Virgin Mary entrusted you to me, and now I have to care for your soul."

A few years later, Padre Pio asked me to be part of the Franciscan Third Order, a religious congregation for lay people. It was founded by St. Francis himself. This congregation allows you to remain in the world while you live out the Franciscan spirit. I liked the idea, and Padre Pio himself prepared me. When you enter the Third Order, you have to choose a new name. Padre Pio chose that of Jacopa for me. "What an ugly name," I said. "I don't like it. Give me the name of Clare." But Padre Pio repeated, "You will be called Sr. Jacopa. Have you read the life of St. Francis? This noble Roman matron had the privilege of being present at the death of the saint from Assisi. One day you will be present at my death."

His words remained engraved in my memory, but I didn't attach much importance to them. In September of 1968, while I was in Rome, I heard Padre Pio's voice telling me, "Come immediately to San Giovanni Rotondo because I'll be going away. If you don't hurry, you'll never see me again." I left with Margaret Hamilton, a friend, the next day. I was able to see Padre Pio and he was able to hear my confession. "This is your last confession with me," he said. "Why?" I asked. "Because my hour has come," he replied. "I'm going away."

After my confession, I went to kiss his hand and I made an offering for his work. "Keep it, you'll need it," he said.

"I have enough to pay for my hotel and my return ticket to Rome," I said. "This money is for the House for the Relief of Suffering."

"Keep it, my daughter," he said. "You'll have to stay in San Giovanni for a few more days and you'll need the money."

In the afternoon, while talking with my friend, I was telling her about my meetings with Padre Pio and what he said. I told her the story about how I became a Third Order Franciscan, about how I was given the name of Jacopa, and the words that Padre Pio had said to me at that time: "One day you'll be present at my death." At that time there were a lot of people who had come to San Giovanni Rotondo to celebrate the fiftieth anniversary of the stigmata on Padre Pio's body. On Sunday morning, September 22, Padre Pio didn't feel well after Mass, but there was no reason to be alarmed about his health.

That night something happened that I wouldn't even dare tell anyone if it hadn't been confirmed in writing by my friend, Margaret Hamilton. We were sleeping in the same room and I couldn't fall asleep. Dogs were howling. Finally I fell asleep.

I don't know what happened immediately afterwards. I don't know if it was a dream, a vision, or something else. Suddenly, I was in Padre Pio's room. I was perfectly conscious of what I was seeing. Padre Pio was sitting in an armchair and was feeling sick and his breathing was laborious. I saw Fr. Pellegrino and some other monks next to him. There were also two doctors there. Everyone was sad and worried. They were bending over Padre Pio. Suddenly I woke up and cried, "Margaret, Padre Pio is dying."

"That's impossible," she said. "He was well this afternoon. It's only a bad dream."

"No, he's dying. I saw him," I answered back. I got up, dressed, and walked down the street to the little piazza in front of the church. When I got there, a monk was leaving the monastery and told me that Padre Pio had died.

In the following days, I was telling Fr. Alberto D'Apolito about this dream or vision. Fr. Alberto knows me very well. I said to him: "If you want, I can describe Padre Pio's cell in detail, just as I saw it that night." I did so and he confirmed that my description was correct. You have to remember that before Padre Pio's death, no photographs were ever taken of his cell, so there was no way I could have seen a picture of it in some magazine. Furthermore, since he was living a cloistered life, there was no way that I, a woman, could have entered there.

SIXTEEN

Some Remarkable Conversions

When Padre Pio was given permission again to exercise his priestly ministry at the Church of Santa Maria delle Grazie, his faithful followers began to organize pilgrimages to the Capuchin monastery in San Giovanni Rotondo once again. Every day hundreds of people arrived from every part of Italy and from around the world. Everyone wanted to meet the friar with the stigmata, share their problems with him, and seek his advice.

Poor people of simple faith were not the only ones to seek him out. The rich, the famous, and the powerful visited him as well. Escorted by policemen, Queen Maria Jose of Italy visited him at length and asked to have her photograph taken with him. The king and queen of Spain, the queen of Portugal, Empress Zita of Austria, together with her son Robert and her daughters Adelaide and Felicity, also visited him. The queen of Bulgaria, Count Lodovico di Borbone Parma, Duke Eugenio di Savoia, and many others visited Padre Pio as well. Several of them eventually became Padre Pio's spiritual sons and daughters. The monastery guest book, which all illustrious visitors were asked to sign, includes the signatures of cardinals, bishops, writers, and even the signature of Pope Pius XII's sister, Maria Teresa Gerini.

When Cardinal Eugenio Pacelli was elected pope on May 2, 1939, Padre Pio's fame grew even greater. Everyone knew that the new pope held Padre Pio in high esteem. While he was Pope Pius XI's secretary of state, Cardinal Pacelli had told the Archbishop of Manfredonia, the Most Reverend Andrea Cesarano: "When you need anything for Padre Pio, come to me." Shortly after he was elected pope, he ordered the Roman Curia "to leave Padre Pio in peace." He once confided to a journalist: "Padre Pio is a great saint, and it displeases us that we are not able to say so publicly." Sr. Pasqualina, Pope Pius XII's housekeeper, stated on several occasions that Pope Pius XII called the Capuchin stigmatist "Italy's salvation."

World War II brought new men, new tragedies, and soldiers in every kind of uniform to San Giovanni Rotondo. Moreover, mothers, wives, fiancées, sons and daughters, brothers and sisters, widows and orphans also came to San Giovanni Rotondo, while searching for soldiers who were dead, missing in action, prisoners of war, or simply deserters. Padre Pio listened to them all and had a word of comfort for everyone. Reports about miracles, clairvoyance, and mysterious interventions guided by "unknown forces" became more and more common.

Many remarkable conversions took place in San Giovanni Rotondo. Right after the war, several noteworthy conversions were reported in the press. Costante Rosatelli, an ardent Italian communist politician who was the Communist Party's chief propaganda architect, was one notable example. Michel Boyer, a hero of the French Resistance who was also a famous spokesman for the French Communist Party, was also converted during a visit with Padre Pio. But the conversion that most deeply impressed people in Italy was that of Professor Italia Betti, who was nicknamed the "Red Passion" of the province of Emilia, and often referred to as "Karl Marx's virago."

Italia Betti had a degree in mathematics but was forced to abandon her teaching career because of her opposition to the Fascist regime in Italy. During the German occupation, she was part of the resistance movement in Bologna. When the city was liberated, she led the local representatives of the resistance in a march against the allied forces. She was dressed in bright red, her hair blowing in the wind, waving a red flag in her fist. When the communists came to power in Bologna, she cut her hair like a man's, thundered through the streets of the city on a bright red motorcycle, and became an untiring proponent of atheistic communism in the city and the surrounding countryside.

When Betti visited San Giovanni Rotondo by chance, she suddenly and unexpectedly had a conversion experience. She abandoned her teaching career and her political activities and moved to San Giovanni Rotondo. There she devoted herself to a life of prayer and penance. She died a very holy woman.

Another conversion experience widely reported in the newspapers was that of Carlo Campanini, one of Italy's most popular actors. "My conversion experience took place in 1950, but Padre Pio had patiently kept his eye on me for eleven years," the actor told me. "When I visited him for the first time in 1939, I did so for selfish reasons. I thought he was some kind of magician or fortune teller, and I hoped to make some money by visiting him. As an actor, I toured the world. It was a hard life. I traveled all year long and lived like a gypsy. I was married and had three children. Since the work I was doing didn't allow me to have a permanent residence, no one wanted to rent me a house. My wife worked with me, and we had to leave our children with a sister-in-law.

"This kind of lifestyle was hard on me. I really wanted to find a job that would allow me to be with my children. I came from a very poor family and only went to school until sixth grade. All that time I was in a school run by the Christian Brothers, and we were forced to go to Mass every morning before classes. This bothered me so much that I never set foot in a church again after I left school."

One day in 1939, when Campanini was talking to a colleague, Mario Amendola, who later became a famous producer, Campanini told him: "Once it was easy to believe in God. There were great saints like St. Francis, St. Anthony, and St. John Bosco, who performed miracles. Saints no longer exist, and there aren't miracles anymore." Amendola told him that it wasn't true. "There's a holy monk in Puglia who does extraordinary things."

Amendola told him about an incident that had happened to his cousin a few years before. "He was poor, without a cent to his name, and out of work. Just to do something, he volunteered to fight in the civil war in Spain. When he returned, his wife told him,

'If you've made it back alive, it's because Padre Pio prayed for you. I made a vow to him that you would go and thank him.' My cousin went to San Giovanni Rotondo and told Padre Pio about his difficult situation. Padre Pio gave him some very precise direction: 'Go to Falconara.'

"'I can't,' my cousin answered. 'At least I have friends in Rome who'll help me. I'd die of hunger in Falconara.'

"'Go to Falconara,' Padre Pio repeated.

"My cousin moved there with his wife and children. He found his mother there. A few months before, she had left Rome so that she wouldn't be a burden on him. Now she was trying to survive by begging outside the door of the church. Together, they went through two months of incredibly hard times.

"One morning a man came from Ancona looking for my cousin. He said to him, 'I'm here on an assignment for the head of a union. He would like to see you tomorrow morning at his office.' My cousin went to his office at the appointed time. The man asked him if he spoke Spanish. 'Yes,' my cousin replied. He offered him a contract on the spot for a hundred lire a day—three thousand lire a month. At that time people felt they were living well when they made one thousand lire a month!"

"His cousin's experience made a deep impression on me. It also made me think," Campanini said.

During Holy Week, I was in Bari with a theater company. They gave us two days off—Thursday and Friday. That was the first time we were given two days off. Normally we only had Friday off. "San Giovanni Rotondo is somewhere around here," I told Amendola. "Why don't we visit that holy monk?"

We left on Thursday morning. San Giovanni Rotondo was poor and almost deserted. We looked for Padre Pio's church. "He can't see you," they told us. "His wounds are very painful. Even though they usually bleed all year long, during Holy Week they leave him in a pitiful state. For this reason, he is unable to see anyone." Nonetheless, we protested: "But we're actors. We've come from far away. We only have these two days free. We have to see him."

We decided to stay and walk around the monastery, hoping to run into Padre Pio. Since I was rather frivolous and could only think about making people laugh, I was even cracking jokes in the monastery. That Thursday afternoon, while Amendola and I were making a lot of noise, a friar who looked like a giant walked out of the church and complained: "So, you won't even let me pray these days! What do you want?"

"Father, we're two poor actors."

"We're all poor."

"We want to go to confession with you," I added, trying to justify our presence. "Go prepare yourselves," Padre Pio replied. "I'll hear your confession tomorrow morning after Mass."

"I remember that Mass as being a nightmare. It never ended. I had to stay on my knees the whole time. Otherwise those behind me couldn't see. The pain from kneeling was unbearable. When Mass was over, I went to confession. Padre Pio wouldn't let me speak. Yet he knew everything about me. He made me promise that I would change my life, and then gave me absolution. I didn't have the courage to ask him for anything. But inside me I kept repeating to myself: "Father, help me to find a job near home, even as a shopkeeper, so that I might live together with my children."

I went back to Bari and then I went to Rome. They were beginning to make a new film, *Addio Giovinezza*. Back in those days the actors' parts were assigned by the Ministry of Public Culture. There were four famous actors who were candidates for the role of Leone in that film: Nino Besozzi, who resembled the famous Italian actor Marcelo Mastroianni; Umberto Melnati, who worked with the famous producer De Sica and who was a hit all over Italy; and two other less-known actors, Paolo Stoppa and Carlo Romano. I was totally unknown in those circles, but for some reason that I'll never figure out, the part was given to me. But that wasn't the end of it. Since that time I've made over 106 films, one after another. Now I'm rich and famous. I was able to buy a house and live with my children, just as I had wanted.

Padre Pio told the actor that he needed to change his life, but Campanini did not do so. Fame and fortune had an adverse effect on his life. "I was leading a dissolute life. I was involved in illicit relationships. I wasn't going to Mass, and I didn't want to hear anything about prayer," he recalls. "Yet, I felt guilty. Padre Pio had answered my prayer, but I had deceived him. For this reason, I didn't want to go back to see him.

This was the situation I was in at the end of 1949. I was at the height of my fame. I had a custom-made American car. Newspapers wrote extensively about me because I was appearing in every film. I didn't lack anything. But morally I was destroyed, empty, tired, demoralized, and tremendously unhappy. I even envied those people who were brave enough to commit suicide.

One evening I returned home and my wife said to me, "The assistant priest at the parish dropped by and asked us to consecrate our house to the Sacred Heart. The ceremony is set for January 8. He suggested that we prepare ourselves spiritually because he would like us all to receive Communion." This made me uneasy. I couldn't receive Communion given the life I was living. My wife and even my little daughter were insistent that we do it, and I couldn't think of an excuse to make up.

While I was walking around Rome restless and unhappy on the morning of January 6, 1950, feast of the Epiphany, I happened to go into St. Anthony's Church on the Via Merulana. The church was crowded with people who were there for Mass, and some people were standing in line to go to confession. A lot of people recognized me and were watching me out of curiosity. The confessional had a glass window on the door, and I spotted a chubby and ruddy monk inside. "That guy enjoys a good meal more than I do," I said to myself. "I'll never tell him my sins."

At that moment I saw another monk praying in front of a crucifix. He looked emaciated, and from his face it was clear that he had suffered a great deal. "That monk is more of a mystic. I think I could open up to him," I thought. Right at that moment the skinny monk stood up, went right to the confessional where the chubby monk was, and took his place. I was perplexed, but I reassured myself by saying, "Look at all the people in front of me. I can't wait." Just as the thought crossed my mind, the man at the front of the line turned to me and said, "Go ahead, sir." I found myself kneeling in the confessional.

I left a half-hour later with tears streaming down my face. I felt like a new man. We celebrated as a family. Joyfully I participated in the consecration of our home to the Sacred Heart and went to Communion. I decided to visit Padre Pio and let him know that my life had changed. Since I had already confessed my past sins, I didn't need to tell him what they were. But when I entered his confessional, he said to me: "Begin in 1936."

"I just went to confession a few days ago," I protested.

"I told you to begin in 1936," Padre Pio said in a thundering voice. He told me that I was a coward if I was ashamed to confess my sins when I wasn't ashamed to offend Jesus.

That confession changed my life completely. When I finished, Padre Pio hugged me and kissed me. He gave me a rosary, urging me to pray the rosary often. Then he added, "I'll always be at your side." It wasn't easy to keep my promise, but I worked hard at it. I haven't missed daily Mass since then."

From that time on Campanini was a frequent visitor to the monastery in San Giovanni Rotondo. "I consider Padre Pio to be my protector," he told me.

I feel him by me every moment of the day, in every situation, especially in the midst of difficulties. He saved my niece who was dying. When my son was finishing his degree at the university, he was suddenly confronted with the possibility of having to do another year of studies. At the last moment, he learned that a section on urban studies was being added to the exam for his degree in architecture. "I know almost nothing about urban studies," my son said. "I'll be able to answer three questions at the most." I told him I would ask Padre Pio to pray for him. He smiled at me condescendingly because he himself didn't believe. He thought that my devotion was a form of fanaticism. But when he came home after the exam, he said, "Dad, would you believe those were the three questions they asked me?"

Once I was on tour in Brazil for six months. The night that I had to catch my plane home, I remembered that I hadn't been to Mass that day. I checked the Mass schedules and saw that there was a Mass at 6:30 in the evening at the cathedral in Sao Paolo. I took a taxi there. I wanted to go to confession, but there was only one priest hearing confessions and a lot of people were waiting in line. Moreover, I don't speak a word of Portuguese. I prayed to Padre Pio: "I have to catch a flight this evening and it might be the last evening of my life. I really want to go to confession before leaving. I beg you to help me find a priest who speaks Italian." At that moment the door of one of the confessionals opened and a priest said to me in perfect Italian, "Come in." When I finished my confession, I could smell the typical fragrance that emanated from Padre Pio.

The plane trip was a nightmare. We flew through a terrible storm, and the radar wasn't working. All the passengers were shouting and crying. The impresario for our touring company fainted, and they had to give him oxygen. Lelio Luttazzi and Fred Bongusto were traveling with me. When we landed, my wife came to pick me up at the airport and they said to her: "Your husband sure is an ascetic soul. Everyone was scared stiff and he just slept."

Campanini had many intimate conversations with Padre Pio, who would hug him like a brother whenever they met. "Padre Pio liked to tell jokes," Campanini recalled.

He was much more clever than me. He had a knack for being concise. And he had a knack for knowing the right thing to say at the right time, like a good actor. One of my friends from the theater was being treated by a famous doctor in Florence. One day my friend told his doctor: "Tomorrow I won't be here for my usual treatment because I'm going to see Padre Pio." The doctor asked him: "Why are you going to see that hysterical old man? That's what science would call him. Why, he caused the stigmata to appear simply by thinking so much about Jesus on the cross." When my friend visited Padre Pio and finished his confession, he told Padre Pio what his doctor had said. "When you see him," Padre Pio replied, "tell him to think intensely about being an ox. Let's see if he grows horns."

A lot of people complained that Padre Pio was rough on sinners and often sent them away. One day I said to him, "Did you know that Fr. Leopoldo of Padova spent sixteen hours a day in the confessional and never turned anyone away?"

"I know," Padre Pio answered. "In fact, he sends the worst ones to me."

Then I added, "But you're taking a big responsibility on your shoulders by sending them away without absolution. What happens if they die after they leave church?" Padre Pio threw up his arms and said: "If I've made a mistake, do you think God would make a mistake? God will take care of things."

Following Carlo Campanini's example, many other famous Italian celebrities sought Padre Pio's advice, including Mario Riva, Tino Scotti, Aldo Fabrizi, Beniamino Gigli, Gino Bechi, Ferruccio Tagliavini, Silvio Gigli, and Lisa Gastoni.

Beniamino Gigli ended up going to Padre Pio by coincidence. One day, when he was talking on the phone with his girlfriend, his wife caught him by surprise and asked him, "Whom are you talking to?" Gigli told her, "With someone who wants to take me to meet

Padre Pio." In order to avoid raising suspicion, he ended up making the trip to San Giovanni Rotondo. While he was in the monastery garden, he laughingly told himself: "Don't think for an instant that I'm going to tell that friar about my affairs." A while later Padre Pio came down. "Giovanotto, change your shirt," he told Gigli. "I put on a clean one this morning," the singer replied. "I don't mean that one," Padre Pio retorted. He took the famous tenor by the hand and led him into the garden. When they came back, Gigli was deeply moved. From that moment on, his life changed and he became one of Padre Pio's spiritual sons.

SEVENTEEN

Francesco Messina's Testimony

A nother conversion experience that caused quite a stir was that of Francesco Messina, the famous Italian sculptor whose popularity in the years following World War II was comparable to that of a movie star.

"Padre Pio played a very significant role in my life," the sculptor confided to me. "My first encounter with him on April 11, 1949, was like a bolt of lightning. It radically changed my way of thinking and of looking at things. It even gave a whole new orientation to my art."

News about Messina's meeting with Padre Pio quickly circulated around the world. Newspapers reported on it at length, although the reports were often exaggerated. "They made it seem like I had been an atheist and vehemently anticlerical up to that time," the sculptor told me. "But that wasn't the case. Until then, even though I believed in God, I had been a big sinner, but Padre Pio changed me. I felt compelled to make a public statement, so I wrote an open letter to the newspapers, thanking God for having met a 'true priest.' I concluded the letter by saying: 'I was born on April 11, 1949.'"

Francesco Messina spoke to me at length about his relationship with Padre Pio. We visited in his studio and museum, located in the ancient Church of San Sisto in Milan, which the artist has restored even though it no longer serves as a church. We were surrounded by statues, plaster molds, drawings, reproductions, and photographs of his works. His sculptures, which rival those of Michelangelo in size, are now part of art history. His statue of Pope Pius XII, which is twelve feet tall, is on display in Saint Peter's Basilica in

Rome, the most prestigious church in Christianity, next to famous works by Buonarroti, Bernini, and Canova.

"I am a man who always has his feet on the ground. I also have an instinctive aversion for anything of a miraculous nature," Messina said. "When I was young and heard my friends talking about some of the phenomena associated with Padre Pio such as miraculous fragrances, bilocation, and reading people's souls, I refused to believe them. I even made fun of them. Nonetheless, I was curious about this monk with his fiery eyes. I was especially baffled by his mysterious wounds. It was hard to doubt that they were genuine since various doctors had examined them. It's for this reason that I wanted to meet him."

Messina was born into an extremely poor family in Linguaglossa, in Sicily. He grew up in Genoa, where his parents had moved to seek their fortune. He was already working by the time he was ten years old.

"I was baptized, but I never had any religious upbringing," Messina told me.

My father never talked about God, and neither did my mother. They never took a concern to see that I made my first Holy Communion or that I was confirmed. Our only link with God was our poverty, since poverty is an authentic relationship with Christ.

From the time I was a child I often thought about Jesus even though I never went to church. I felt as though he was a friend who understood me. I wanted to follow his teachings, but I was a sinner, waylaid by vanity, pride, and all other kinds of human vices.

I lived this way for forty years. I was in a relationship with a woman whom I couldn't marry since she was not free to marry. Cardinal Schuster of Milan, who took a concern for me and was a good friend, always reminded me: "The Church can't do anything for you." However, her situation changed during the war, and we were able to obtain permission to get married in the Church. First of all, though, I had to receive the other sacraments: the Eucharist and Confirmation. These sacraments had a liberating effect on me. For the first time in my life, I felt I was at peace. But this peace only lasted a very short time.

I returned to my former ways. I had faith, but I didn't have anyone to guide me, a teacher who could be a point of reference for me in the midst of so much uncertainty and so many spiritual struggles.

It was during this time in my life that I had a great desire to meet Padre Pio. As I've already said, I wasn't attracted by the miracles people attributed to him. What attracted me were the stigmata, which for me were a sign of true holiness.

In the spring of 1949, an exhibition of Messina's work was held at a prestigious art gallery in Genoa. It won the applause of all the art critics. The press praised his art, but Messina himself was feeling empty and dissatisfied.

On the last day of his stay in Genoa, something strange happened. "That evening," the artist told me,

I went with my wife to have dinner at the home of some friends. All of them were followers of Padre Pio. They spoke to me at length about Padre Pio. Our host had a biography about him with a very expressive photograph of him inside. I held the book in my hands and looked at his eyes for a long time. "I have to meet him," I said to myself.

When dinner was over, my wife and I went back to the Hotel Bristol where we were staying. That night I couldn't sleep. I tossed and turned in bed, thinking about Padre Pio. His image seemed to follow me.

At five o'clock in the morning the phone rang. "Who's calling at this hour?" I asked. The desk clerk apologized, and told me that someone was insisting on talking to me—a man named Ezio Saltamerenda.

I knew Ezio. When I was young, we lived next door to each other and we often went swimming together. Ezio told me a rather unusual story. "Yesterday evening, while I was walking across the Piazza De Ferrari, I suddenly smelled the sweet and miraculous fragrance that I associate with Padre Pio." I brusquely cut him off: "What are you up to? Are you peddling Padre Pio's perfume?"

"Don't think I'm a fool," Saltamerenda replied. "Well, maybe I am, but not this time. As I was saying, I was walking across the Piazza De Ferrari, when I suddenly smelled Padre Pio's sweet fragrance. Generally people smell that fragrance when Padre Pio wants something, and I wondered why I was smelling it then and there. I took a few steps and the fragrance disappeared. I went back to where I had been standing, and I smelled it again. I looked around. In front of me was a large poster advertising your exhibition. The fragrance was coming from that poster! I did a few experiments, and there was no doubt about it. I smelled Padre Pio's fragrance only when I was in front of the poster announcing your exhibition. When I got home, I couldn't fall asleep. I felt I had to call you and let you know. I resisted until now."

Angrily I asked him, "So, what do you want now?"

"Nothing," he answered. "It's Padre Pio who wants something from you."

I felt a strong urge to cut off such a ridiculous conversation by slamming down the phone, but the strange coincidences concerning Padre Pio that had occurred within a few short hours prevented me from doing so. "You should go see Padre Pio," Saltamerenda repeated. "I have a lot to do," I answered. "I'm going back to Milan today. Call me next week and I'll see if I find the time."

The next day I found out a little more about my childhood friend. He was highly respected. He had a degree in medicine and was director of the Biotherapeutic Institute in Genoa. He had been a sincere atheist as a young man, and always fought for what he believed in. During the war, he went through some rather painful ups and downs. Because of Padre Pio, he had a conversion experience, became his spiritual son, and never lost an opportunity to tell people about Padre Pio."

When he returned to Milan, Messina immersed himself in his work, but he still could not sleep at night. The thought of Padre Pio became an obsession. A week later, he called Saltamerenda. "I have to see Padre Pio," he told him. "That friar doesn't let me sleep anymore." He decided to leave immediately.

"We arrived in San Giovanni Rotondo late in the evening," Messina recalled.

At that time of night, Padre Pio wasn't seeing anyone. However, the monks at the monastery knew Saltamerenda and let us in. When Padre Pio saw us, he said to Saltamerenda: "Oh, you're here again, you pain in the neck!"

"Father, I felt I had to bring this friend to you," Ezio answered.

"You're a real fanatic," Padre Pio said. Then he turned to me and said, "What do you want?"

"I wanted to meet you," I said. "This has been my desire for a long time. I'm happy to be here. I put myself into your hands."

Then Padre Pio said, "You're in good hands." He told us to go to the church so that we could go to confession. I didn't want to go to confession, because I didn't feel prepared to do so psychologically, but I didn't have time to protest. Padre Pio had already left.

When he returned, I went up to him to tell him that I didn't feel ready. But he told me in a voice that left no room for a reply: "Don't say anything to me. Just answer." Then he began to list my sins with incredible precision. It was as though he could read my soul.

The next morning I went to Mass and received Communion.

When I went to say good-bye to Padre Pio, he said to me: "What? You just arrived and you're already leaving?"

"I have business in Milan, but I'll be back soon" I replied. From that moment on, Padre Pio was an extraordinary spiritual director for me, truly a "father." Whenever I had the chance, I would visit him.

Francesco Messina became Padre Pio's faithful spiritual son from that moment on. He visited San Giovanni Rotondo frequently. He regularly visited the Capuchin friar in his cell, went to confession to him, spoke with him at length, and occasionally brought other friends along who needed some words of comfort.

"As I said, I never thought a lot about Padre Pio's miracles," Messina explained.

The miracles that people talked about and that the newspapers wrote about left me feeling indifferent. They might be true, but in my opinion Padre Pio's true holiness was found in his way of thinking and living. One day, though, I too witnessed an inexplicable event that I've never wanted to talk about. But maybe it's good for people to hear about it.

I was a good friend of Giovanni Papini, the famous Italian writer who died in 1956. For a long time he was completely paralyzed. Even his tongue was affected, and he communicated with whimpers that only his niece was able to decipher. The only contact that this famous writer had with the outside world was through a ray of light that he could see through his right eye. To see a little light and read a few words, even with great difficulty, was a source of immense joy for him.

One morning Papini's wife called me and said: "A while ago Giovanni fell in the bathtub, hit the right side of his head, and can't even see the little ray of light that he could see before. Now he's completely blind. We've taken him to the best specialists, but there's nothing they can do. The sight in his eye is gone. Giovanni's very sad. Since you're Padre Pio's friend, I would like you to ask the monk to pray for him."

I was very upset. I wanted only the best for Giovanni, and I wouldn't hesitate to make any sacrifice that might alleviate his suffering. "What can we do?" I asked Mrs. Papini.

"I was thinking that if I give you a photo of Giovanni and you take it to Padre Pio, maybe he can do something," she answered.

"I think that's a good idea," I told her. I made arrangements for the trip.

I stopped in Florence, picked up the photo of Papini, and went to San Giovanni Rotondo. I had visited Padre Pio a week before, so when he saw me he said dryly: "Are you still here?"

"Something sad happened," I told him, "that medicine can't resolve and that involves my dear friend, Giovanni Papini. He's a famous writer. Even you must know about him."

"What should I know about Papini?" Padre Pio answered.

"He's the one that wrote the *Story of Christ,*" I insisted.

"A lot of people have written on that topic," he said. I went on to explain: "My friend is very ill. He was only able to see very little out of one eye, but then he had a fall and hit his head and now he can't see anything." I took out the photograph of Papini and handed it to him. Padre Pio looked at it for a while. Then, putting it in the pocket of his shirt, he said to me in all earnest: "If that's what happened, I'll think about it. Go tell his family not to worry. I'm thinking about it."

I went back to Florence and told them everything that Padre Pio had said. I was anxious and discouraged. I saw the immense sorrow of Papini's wife, and inside me I was sure that nothing would happen. During the next few days I didn't have the courage to call her in Florence. But a week later Mrs. Papini called me. "Did you hear that Giovanni can see as well as he did before the fall?" she asked happily.

"So the fall didn't affect his eye," I answered.

"No, no," she insisted. "Something strange happened. All the doctors who saw Giovanni said that his eye had been damaged forever. They can't explain how he can see again. But you and I know what really happened."

"Well, maybe it's better that we don't say anything," I said. "Otherwise they'll think we're some kind of fanatics."

Giovanni Papini continued to see to the very end of his life. Following my recommendation, his wife never said anything about what happened, but I think the time has come to talk about it. I don't know why Papini was able to see again. However, I'm sure that Padre Pio took an interest in him and prayed for him.

Francesco Messina is the creator of a monumental sculpture called *Via Crucis* that is now located in San Giovanni Rotondo, between the convent of Santa Maria delle Grazie and the House for the Relief of Suffering.

"It was my last work," the sculptor told me.

I didn't want to do it. When the Capuchins commissioned me to do it in 1967, my hands were already crippled from arthritis. But they told me that Padre Pio wanted me to do it, so I accepted the job.

While I was preparing the first designs, I often visited San Giovanni Rotondo. I would stop and talk with Padre Pio when I was there. He was already quite sick, and he walked with great difficulty. He felt shooting pains in his feet. I would ask him, "How are you, Father?" He would answer, "Not very well, not very well at all."

Padre Pio was not able to see the *Via Crucis* when it was finished, but he was there to bless it when we laid the first stone. They've placed my bronze statue of Padre Pio, which is seven feet tall, on the spot where he stood during that ceremony.

EIGHTEEN

Miracles Every Day

E very biography of Padre Pio dedicates at least one chapter to his miracles. In fact, the biographies that were published while he was still alive were based mainly on these miracles, which were described in great detail. Consequently, the Holy Office regularly put them on the index of forbidden books, in accordance with Canon 1399 of Canon Law. But Padre Pio's followers read them and circulated them nonetheless.

In 1952 the Holy Office condemned eight different books on Padre Pio and his miracles all at the same time. Today these books are considered "historical sources" and are quoted at length in the official biographies that have been prepared for the cause of his beatification.

For the Church, a miracle is a "sign" that draws people's attention to the spiritual world. Theologians define it as a "noteworthy event produced by God's specific intervention, which lies outside the course of nature and which serves some supernatural purpose."

The Church has instituted a long process for determining whether something is an authentic miracle. We will be able to talk objectively about Padre Pio's miracles only when he has been named a saint. When referring to Padre Pio's miracles in this book, we are speaking about those numerous, mysterious, inexplicable, and extraordinary events that continually occurred in his presence and involved him. We will describe them by citing first-person testimonies or the testimonies of interested parties whenever possible. However, we have no desire to pass judgment on the miraculous nature of these events.

The first newspaper article about Padre Pio, which was published in Naples' *Mattino* on June 21, 1919, mentioned his miracles. Its headline was spread across six columns: *Padre Pio, the "Saint" of San Giovanni Rotondo, Works a Miracle for the Region's Chancellor.* It described the experience of Pasquale Di Chiara, thirty-six, who was chancellor of the Prefecture of San Giovanni Rotondo. De Chiara had been forced to use a cane in order to walk after suffering a fall several months earlier. Padre Pio commanded him to walk when he saw him. Di Chiara described his experience to the journalist: "I felt a strong burning sensation in my foot, that soon spread throughout my body. I began to walk perfectly without any need for assistance."

The newspaper also referred to the fact that Pasquale Di Chiara's daughter had also experienced a miraculous healing. A victim of infantile paralysis, she had been using braces on her legs. But when Padre Pio told her to take them off, she was able to walk and never used them again.

Pasquale Urbano from Foggia was sixty-two years old in 1919. He needed to support himself with two canes whenever he walked, after having fallen out of a carriage and broken his legs. The doctors were never able to help him. After hearing his confession, Padre Pio said to him: "Get up and go. But you have to throw away those canes." To everyone's amazement, Pasquale Urbano obeyed and walked away.

Another noteworthy event that caused a stir in the area around Foggia also took place in 1919. It involved Antonio d'Onofrio, who was fourteen at the time. When he was four years old, Antonio came down with typhoid fever. Afterward he suffered a form of rickets, and his body was deformed by two large humps. One day Padre Pio heard his confession and then touched him with his wounded hands. The boy got up from his knees and walked as straight as an arrow. Likewise, Francesco Vicio, a seventy-five-year-old man known as "the little saint," also was deformed. He moved about on all fours with his chin almost touching the ground. News about his complete and miraculous healing spread quickly.

In his books on Padre Pio, Alberto Del Fante, another of Padre Pio's famous converts, collected documentation concerning thirty-seven miraculous healings that were attributed to Padre Pio during the 1920s. His own personal conversion experience occurred after a miracle. Del Fante had been a Mason who despised Padre Pio. He wrote several articles in the Florentine magazine *Italia Laica,* accusing him of being a swindler, "capable of duping naive people who are prey to outbursts of enthusiasm." A few years later, his dearly loved grandson, Enrico, was suffering from kidney disease and showed symptoms of tuberculosis of the lungs and of his bones. Doctors gave little hope for his recovery. Two of Del Fante's relatives went to see Padre Pio. When they returned, they told everyone that Padre Pio had said that everything would be well. Alberto Del Fante was still skeptical. "If Enrico gets well, I, too, will make a pilgrimage there." He was convinced that nothing would happen. Instead, the child recovered. Totally bewildered, Del Fante went to San Giovanni Rotondo, where he had a conversion experience, and subsequently became a fervent proponent of Padre Pio's life and work.

It was an extremely emotional experience to live in daily contact with Padre Pio, especially at the beginning of the twenties when his fame was still limited and there were no rules or regulations that kept him away from people. Every day extraordinary things happened that were connected to him in some way. It seemed as though the laws of physics that governed the life of every human being did not apply to him.

Emanuele Brunatto had the good fortune to be in regular contact with Padre Pio during this period. As we have already noted, Emanuele Brunatto was one of the first people to have a conversion experience because of Padre Pio. Later, he led the life of a "secret agent" in his attempts to defend Padre Pio during the first wave of persecution that Padre Pio had to endure.

Immediately after his conversion experience, Brunatto went to live in San Giovanni Rotondo so that he could spend as much time as possible near Padre Pio. Every morning, at four o'clock, he went to church to hear Mass. He remained there until evening. He often ate dinner with the monks. For a while he taught at the local high school for boys aspiring to religious life. Brunatto did not doubt Padre Pio's sanctity. He kept a diary in which he noted everything he observed. These eyewitness reports are extremely valuable because they relate events that were witnessed by a person who was both cunning and cynical. Here are some "little flowers" from Brunatto's unpublished diary:

The monks at the monastery used to play a form of lawn bowling, but Padre Pio was not a very accomplished player. One day a cat was walking by at the very moment when Padre Pio was throwing his ball. The cat became frightened and ran right into the ball's path. He was about to be hit when the ball stopped in midair and fell to the side.

I was splitting logs in the monastery garden when I got a splinter deep in my thumb. A couple of monks tried to get it out, but neither could manage to grab hold of it. Then Padre Pio came up to me smiling. I knew what he was about to do, so I extended my hand without saying a word. He took my thumb between his fingers and, with a swift, precise, and painless gesture, pulled the splinter out.

Once I had an infection in my left toe. On Sunday I was unable to walk, so I went to the monastery riding on a mule. After Mass, I sat down in the garden. Padre Pio came up to me and asked: "Who are you waiting for?"

"Antonio's mule, because I can't walk."

"No, you're going to leave walking. The walk will do you good," he replied, smiling but making a command at the same time. I obeyed. As I walked along, the pain gradually subsided, and by the time I arrived at my home, it had completely disappeared. I took off the bandages. The gauze was soaked with blood and pus. But instead of an infection, there was a white scar without even a ring of infection around it. I was healed!

Angela Serritelli was reading a letter from Padre Pio by the side of the road. The wind blew the paper from her hand, carrying it down the side of the mountain. It was already quite far away when it suddenly came to a complete stop on top of a rock, and Angelina was able to grab it.

The next day Padre Pio said to her: "Be careful of the wind next time. If I hadn't put my foot on top of it, my letter would have ended up in the valley."

I was writing a religious play, *"Brother Son,"* in a cell at the monastery. It was going to be produced at the Adrian Theater in Rome. I came to the final scene in which St. Francis was being told: "Whoever has spoken through the mouth of the ass of Balaam has not met a more vile creature on earth than me." At that moment Padre Pio came knocking at my door: "Giovanotto, come. It's recreation time."

"I'm coming, Father," I answered without opening the door. I finished writing down the line and went to the garden. Padre Pio greeted me with a mischievous little smile. "So, what does the ass of Balaam say?" he asked.

Winter of 1922 was especially harsh. Throughout the month of January I had to walk a mile and a half every morning to the monastery with snow up to my knees. When I arrived at the sacristy, Padre Pio was there, squatting down by the stove and warming his hands. For three or four days in a row he greeted me with the same words: "You're going to get sick!" Each time I would laugh.

One evening as I was going into my hermitage, I suddenly began to shiver from the cold. I kindled a fire in the fireplace so I could warm up. But then I had a hard time breathing. My head, my chest, and my back began to hurt.

I spoke to Padre Pio, pretending he was there: "If I'm going to get sick, Father, let me get sick in the monastery and not here, far away from you!" Then I dragged myself to my bed and lost consciousness.

During the night, I came to, and instinctively I grabbed one of Padre Pio's checkered handkerchiefs that I kept under my pillow. I pressed it to my nose. I coughed so hard into it that it cleared out my lungs. My temperature went down.

At about four o'clock in the morning I began to walk to the monastery as usual. I arrived there in the middle of a big snowstorm. Padre Pio was in the sacristy by the stove, with his back turned to me. Without turning around he asked: "What happened to you last night?" Deeply moved, I told him what had happened and about the providential cough.

"It won't be the last one," he said. "You'll have others." In fact, a second big cough caught me by surprise on my way home, and a third one at home in the evening. After that, I felt completely well again.

A few days went by. One morning, before leaving the monastery, I went to one of the common rooms to warm up. I found Padre Pio sitting there next to the fireplace. I sat down next to him and extended my hand toward the flames that were leaping up. I was in the same position that I was in that evening when I was sitting by the fireplace in my hermitage and cried out to Padre Pio for help. Suddenly, the fever, the tightening in my chest, and the pains reappeared exactly as they did that evening. Padre Pio raised his head and said to me very simply: "Well, here's what you wanted!" Then he turned to the guestmaster and said: "Emanuele has a fever of 104 degrees. He needs to spend a couple of weeks in bed. What do you think? Can we prepare cell number six for him since it's empty?"

Indeed, the thermometer registered 104 degrees. I spent exactly fifteen days in bed with double bronchitis and an intestinal infection.

I had a pleasant surprise when I was better. The guestmaster offered me a position as a teacher in the little boarding school for candidates to the Capuchin order that was annexed to the monastery.

Grazia, a peasant woman who was twenty-nine years old and who had been blind from birth, had been coming to the small church at the monastery for some time. One day Padre Pio suddenly asked her if she would like to see. "Of course I would," she answered, "as long as it won't be an occasion for sin." Padre Pio told her that she would get well and sent her to Bari. He asked the wife of a leading eye doctor, Dr. Durante, to watch out for her. After the eye doctor had examined the woman, he said to his wife: "I can't do anything for her. Padre Pio might be able to perform a miracle and heal her, but I can't. I have to send her home without operating on her."

But his wife insisted: "Since Padre Pio sent her to you, you could at least try to operate on one of her eyes." His wife finally convinced him. First he operated on one eye, and then the other. Both were healed.

Upon returning to San Giovanni Rotondo, Grazia went to the monastery. I was in the sacristy when she threw herself at Padre Pio's feet. He stood there in silence looking about while she lay at his feet. Then he told her to get up. Grazia got up and looked at him for the first time in her life. You could see only love, wonder, joy, and gratitude in those eyes that were seeing light for the first time. Padre Pio stood there without moving and smiled at her.

"Bless me, Father, bless me," she implored. He traced the sign of the cross above her. But Grazia remained there motionless. When she was blind, Padre Pio would bless her by putting his hands on her head. "Bless me, Father, bless me," she repeated, disappointed. "What kind of blessing do you want?" Padre Pio replied. "A pail of water on your head?"

Emanuele Brunatto also relates the conversion experience of a famous lawyer from Genoa, Dr. Cesare Festa, president of the

Italian veterans association, mayor of Arenzano, counsellor to King Victor Emmanuel III of Italy, and a high dignitary in the Freemasons. His conversion experience caused quite a stir in Italy, and the newspapers reported it at length. Emanuele Brunatto described Festa's experience in the following words:

Cesare Festa was a very well educated and intelligent lawyer. A leading jurist and public speaker, he was convinced that the Catholic Church was preventing social progress. He fought against the Church passionately in the political arena.

Because of his position, he was always engaging in lively conversations with his cousin, Dr. Giorgio Festa, who had discovered some solid reasons for defending the Church because of Padre Pio.

One day Dr. Festa said to his cousin the lawyer: "What purpose does it serve to keep on fighting? There's someone who will put an end at once to all your objections: Padre Pio. Go visit him. Then we can take up our discussion again."

"OK, I'll go," the lawyer responded. He kept his promise.

When he arrived at the monastery, a monk welcomed him with these words: "Why are you, a Freemason, coming here to be with us?" He was a bit shaken by this welcome and tried to explain. While he was speaking, Padre Pio opened the door of the sacristy and showed him the way to the confessional. The lawyer obeyed without a fight. He went to confession for the first time since he was a teenager.

He stayed at the monastery as a guest for a few days, where he received the scapular of the Third Order Franciscans. Upon returning to Rome, he went to thank his cousin. "From now on I don't want to burden my brain with philosophical or scientific texts. Tell me what good and holy book to read," he said to his cousin. Dr. Festa suggested a two-volume work on the life of the Holy Family written by Fr. Pietro Bergamaschi. "But I don't have it." Dr. Festa explained, "Padre Pio gave it to me to read while I was in San Giovanni Rotondo. But you can probably find it in a bookstore on the Via Cavour that specializes in such works. It's on your way to the train station."

The lawyer, who was returning that evening to Genoa, discovered that the bookstore was closed. So he was unable to buy the book. When he arrived at home the next morning, he went straight to bed. While he was sleeping, a young man whom he did not know came to his apartment and handed his servant a package saying, "For the commander." Then he left. It was a package containing the two volumes by Bergamaschi, old and covered with newspaper.

When I met the lawyer for the first time in Genoa, he told me what had happened. He said that the two volumes were still in his study. He found them in the bookcase and showed them to me. I immediately recognized them, since on the spine of the cover, in red ink and in my handwriting, were the call numbers of the monastery library at San Giovanni Rotondo, to which they belonged.

The Italian comedy writer Luigi Antonelli, author of such works as *L'uomo che incontro se stesso, La fiaba dei tre maghi,* and *L'isola delle scimmie,* also experienced one of Padre Pio's miracles. He described his experience to an Argentinean writer, Dino Segre, known as Pitigrilli, who also experienced a conversion because of Padre Pio.

The doctors discovered that I had cancer extending from my ear to my back. They told me what they told everyone. When it comes to cancer, modern science is where it was two thousand years ago. Back then, the motto was *opium et mentiri*: give the victim some opium and hide the truth from him. Today, though, the doctors' lies are more sophisticated. Instead of putting opium in your drinks, they inject you with painkillers. I said to my surgeon: "At this point, I've lived half of my human life.

Anything more is extra, and I'm not about to give it up. Tell me the truth. How much more time do I have?"

"With the operation, six months; without the operation, three months."

"Operate, then," I said. "Three months of life isn't something to throw away."

I was about to be operated on when someone suggested, "Why don't you go and see Padre Pio?" I checked with various people and everyone told me about a monk who worked miracles who lived at the Capuchin monastery in San Giovanni Rotondo. I'm not sure that the word "miracle" is exact from a theological point of view. I went to see Padre Pio, attended a Mass that he celebrated, and had a long talk with him in the confessional. I cannot repeat what he said to me, because while he was speaking to me I seemed to be living in a supernatural world!

My cancer was arrested. Now I am writing an article every Sunday for the newspaper *Giornale d'Italia*. I go hunting. For the past month I've been working on a comedy which will be produced at the Manzoni Theater in Milan. I don't know what the doctors think, and I don't know what X rays and a histological examination might reveal—which I wouldn't let them do anyway—but I feel like I have been miraculously cured.

During World War II, many who were suffering, frustrated, discouraged, and penniless came to the monastery of Santa Maria delle Grazie, seeking a word of hope from Padre Pio. The heartrending scenes that occurred in Padre Pio's confessional during that period of his life defy words. Padre Pio was a very sensitive man, and their anguish often upset him. He would burst out in tears when he was talking to them. During such moments a mysterious strength surged from his soul, accompanied by a miracle.

Cleonice Morcaldi, the aunt of the mayor of San Giovanni Rotondo and an administrator of the hospital that Padre Pio established later in his life, recounted the following story:

During World War II, my nephew was a prisoner. We hadn't received any news about him. Everyone thought he was dead. His parents were going crazy with grief. One day his mother flung herself at Padre Pio's feet when he was in the confessional. "Tell me if my son is alive," she said. "I won't let go of your feet until you tell me." Padre Pio was deeply touched and, with tears streaming down his face, said, "Get up and go in peace."

A few days later, my heart could no longer bear the sorrowful tears of his parents, so I decided to ask Padre Pio for a miracle. Full of faith, I said to him, "Father, I'm writing a letter to my nephew, Giovannino, with only his name on the envelope since I don't know where to send it. You and your guardian angel have to get it to wherever he is."

Padre Pio didn't answer me. I wrote the letter that evening, and set it on my nightstand before going to bed. The next morning, to my great surprise, amazement, and fear, I noticed that the letter wasn't there. I was shocked. I went to thank Padre Pio. "Thank the Virgin Mary," he said. Two weeks later, the family was weeping with joy and thanking God and Padre Pio. My nephew, whom everyone had feared was dead, sent a letter in reply.

Luisa Vario was a woman of Italian and English origins who was well known by Europe's best families. She was very rich and married when she was young, yet she was dissatisfied with the life she was leading. She met someone at a party who told her about Padre Pio. Out of curiosity she went to San Giovanni Rotondo. She was annoyed when she saw how barren and poor the countryside was. She went to the church in San Giovanni Rotondo and felt no emotion. She approached the confessional where Padre Pio was hearing confessions, but he sent her away, saying that he would hear her confession later.

"When it was my turn for confession," Luisa Vario said, "I was anxious and confused. I said to Padre Pio, 'I don't know what to say.' His answer was, 'Then I will speak.' Then he proceeded to tell me my whole life's story as though he was reading from a book. At the end, he asked me if I had something to add. There was still one sin that he hadn't mentioned. I felt very ashamed. I couldn't decide whether I should say something. Yet, if I kept silent, my confession wouldn't be valid. I said to myself, 'Why should I confess something that he didn't mention after having told me everything?' Padre Pio was waiting in silence for me to answer. Finally I found the strength to confess even that sin. 'That's the one I was waiting for,' he said. 'You've won the victory. Don't get discouraged.'"

Luisa Vario had a son who was an officer in the British Navy. Every day she prayed for her son's conversion and for the salvation of his soul. One day an English pilgrim arrived in San Giovanni Rotondo with a bundle of British newspapers. Luisa asked if she could read them. A news item reported that the ship on which her son was sailing had sunk. In tears, she ran to Padre Pio. The monk consoled her by saying, "But who told you that your son is dead?" He then told her the exact name and address of the hotel where her son was staying. He had escaped the shipwreck. Luisa Vario wrote to him immediately, and received a reply a few days later.

Savino Grieco was an atheist who was noted in Puglia for his fervor in combatting religion. His wife, on the other hand, was very religious. Savino Grieco had strictly forbidden her to go to church or to talk to their children about God.

In 1950 Savino fell sick. The doctor's diagnosis was dismal: a brain tumor and another tumor behind his ear. There was no hope for recovery. Savino Grieco himself told me his story:

> I was taken to the hospital in Bari. I was very afraid of being sick and of dying. It is this fear that stirred within my soul a strong desire to turn to God, which I had not done since childhood.
>
> From Bari I was taken to Milan to undergo surgery in an attempt to save my life. The doctor who examined me told me

that the operation was very delicate and the outcome was rather doubtful.

One night, while I was in Milan, I saw Padre Pio in a dream. He touched my head and I heard him say, "Watch, you'll get well with time." By morning I was better. The doctors were amazed at my rapid recovery, but maintained that the operation was indispensable. However, I was terrified. Just before I was supposed to go to the operating room, I fled from the hospital and went to the home of some relatives in Milan, where my wife was also staying.

After a few days, though, the pain returned, worse than before. I couldn't bear it. I went back to the hospital. The doctors were upset and didn't want to treat me, but their professional conscience prevailed. Before proceeding with the operation, though, they thought it would be best to do one more test.

After they did the test, they realized there was absolutely no trace of the tumors, much to their amazement. I too was amazed, not so much by what the doctors told me but by the fact that during the tests I smelled an intense fragrance of violets, and I knew that that fragrance announced Padre Pio's presence.

Before leaving the hospital, I asked for my bill. "You don't owe anything," I was told, "since we didn't do anything to save you."

Upon my return home, I wanted to go with my wife to San Giovanni Rotondo to thank Padre Pio. I was convinced that it was because of him that I was healed. But when I arrived at the church at the monastery of Santa Maria delle Grazie, the pain returned with a vengeance, so much so that I fainted. Two men carried me to Padre Pio's confessional.

When I came to and saw him, I said to him, "I have five children and I'm very sick. Save me, Father. Save my life."

"I'm not God," he answered, "nor am I Jesus Christ. I'm a priest like any other priest, no more and perhaps even less. I don't perform miracles."

Crying, I implored him, "Please, Father, save me."

Padre Pio remained silent for a while. He lifted his eyes toward heaven, and I noted that his lips were moving in prayer. At this point, I once again smelled an intense fragrance of violets. Padre Pio told me, "Go home and pray. I'll pray for you. You'll get well." I went home, and since then every symptom of the illness has disappeared.

Padre Pio was not always a sweet and smiling saint who was ready to heal the sick and comfort them with his words. At times he was even the bearer of sad news. His mystical gifts freed him from the barriers of space and time. He would tell those who were interested in knowing when they would die, with the same calmness and clarity that he had when he would prophesy a sudden healing.

Giancarlo Pedriali remembers the following episode:

During those times when people were flocking to see Padre Pio, two policemen were asked to remain by his side for protection. One day when he was in the sacristy taking off his vestments after Mass, Padre Pio turned to one of the policemen and said with a smile, "As soon as I finish here and make my act of thanksgiving, come up to my cell because I need to talk to you."

The policeman was happy and waited until Padre Pio finished. Then he went to his cell. "I sense," Padre Pio said, "that within a week at the most, you're going home to your parents and you're going to die, my son."

"But, Father, I'm perfectly well," the policeman replied.

"Don't worry about that," Padre Pio said. "You'll be even better in a week. What's life? A pilgrimage. We're all on a pilgrimage, my son. Ask for a leave of absence and go home to take care of your affairs. Tomorrow you're going to die, and what do your parents know?"

The policeman was disturbed by his words and asked, "Father, can I tell people what you've told me?"

"Not now," Padre Pio answered. "But you can tell them when you get home."

The young man went to San Giovanni Rotondo and asked for a leave so that he could go home. They didn't want to give him one because he didn't have a good reason. Padre Pio, who knew his captain, intervened: "Let him go home to his mother for a while, the poor guy. Let him go." The captain gave him the leave.

When he got home, the policeman told his parents: "Padre Pio told me that I'm going to die so I came to say good-bye to you." A week later he died.

NINETEEN

Defying the Laws of Nature

Among the various healings attributed to Padre Pio, some are so unique that they have been the subject of controversy in medical circles. In these particular cases, the person who has been healed lives a completely normal life afterward. However, they continue to have all the physical symptoms of their illness in their bodies. From a scientific viewpoint, they are still sick.

I personally met two people in this situation who were healed by Padre Pio. I asked them to share their extraordinary experiences with me.

Gemma Di Giorgi, a woman from the Sicilian town of Ribera in the province of Agrigento, has been able to see for more than thirty years even though she has no pupils in her eyes. "If you look at me closely, you will notice that my eyes are a little strange. I don't have any pupils," she told me when I met with her in her hometown. "According to medical science, I shouldn't be able to see anything. Instead, I see and write like a normal person."

Gemma Di Giorgi is part of the Auxiliaries of Divine Mercy, founded by Fr. Domenico Labellarte under the direction of Padre Pio. Usually she resides in the town where she was born, but she often travels around the world telling her story. A documentary film has also been made about her.

"I was born on Christmas Day in 1939," she said.

Almost immediately my mother realized that my eyes were different from other children's eyes. When I was three months old, she began to suspect that I would not be able to see. She took me to a doctor in Ribera, who was unable to determine the

gravity of my condition, so he had her take me to two specialists in Palermo, ophthalmologists named Dr. Cucco and Dr.
Contino. They said that I was blind because I didn't have any
pupils.

My family was desperate, but there was nothing they could
do. My parents told me that they often took me in front of
Mary's altar in the church because it would take a miracle to
heal my eyes.

One day, when I was about seven years old, a relative who
was a nun came to our house. When she realized my condition,
she advised my parents to seek out Padre Pio, a very holy
Capuchin monk who also bore the stigmata. Her advice gave a
lot of hope to my grandmother. She began to pray and asked
this nun to write a letter to Padre Pio on my behalf.

When she returned to her convent, she wrote to him asking
him to pray for me. One night she saw him in a dream. Padre
Pio asked her, "Where is this Gemma for whom so many prayers
are being offered that they are almost deafening?" Still dreaming, she introduced me to him. Padre Pio made the sign of the
cross on my eyes and disappeared. The next day this nun
received a letter from Padre Pio in which he wrote: "Dear
daughter, I assure you that I prayed for the child. I send you my
best wishes."

She was struck by the coincidence of the dream and the
letter that followed, so she wrote to us exhorting us to go at
once to San Giovanni Rotondo. At that time, right after the
war, travel was difficult. But we left that very day, together with
some other people from our area. The train there followed the
tracks by the seaside, and it seemed to me that I could see something. I told my grandmother, but she didn't believe me. When
she checked my eyes, there still were no pupils.

In San Giovanni Rotondo, we went to confession to Padre
Pio. My grandmother, told me to request that I might be
blessed with a healing, but I forgot. I remember, though, that

as soon as I knelt down in front of him, Padre Pio touched my eyes with the wounded part of his hand, tracing the sign of the cross.

My grandmother was very upset that I had forgotten. She was crying. She stayed in church all day long so that she, too, might go to confession to Padre Pio. She was the one who asked him for a blessing for me. "Have faith, my daughter," Padre Pio told her. "The child shouldn't cry, and neither should you be worried. Gemma sees, and you know it."

I had not yet made my first Communion, and I was fortunate enough to receive my first Communion from Padre Pio's hands. My grandmother prepared me for it. When it was time for Communion, a man took me in his arms and carried me to Padre Pio. He gave me the host and then traced a second sign of the cross on my eyes with his finger.

We left San Giovanni Rotondo full of hope. The shadows that I had seen during the train trip became clearer and clearer. I had the impression that little by little I was beginning to see. When we arrived in Cosenza, my grandmother got sick and had to be taken to the hospital. We had to spend several days there. Before leaving, though, my grandmother had the eye specialist at the hospital examine me. Right away the doctor said that someone with my condition would not be able to see. But since my grandmother insisted, he did some simple tests on me. After doing so, he said: "There's no explanation for this. Without pupils a person should not be able to see. I don't understand why this child sees." Four months later, Dr. Caramazza from Perugia examined my eyes carefully. He, too, declared that my eyes were in no condition to see. There was no way to explain what was happening to me.

From then on, my sight got better and better. I was able to go to school and learn how to read and write. Today my life is as perfectly normal as any other person's life.

Giuseppe Canaponi, a former railway worker from Tuscany who died in 1983 at the age of seventy, experienced another healing attributed to Padre Pio that people consider a miracle. "I am a living challenge to the laws of nature," Canaponi was always saying. From a scientific point of view, his left leg should have been completely stiff. Yet, he was able to bend it as though it were completely normal.

A few months before he died, I went to visit him in Florence. Canaponi was still feeling well. He accompanied me around town in his sports car. We also covered a lot of ground on foot. I could hardly keep up with him. Canaponi's stride was quick and vigorous. You had to look at him closely to notice that he walked with a slight limp. "My left leg is two centimeters and four millimeters shorter than my right one," he said. "I should be wearing orthopedic shoes, but after the miracle that I obtained from Padre Pio, I've never used them."

In 1945 Giuseppe Canaponi was living in Sarteano, in the province of Siena. He was married and had a little son. He was an electrician for the railroad. On the morning of May 21, while he was on his way to work on a motorcycle, a truck hit him. He was on death's door when he arrived at the hospital. The doctors found he had a fractured skull, a fracture above his eye, a broken eardrum, several broken ribs, and five fractures in his left leg. He hung between life and death for several days before the doctors said he was out of danger.

"My recovery was long and satisfactory, except for my leg." Canaponi told me.

It was so bad that the doctors weren't able to fix it. I went from one hospital to another. I spent time at hospitals in Sarteano, Chiusi, and Montepulciano. Then on May 10, 1946, I was taken to the Orthopedic Clinic in Siena, where I remained under Dr. Leopoldo Giuntini's care for a year and a half. Then I was sent to the Rizzoli Hospital in Bologna. After the first few operations, the fractures to my femur were partially repaired, but because of a series of complications, my leg was completely rigid. Doctors said it was a "fibrous ankylosis of the left knee" and weren't able to help me. Moreover, the wounds caused by so many surgeries never healed over.

Since all attempts to bend the leg were futile, doctors at the Orthopedic Clinic in Siena decided to try to forcibly flex the knee under general anesthesia, using a Zuppinger device. A general anesthetic, besides preventing me from feeling the pain of the forced flexing, would also help to relax the muscles of my leg so that my knee would be freed up. But the muscular adhesions and the ligaments that blocked it from bending were so resistant that even this procedure was useless. In fact, when the doctors applied even greater force, the femur broke once again and I had to spend another three months with my leg in a cast.

At the beginning of 1948, I was discharged from the Orthopedic Clinic in Siena and declared incurable.

Giuseppe Canaponi showed me the original document issued by the *Ospedali Riuniti di Santa Maria della Scala*, signed by the director, Dr. Giuntini. It reads: "This is to certify that Mr. Giuseppe Canaponi was treated in this clinic in 1948 for a stiffening of the left knee as the result of a fracture to his femur. Since medical and physical therapy proved unsuccessful, an attempt was made to move the rigid joint by force under general anesthesia. This procedure was of no avail, and a fracture of the femur occurred once again. Therefore, he was released with his knee as rigid as it was after his recovery."

"I was going to have a stiff leg for the rest of my life," Canaponi continued.

I was thirty-five years old, and I couldn't resign myself to such a fate. Therefore I decided to consult other specialists. I went back to the Rizzoli Hospital in Bologna for treatment. After various examinations, X rays, and consultations, the doctors there told me they could attempt an operation. But, they added, any hopes for a successful outcome were very limited, and any improvement, if there was one, would only be partial. When faced with the prospects, I felt like I couldn't face another operation.

I was totally demoralized. I was as mean as a wounded animal. I didn't want to see anyone. I didn't want to live anymore. I vented all my anger on my wife, who was trying to encourage me. In order to get around, I started using crutches, but I was only able to drag myself for a few yards because my leg, besides being stiff, still had several open wounds and was very painful. Often I would try to walk alone, but I would fall. Then I would scream and vent my anger, cursing God and cursing everyone.

My wife was a believer, but I wasn't. She would go to church, and I would scold her for doing so. I would swear just to spite her, and she would cry.

One day a priest came to our parish to give a talk. He was from Sarteano, and when he heard about me, he wanted to talk with my wife. "Why don't you take your husband to Padre Pio in San Giovanni Rotondo? He's a Capuchin monk who works miracles." Full of hope, my wife told me what he said. All I did was laugh, swearing and cursing even Padre Pio.

My wife didn't want to give up this ray of hope. She wrote to him several times but never received a reply. Then she started telling me about him and asking me to make her happy by going to visit him. My health was getting worse and worse. I realized that my life was drawing to an end. Hopelessness finally had the upper hand in my life. Toward the end of the year I gave in. "OK," I said to my wife. "Let's try even that."

We decided that we would leave on Christmas Eve. But two days before departure, I came down with a terrible kidney infection. After spending a night in tremendous pain, I recovered, and we left on December 24, 1948. The trip was hard. I was stretched out on a stretcher in the train, but when I had to enter or leave our compartment, I experienced incredible pain. The first stop was Rome; the second was Foggia. There was only one bus to San Giovanni Rotondo, and it left first thing in the morning. We decided to spend the night in a hotel. While I was walking with my crutches, I slipped in a puddle and had quite a bad fall. Some railway workers helped me up, and when they learned that I was a railway worker too, they found a place in an office in the train station where I could spend the night. First thing in the morning, my wife, my son Augusto, and I took the bus to San Giovanni Rotondo. I was able to stretch out in the train. In the bus, I did what I could to make myself comfortable, but the whole trip was a nightmare.

Back then, San Giovanni Rotondo was a small town without any conveniences. The bus stopped about two kilometers from the Capuchin church. The streets weren't even paved. I don't know how I ever managed to get to the church. When I walked in, I lay down on a bench half-conscious.

I had never seen a photograph of Padre Pio, so I didn't know how I would recognize him. There were several Capuchin monks in church. One was near me hearing the women's confessions. The curtain that was used to hide the priest who was hearing confessions was partly open. The eyes of the monk who was sitting there were cast down, and his hands were hidden in his tunic. When he raised his right hand to give absolution, I realized he was wearing half-gloves. "It's him," I said to myself. At that very moment, Padre Pio raised his eyes and stared at me for a couple of seconds. My body began to shake when he looked at me, as though I had been struck by a powerful bolt of electricity.

A few minutes later Padre Pio walked out of his confessional and left. We asked the sacristan when he would be back. "At four o'clock in the afternoon, to hear the men's confessions in the sacristy," he replied. We went to church again at four o'clock. My son accompanied me to the sacristy. Padre Pio was already hearing confessions. There were only a few people in front of me. After about fifteen minutes, it was my turn. Propping myself up on my crutches, I walked up to Padre Pio. I tried to say something, but he didn't give me a chance. He started talking, painting a perfect portrait of my life, my personality, and my behavior. It seemed as though he had always lived with me. He spoke in a soft voice, and didn't scold me in the least. He helped me to see how ridiculous my behavior was. I was completely enthralled with his words and wasn't even thinking about my leg.

When Padre Pio raised his hand to give me absolution, once again I experienced my body shaking like it had earlier that morning. Without noticing it, I knelt down and made the sign of the cross. Then, without thinking about my leg, I got up, took my crutches in my hands, and walked away as though I was normal. I did this without realizing that I was walking normally. My wife, who was there in church, saw me coming with the crutches in my hands, and she didn't even realize it. She only said, "How peaceful your face looks." We stopped to pray a while, and then we went to the door.

It was only at this point that my wife realized what had happened. "Giuseppe, you're walking!" she said. I stopped and looked at the crutches I was holding in my hands. "It's true. I'm walking. And I don't feel the slightest pain," I replied. "Dad," my son added, "you were kneeling down when you were with Padre Pio."

I was deeply moved. My eyes were filled with tears. "What happened?" I asked myself. I couldn't believe it so I kept bending my leg. I walked from the church to the hotel at a rapid pace. I immediately went up to my room, took the pillow from my bed, threw it on the ground, and knelt down on it. Then I got up and knelt down again. I was able to perform these movements without any pain or discomfort. I took my pants off and looked at my leg. The wounds, which had been very painful and bleeding, had healed over. Now you can see only some small scars. "I've really been healed," I cried out to my wife, and broke down in tears.

News spread rapidly. Back at the hotel, everyone remembered the condition I was in when I arrived in the morning. We celebrated the whole afternoon. That night I couldn't sleep. The next day I went back to thank Padre Pio. When he saw me, he smiled. Then, raising his eyes to heaven, he said: "I didn't do the miracle. I only prayed for you. The Lord healed you."

My return home was like a triumphal march. Several times I stopped and shared what had happened to me. I arrived back home on New Year's Eve. It was almost midnight. There was a New Year's Eve party at the theater. My wife and I went to it, and I began to dance. Everyone knew about my accident, so they were taken aback to see me dancing. They cleared the floor and let me dance alone so they could observe me better. Then they broke out in resounding applause. I danced for two hours. Since then I haven't had any problems.

I went back for a checkup at the Orthopedic Clinic in Siena. The doctors were shocked. First, they were shocked to see me walking. Then, they were shocked to see that nothing at all had changed in the X rays of my leg. The fibrous ankylosis of the left knee was still there, and there is no way in which I should have been able to walk.

My case was presented at a medical congress in Rome. Many of the illustrious specialists who were there from all over the world examined me and were amazed.

Giuseppe Canaponi showed me an affidavit from Dr. Leopoldo Giuntini, signed on letterhead from the Orthopedic Clinic of the University of Siena. The doctor noted: "There is reason, then, to believe that in Canaponi's case his sudden ability to move his joint constitutes an extraordinary event that has no logical explanation within the limits of present scientific knowledge."

After his accident, Canaponi had been declared permanently disabled and given an adequate pension to live on. After his healing, he tried to be reassigned to the workforce. But the doctors, noting that the physical causes of his disability were still there, simply reconfirmed him as disabled. From a legal point of view and from a scientific point of view, Giuseppe Canaponi remained an invalid until the day he died.

TWENTY

The House for the Relief of Suffering

Padre Pio was a man of suffering. His entire life was a life of continual suffering and sickness, accompanied by moral and spiritual trials that challenged his soul. Physically he was crucified for fifty years; spiritually he was crucified for his entire earthly existence.

In his priestly ministry, Padre Pio was the "doctor" of suffering. He exercised this mission in the confessional, where he spent as many as eighteen or nineteen hours a day, healing spiritual illnesses. He also exercised this mission by constructing a large hospital that was primarily intended for sick people who were poor. He wanted to call this hospital *Casa Sollievo della Sofferenza*, that is, House for the Relief of Suffering.

Padre Pio first began to think about this project when he was young. Some people have said that Jesus himself commissioned him to do this project during a mystical vision.

At the beginning of the 1920s, thousands of sick people began to arrive in San Giovanni Rotondo seeking miraculous cures after they heard about Padre Pio's stigmata. Padre Pio knew that he was not able to help everyone, so he decided to provide as much relief as he could for their suffering with adequate medical care. This medical care would be performed out of deep Christian love.

At the time there was not one hospital in the entire region. The closest hospital to San Giovanni Rotondo was in Foggia. To get there people had to travel for twenty-five miles on roads that were nearly impassable, using the most primitive means of transportation.

In January of 1920, Padre Pio turned an old convent of the Poor Clares in the center of San Giovanni Rotondo into a minuscule but functional hospital with two wards, twenty beds, and an operating room with some basic equipment. It was called St. Francis Hospital. Various doctors who were friends of Padre Pio enthusiastically donated their services to the hospital, but eventually they were too overwhelmed to continue. After a short time, the little hospital had to close down for a lack of personnel.

But Padre Pio never gave up on his idea. He realized that such a work needed a solid economic base in order to be successful. Many of Padre Pio's biographers say that he began to talk about the House for the Relief of Suffering in the 1940s. But by that time he had already been secretly working on his plan for more than ten years. These ten years of activity are rarely mentioned, yet they are interesting because they demonstrate Padre Pio's enterprising spirit and his knack for making dreams come true. I have checked numerous biographies of Padre Pio as well as books on the House for the Relief of Suffering, and none of them mention these ten years of exhausting work that he spent searching for the funds needed to begin construction.

It is very likely that their silence on this point is due to the presence of Emanuele Brunatto on the scene, the man who, with his instincts of a detective, was able to expose Padre Pio's critics, thwart their diabolical schemes, and force Church authorities to rescind their condemnations of the Capuchin monk.

As we have already noted, Brunatto was forced to publicize the misdeeds of some well-known people in the Church in the process, thereby earning him the reputation of being a troublemaker. Even today some people in Church circles prefer to maintain absolute silence on his activities. Yet, Padre Pio loved him dearly. Padre Pio was well aware of his defects, but he was also well aware of his absolute loyalty. In the midst of trials, he would seek out Brunatto. Thus, he sought out Brunatto in the 1930s, when he had the idea for an "economic coup" that would enable him to make his dream of helping the sick come true. Here is the story behind that "coup," reconstructed from unpublished documents, that enabled Padre

Pio to find the money needed to begin building the hospital.

In 1929, the Countess Oliva Bajocchi was miraculously healed through Padre Pio's intervention. Out of gratitude, the noble-woman gave Padre Pio the profits that would be forthcoming from a series of patents that would revolutionize the world's railroad system by substituting steam engines with diesel engines. The patents were the property of two inventors, Fausto Zarlatti and Umberto Simoni, and a company was formed called the Zarlatti Company in order to exploit them. The company was made up of Count Vincenzo Bajocchi; Count Alessandroni; a lawyer named Antonio Angelini Rota; Umberto Simoni, one of the two inventors who was also an engineer; and Count Edoardo Aluffi, a member of the papal nobility. Through the intervention of Countess Bajocchi, Padre Pio was also invited to join them. He chose his friend, Emanuele Brunatto, to represent him.

The first tests on the new engines were very promising. Between April 15 and November 15 of 1930, some railroad engines equipped with the Zarlatti engine had already made numerous trips between Rome and Ostia—a total of two thousand miles—thereby demonstrating that the engine could work. It would be necessary, though, to publicize this new diesel engine abroad if it were ever to be sold internationally, and this task was entrusted to Emanuele Brunatto.

In order to bypass the usual misunderstandings and delays of Italian bureaucracy, Padre Pio suggested that Brunatto move to Paris, where a French affiliate of the Zarlatti Company was set up. Padre Pio closely followed his friend's every move. Several hand-written letters that Padre Pio sent to Brunatto with detailed instructions attest to this fact. Other friends of Padre Pio, such as Francesco Morcaldi, the mayor of San Giovanni Rotondo, and Antonio Massa, were also aware of these developments.

On March 4, 1931, Antonio Massa wrote a letter to Morcaldi, referring to Padre Pio simply as "our friend":

"I hadn't gone to see our friend because there was so much

snow, but yesterday I did have a long talk with him. As regards reselling the Zarlatti shares immediately, he told me that it was a very dangerous move. The sale should take place when Emanuele Brunatto returns from abroad. You told me that the engineer, Simoni, would sell fifty shares for 1,500 lire. If he hasn't sold them to anyone else yet, stop him because our friend will find another buyer from among us who will acquire them so that they don't fall into other hands. Father was extraordinarily insistent, so don't waste a minute."

Brunatto, who was out of the country, devoted himself to this task. From Paris he went to Berlin, since the Machinenbahn Company and the Krupp Company were interested in the patent. In the meantime, the Holy Office had forbidden Padre Pio to have contact with people outside the monastery. From that moment on, Padre Pio was unable to take a direct role in the venture, and Brunatto continued on his own.

However, Padre Pio's faithful friend encountered more and more difficulties. He needed more funds. Through Morcaldi, he asked for a loan of twenty thousand francs, an enormous sum at the time, thereby stirring up discontent among the other partners of the Zarlatti Group.

In 1931, Brunatto went to Brussels to sell shares in Belgium. Since he needed money to live on and was unable to obtain any help from Italy, he started working as an impresario in film and theater, and as a playwright. In 1932 he returned to Italy, where he had a stormy meeting with Morcaldi and some other shareholders in the Zarlatti Group, who accused him of fraud. Brunatto did not become discouraged as he faced these new difficulties. On the contrary, he strengthened the position of the Paris office of the company by relocating it to new and more dignified headquarters.

In 1935 he attempted to close a huge deal with the Soviet Union on behalf of the Zarlatti Group. In 1937 Padre Pio reappeared on the scene. He sent Morcaldi to Paris with a very friendly letter for Brunatto, thereby demonstrating that he continued to have full confidence in his friend: "My dear friend in Christ," Padre Pio wrote. "May Jesus be all your support and comfort, and may he come to you with his grace. Our mutual friend, Ciccillo, will be coming to visit you, and I asked him to give you a fatherly hug from me. He's lucky to have such a pleasant task! What I wouldn't do to have such a task. But may the Lord's will always be done. I come to you with hands joined in prayer, asking you not to place any obstacles in selling a license to do business with the United States. Please, my son, do not leave these poor people who are absolutely unable to make even the most minimal sacrifices in desperate straits. Moreover, a 3 percent share is nothing to look down on. Pay heed to my request and deal with Ciccillo right away in order not to lose any time or the right moment. I always remember you with genuine and holy affection in the Lord, and I also send you a fond hug."

From a letter that Brunatto wrote to his partners in Rome at the beginning of 1935, we can gather that the sale of licenses abroad had begun to bear fruit, since he was asking them to pay him the shares that were due to him.

In the meantime, Padre Pio, aware of the fact that the licenses had begun to generate some revenue, moved ahead with his plans in Italy. At the end of 1939 he gathered a group of friends together in San Giovanni Rotondo and entrusted them with the assignment of laying the foundation for his project.

These friends were prepared to listen to Padre Pio, even though his plans defied all logic and common sense. Among them was Dr. Guglielmo Sanguinetti, an ex-Mason who, after a conversion experience with Padre Pio, moved to San Giovanni Rotondo, where he built a small house near the Monastery of Santa Maria delle Grazie, devoting his life to caring for the poor and the sick. Another was Dr. Carlo Kiswarday, a pharmacist from Yugoslavia. One day he and his wife were on their way to Bavaria, where they were going to visit the German stigmatic, Teresa Neumann. But without knowing why, they changed their plans and went to San Giovanni Rotondo to see Padre Pio. Once there, they never left. He too built a small house near the Capuchin monastery. The third person was Dr. Mario Sanvico, a veterinarian who owned a thriving beer factory in Perugia, but who preferred to live in San Giovanni Rotondo to be close to Padre Pio.

The three men, after a long conversation with Padre Pio about his project, formed a council and held the first meeting of the founding members of Padre Pio's work. They recorded the minutes of that meeting: "On January 9, 1940, at 4:30 P.M., Miss Ida Seitz, Dr. Carlo Kiswarday, Dr. Mario Sanvico, Mrs. Maria Antonietta Sanvico, and Mrs. Mary Kiswarday met at the Sanvico-Sanguinetti residence and formed a committee to establish a clinic according to the wishes of Padre Pio of Pietrelcina. Those present, after hearing Dr. Mario Sanvico speak about Padre Pio's wish, set some rough guidelines to follow. With the help of Divine Providence, the committee was established as follows: founder of the work, Padre Pio of Pietrelcina (who wishes not to be nominated at the present moment); secretary, Dr. Mario Sanvico; treasurer, Carlo Kiswarday; medical and technical director, Dr. Guglielmo Sanguinetti; director of internal organization, Miss Ida Seitz. It was agreed that every decision to be made should be submitted to Padre Pio for his advice."

Two hours later, Padre Pio was informed of the decisions made during that meeting. Dr. Mario Sanvico wrote in his diary: "At 4:30 P.M., Dr. Carlo Kiswarday and I visited Padre Pio and submitted the organizational plan for his work. We asked him if it corresponded with what he was thinking. Padre Pio joyfully approved the initiative and blessed the nascent work. He told us: 'This evening is the beginning of my great earthly work. I bless you and all those who donate to my work, which will grow to be more and more beautiful and even greater.' Then Padre Pio handed Dr. Carlo Kiswarday, the treasurer, the first donation of a ten franc gold coin, saying, 'I too want to donate my own small offering....'"

Five days later, Padre Pio had already decided upon the name he intended to give his work, a name that fully captured his commitment to the sick and the noble mission that he hoped to carry out. As Dr. Sanvico wrote in his diary: "Sunday, January 14. This evening at 7 P.M. I asked Padre Pio what name he was planning on giving the Work, and he immediately answered, 'Casa Sollievo della Sofferenza' (House for the Relief of Suffering)."

The committee in San Giovanni Rotondo was aware of Brunatto's activity in France. In fact, Dr. Sanvico made the precise notation in his diary: "Padre Pio thinks that the Zarlatti license is working out well for financing his Work."

During this time France was involved in World War II, and Brunatto had had some political mishaps. At one point, he even ended up in prison: before the German occupation, he had been considered a foreign enemy since he was an Italian citizen! Realizing that things were getting worse and that anything was possible, Brunatto took special care to see that Padre Pio's funds were safe. On June 9, 1941, he sent a wire transfer to San Giovanni Rotondo from the French-Italian Credit Bank to the Italian Credit Bank of Florence with precise instructions: "Committee for the construction of the clinic in San Giovanni Rotondo." The transfer was for three and a half million French francs, a sum that would allow Padre Pio to begin work on the clinic.

In the meantime, Italy became involved in the war and Padre Pio had to postpone work on his project. He started working on it again after the war. On October 5, 1946, the founding members of the committee for building the clinic organized a legal corporation and began work.

Blueprints were needed. Padre Pio examined those that were presented to him. He was pleased with only one design, submitted by an engineer named Candeloro from Pescara. He chose this plan for the clinic. When the designer of the blueprints was summoned by the committee, they discovered that he did not even exist. The plans had been drawn up by a Mr. Angiolino Lupi, whose only credentials were those of a surveyor.

Angiolino Lupi was a native of the province of Abruzzi. He was from a very poor family, and had only finished five years of elementary school. He was a difficult personality to deal with. He had never held any one job for long. Whenever a position opened up, he would take his chances and claim to be an expert in the area. As a young man in Castelfreddone, he photographed corpses in order to make a living. The people in that area were so poor that they never spent money on having their photos taken when they were alive. So every time someone died, relatives would bemoan the fact that they had no pictures of their beloved deceased. Angiolino would come forward with his Kodak camera and offer to take some pictures for a few lire. He would rub the face of the corpse with a wet handkerchief to open its eyes for a few moments, the time needed to take a picture.

Having left home, Angiolino worked in Chieti, Lanciano, Pescara, and Rome, as well as in Syria and Egypt. During his career he had been a carpenter, interior decorator, machinist, and set designer. He was a tall and heavy man who wore knickers, a jumper, and big boots. He had a fierce temper. Once when he was working in a monastery, he had a quarrel with some monks. In a rage he tied eight monks to some scaffolding. Nonetheless, Padre Pio liked this rather exotic and eccentric man, and he chose to work with him.

Angiolino Lupi became the architect, builder, and supervisor of the work on the House for the Relief of Suffering. Within a short period of time, he had organized a construction site that was a work of wonder. He transformed simple farm laborers from the region into carpenters, blacksmiths, bricklayers, woodworkers, decorators, and painters. Overcoming enormous technical difficulties, he was able to build a work that eminent architects have since called "a genuine miracle."

At one point an electrical engineer from Foggia denounced Angiolino to the civil authorities for "abusing his profession." When Angiolino informed Padre Pio about this, he also asked him anxiously: "Will they throw me in jail?"

"Do not be afraid, my son," Padre Pio answered. "The authorities have good common sense. The man who denounced you will have his reward from other men. You, on the other hand, will have your reward from God." The whole incident quietly blew over.

Work on building the clinic lasted ten years. It was interrupted whenever there were no more funds, and started up again when more donations came in. Padre Pio rejected any offers from credit institutions to finance construction with large loans. He would always say, "This is the house of Providence; when Providence doesn't have any funds available, let work be stopped."

Padre Pio anxiously watched his work grow from the window of his monastery. Don Giuseppe Orlando, his good friend from home, had moved from Pietrelcina to work at the construction site. He later observed: "Padre Pio watched me every day from the window of the monastery. In the evening he would shake the dirt off my apron that had accumulated when I was working. How happy he was!"

On the list of donations that were gathered for building the clinic, some gifts especially stand out. Side by side with the exorbitant donations from the rich are gifts from the poor: a thousand-lire gift from a retired school teacher, a gift of ten lire from a deaf boy, and fifty lire donated by a young widow with children.

Through the efforts of an English journalist, Barbara Ward, and her fiancé, Commander Robert Jackson, the United Nations Relief and Rehabilitation Administration (UNRRA) sent 400 million lire to Padre Pio for his hospital. However, only 250 million made it to its destination, since the other 150 million was mysteriously sent elsewhere by the Italian government. At the same time, Mario Gambino, an Italian-American worker who was in charge of maintenance at Hunter College in New York, sent five dollars. A few days later Mario Gambino sent another envelope to Padre Pio with ten dollars: a dollar for each of his ten children. This gesture deeply moved Padre Pio and his friends. With the fifteen dollars, they set up the "Mario Gambino Fund," which eventually became the

"Fund for the Poor," a fund that allowed those who did not have any money or who were not covered by insurance to still receive treatment at Padre Pio's hospital.

The House for the Relief of Suffering was finally finished in 1956. It was inaugurated on May 5. Cardinal Giacomo Lercaro of Bologna presided over the solemn ceremony. Many prominent personalities were present, including the Italian minister of state, the president of the Italian senate, and the president of the Italian chamber of deputies. Famous doctors from all over the world also attended. Italy was represented by Drs. Valdoni, Alonzo, Condorelli, Ascenzi, Chini, Cassano, and Pudu; the United States by Drs. White and Wangesteen; Sweden by Drs. Olivecrona and Nylon; Spain by Dr. Cibert-Queraltò; Argentina by Dr. Tarquini; Belgium by Dr. Lequime; Switzerland by Dr. Mahaim; France by Dr. Lian; and England by Dr. Evans. Everyone had unconditional admiration for the great work that had been accomplished in such an isolated area, far removed from Italy's main centers of communication.

Pope Pius XII received the doctors who were there in a private audience a few days after the inauguration. He told them: "The hospital of San Giovanni Rotondo, which has just opened its doors, is the fruit of one of the highest intuitions, of an ideal long matured and perfected by contact with the most varied and cruel aspects of the moral and physical suffering of humanity."

In the spring of 1957, Padre Pio wrote a letter to the pope, describing some of the problems that he had encountered regarding his work.

Padre Pio was a member of a religious order and had taken a vow of poverty. Since he was so scrupulous in observing this vow, he felt he was unable to be involved in the administrative affairs of the hospital. Yet he was receiving offerings from around the world, including inheritances, gifts of stock, cash, and real estate. On a few occasions the heirs of a deceased benefactor would contest the deceased person's will, claiming that Padre Pio could not be named a beneficiary since he was a member of a religious order. How should he respond in such situations?

On April 4, 1957, Pope Pius XII, through his Substitute of State, Archbishop Dell'Acqua, granted Padre Pio a dispensation from his vow of poverty insofar as it related to the House for the Relief of Suffering. His vow of poverty was not totally suspended. As a Capuchin, Padre Pio continued to be submitted to the same vows as his fellow monks. But he was no longer under the jurisdiction of his superiors in matters pertaining to the administration of the hospital. In these matters, he would answer solely and directly to the Holy See.

The House for the Relief of Suffering was Padre Pio's main work. He called it "the apple of my eye." He worked and he suffered enormously to make it a reality. Padre Pio only saw the construction of a part of the present buildings when he was alive. Few people believed that a hospital could have a future there on that desolate mountain. But Padre Pio saw things differently. In the speech he gave for the inauguration of the first building of the clinic, he said: "Now the House for the Relief of Suffering is a small seed, but it will become a mighty oak, a hospital that is a small city and a center for clinical studies of international importance." At the time, his words seemed rather absurd. Right after Padre Pio's death, many people prophesied that the clinic would close within a short period of time. Instead, that "seed" has been growing and thriving. The present complex already resembles a small city.

"The work isn't finished yet," Msgr. Riccardo Ruotolo, president of the clinic, explained to me. "There are other projects to carry out. Padre Pio wanted to build a hospice for the elderly, and we're already thinking about this. Our complex is continually expanding. On the mountain, behind the clinic, there's a secret city: new construction, streets, building sites, trucks coming and going, excavators, bulldozers, workers, engineers, and technicians. This exceptionally vital flurry of activity is Padre Pio's ongoing miracle."

Msgr. Ruotolo spoke to me while consulting a modern computer containing all sorts of data. "As you can see," he said, smiling, "this piece of electronics keeps me abreast of every small detail. I can keep an eye on every activity in the clinic right here in my office. We have a data center with the most up-to-date equipment. We have terminals in every ward and even in the gatekeeper's office so that he is aware of appointments. We can keep track of visitors, people who are admitted, and even payment records. Everything is noted quickly so that a patient's discomfort is reduced to a minimum."

Msgr. Ruotolo accompanied me on a visit to the famous clinic. The wards were bright, beautiful, and spacious. Outside the emergency room were numerous ambulances, including a special mobile reanimation unit. There was a large outpatient health center. We then visited the surgery department with its fiber-optic endoscopes, special cameras to enlarge images during surgery, as well as specialized equipment for studying diseases of the esophagus.

The intensive care unit was equipped with the latest technology, including a central computer that monitored the condition of each patient. The general medicine unit had eighty-four beds and was equipped with electrocardiograms, glucometers, oscillometers, ophthalmoscopes, electroencephalograms, defibrillators, mechanical respirators, and microinfusers.

We continued our visit to other wards: geriatrics, gastroenterology, hematology, oncology, otorhinolaryngology, ophthalmology, nephrology and dialysis, obstetrics and gynecology, the neonatal unit, pediatrics, orthopedics, dermatology, cardiology, nuclear medicine and radiology, the anatomy lab, and pathological histology. We also visited buildings that housed the laundry, the housekeeping department, the power plant, the central heating unit, boarding schools for obstetricians and obstetrical nurses, and finally the administrative offices.

"This is one of the biggest hospitals in Italy," Msgr. Ruotolo noted. "It certainly is the biggest in the south of Italy. We serve the entire region of Gargano, and we even admit people from all over

Italy as well as from abroad. The region around Puglia requested that we send our equipment outside the clinic, and we've agreed to do so. There is a great need for dialysis units. We have eighteen in our dialysis department, and they're always in use. In 1983 we served over 7,200 people. In order to serve as many people as possible and avoid tiring trips to San Giovanni Rotondo, we've opened a center in Rodi Garganico, in Vieste, in San Severo—all with our own equipment and our own specially trained personnel.

"On April 18, 1983, the School of Medicine at the Catholic University of the Sacred Heart and the House for the Relief of Suffering signed an agreement whereby students at the university's medical school can do their internships and residencies at our clinic."

TWENTY-ONE

Padre Pio and His Friends

People have a tendency to emphasize Padre Pio's gruff character, his harsh words, the severity with which he dealt with sinners, and his intransigence when it came to principles. But this is only one aspect of his personality. Padre Pio had a very kind heart, deep feelings, and an ability to love people with tenderness.

"I was fortunate to enjoy his friendship for over twenty years, and I can truly say that I haven't known anyone who was capable of so much tenderness," Giovanni Gigliozzi told me. Gigliozzi is an Italian journalist and writer, the author of numerous theatrical reviews and magazine articles, and one of Italy's most popular radio personalities for more than forty years. He has been responsible for producing programs for one of Italy's largest radio stations and has been the inspiration and host for many popular and successful programs.

"I was the first person to bring Padre Pio's voice to radio," Gigliozzi told me. "One day I took part in a radio marathon for the sick, which was transmitted directly from the House for the Relief of Suffering. I managed to corner Padre Pio on the doorstep of the monastery and convince him to say a few words into the microphone. He only said a few words—a prayer—but his voice deeply impressed our listeners. They called me from all over the country afterward—and even from abroad."

For more than thirty years, Gigliozzi has been the editor of a semimonthly magazine that is put out by the hospital. It's called *Casa Sollievo della Sofferenza,* and it contains the latest news and developments from the clinic. "It was Padre Pio who personally entrusted this job to me in 1947, when I began to visit him,"

Gigliozzi recalled. "Work had just begun on the hospital. Friends and followers of Padre Pio were sending letters with donations and were always asking for news on how construction was going. Padre Pio had already set up an office to respond to their requests, but it was difficult to keep up with the increasing volume of mail. It was at that point that Padre Pio thought about sending out a periodic newsletter. Since I was a journalist, he put me in charge of editing it. I'm still the editor, but it's only an honorary title now since the magazine no longer needs my close supervision."

Giovanni Gigliozzi met Padre Pio through a series of strange coincidences. "I first heard people talk about this extraordinary monk right after the war," he said,

Especially from a friend, Carlo Trabucco, who was also a journalist. He was the theater critic for *Popolo*, one of Italy's leading newspapers, and I was the theater critic for *Avanti*, another leading newspaper. We would see each other at all the opening nights. Since Trabucco knew Padre Pio quite well, he would talk about him with an enthusiasm that bordered on the excessive. My attitude was one of indifference and unbelief, especially when my friend would tell me about certain phenomena, such as the fragrance that would emanate from him, even in places far away from him.

At one point, however, strange things started to happen to me too. Out of the blue I would smell a strong fragrance of violets in unusual places. I would think often about Padre Pio. But then my mind would rebel, and I would tell myself that I was just a victim of suggestion.

One day the phenomenon occurred when I was on vacation with my wife in Francavilla a Mare, in Abruzzo. I went to the train station to send a letter by special delivery, and there, in a place that smells anything but sweet, I could smell the unmistakable fragrance of violets. While I was reflecting on this, my wife said, "Where is that fragrance coming from?" I was astonished. "You smelled it too?" I asked. Then I told her about Padre Pio, my conversations with Trabucco, and about the fragrance that had been pursuing me for some time now. "If I were you," my wife said, "I'd leave right away for San Giovanni Rotondo."

The next day we were on our way. When we were finally standing in front of him, Padre Pio said: "Finally, our hero is here. What I had to do to get him here!" That same day I was able to speak with him at length, and from that moment on my life was changed.

Gigliozzi became a regular visitor to San Giovanni Rotondo. After being named editor of the clinic newsletter, he would meet regularly with Padre Pio for work reasons. He was able to meet his friends, see how he related to them, see how affectionately he spoke with them, and observe how quick he was to take an interest in their problems. His testimony is very valuable for getting to know Padre Pio's private side, when he was far away from the crowds.

"When Padre Pio would meet someone, that person was transformed," Gigliozzi recalled.

In order to carry out his projects, he wouldn't choose people who were noted for their knowledge or even for their piety, but simple, ordinary people and often people who were quite messed up. His closest collaborators on the House for the Relief of Suffering were Dr. Guglielmo Sanguinetti, a retired doctor; Dr. Mario Sanvico, who was a veterinarian; Dr. Carlo Kiswarday, a pharmacist; and Angiolino Lupi, a laborer who had only finished the fifth grade in school.

Dr. Sanguinetti hated priests, belonged to the Masons, and was an atheist. He retired after having worked for many years as a doctor in Florence for the railway workers' union. Since his wife wanted to meet Padre Pio so much, he finally agreed to accompany her to San Giovanni Rotondo in 1948. Sanguinetti had no interest at all in meeting Padre Pio, and made it clear that he was going on the trip only as his wife's "chauffeur."

The day after arriving at the monastery, Sanguinetti went with his wife to Padre Pio's Mass. After Mass he gathered in the sacristy with the men who were there to meet Padre Pio. He was curious to see up close the monk that so many people were talking about. When Padre Pio turned to address the group, he looked right at Sanguinetti and called him by name, as if he had known him for years. He said, "You should come here and help me build a great hospital." Dr. Sanguinetti just laughed, but he was deeply impressed by the fact that Padre Pio had called him by name. "Who in the world told him about me?" he asked himself anxiously.

The Sanguinettis were supposed to stay in San Giovanni Rotondo for only a few days, but Dr. Sanguinetti decided not to leave. He saw Padre Pio several times afterward. One day Padre Pio brought up the whole matter of the hospital. "Sell the few things you have in Florence, and come live here by me," he said. "That's impossible," Sanguinetti replied. "I'm retired now, and I don't have enough money saved to build a house here." Then Padre Pio prophesied: "You'll receive a letter soon that will solve all your problems."

Sanguinetti returned to Florence. He kept thinking about Padre Pio's words to him but wasn't able to figure out what they meant. Then one day he received word that he had won a considerable sum of money in a lottery drawing. At once he understood what Padre Pio had meant, and he decided to move to San Giovanni Rotondo.

With the money he won he built a small house and became Padre Pio's right-hand man in building the clinic. Padre Pio loved Sanguinetti dearly and considered him somewhat like a brother. When Sanguinetti died, Padre Pio wept like a small child.

I heard the sad news when I was in Rome, so I left immediately for San Giovanni Rotondo. When I arrived at the monastery, I headed toward the stairway to go up to Padre Pio's cell, but I had to stop in my tracks. Padre Pio was standing in the middle of the stairway, leaning on a large wooden crucifix. His shoulders were heaving up and down as he sobbed. I found myself the unwilling spectator of a rather disturbing scene. Through his tears, Padre Pio repeated these rather incredible words: "Jesus, if you had told me that he was going to die, I would have taken him away from you." His words seem rather shocking, but they indicate the intimacy of Padre Pio's relationship with Jesus and the great love that he had for his friend.

Dr. Sanguinetti told me about another incident, which he personally witnessed. One day a woman came to San Giovanni Rotondo with a wicker suitcase. She went into the church and waited in line to go to confession with the other women. When it was her turn, she opened the suitcase in front of Padre Pio and broke out in tears. Wrapped in some old clothing in the suitcase was the body of a baby that was about six months old. The woman was coming to San Giovanni Rotondo with her sick son, hoping that Padre Pio would heal him. But the poor boy died on the train. The woman, who was overcome with anguish but still had immense faith, hid the child in her suitcase and continued on with her journey. Dr. Sanguinetti told me that if the child had been hidden in the suitcase while he was still alive, he would have certainly died from suffocation. Therefore, there was no doubt that the child was dead when she opened her suitcase for Padre Pio.

As the woman cried out in desperation, Padre Pio took the little body in his hands and prayed for a few moments. Then he turned to the mother and asked her with a firm voice, "Why are you yelling so much? Don't you see that your son is sleeping?" The woman looked at the baby and realized that he was tranquilly breathing.

Emilia, Dr. Sanguinetti's wife, told me about another incident that happened to her. They lived in a small prefabricated house in San Giovanni Rotondo with a wood floor. Underneath the kitchen, in the basement, Dr. Sanguinetti had set up a little clinic for the sick. Every day he and his wife went to Padre Pio's Mass at dawn. One day, when they were already in church, Emilia remembered that she hadn't turned off the water faucet in the kitchen. Although she wasn't entirely sure, it would be a disaster if she had left it on. The sink had a blocked drain, and the water would spill out of the sink, penetrate the kitchen floor, and flood her husband's clinic. What should she do? Attend Mass or go home and check? In her mind she turned to Padre Pio, who had begun Mass, and said, "I'll attend Mass, and you'll have to worry about the faucet." When Mass had ended, she ran home. When she walked into the kitchen, the water began to gush out of the faucet in a torrent. The faucet was still on, but not one drop of water had poured out while she was gone.

Another person who was able to approach Padre Pio rather easily in private was Giuseppe Canaponi, the Tuscan railway worker who was converted and cured by Padre Pio in 1948. "I spent all my free time in San Giovanni Rotondo," Canaponi told me.

I only was happy when I was with him. Besides being the instrument of my healing, I considered him a real father. I felt that he loved me. Often he would give me some rather sensitive jobs to do, which demonstrated to me how much faith he had in me. I was one of the few people who could go up to his cell without asking anyone's permission. I would go and see him at all hours of the day, and he always welcomed me with a smile. Jokingly he called me, "Canapone, the Grand Duke of Tuscany."

When word got out about how I was healed, parishes, clubs, and even universities began to invite me to tell them in person about my miraculous healing, not only in Italy but even abroad. I didn't know what to do. I asked Padre Pio for his advice. "Can

I tell them in all sincerity what happened to me, or should I keep quiet?" I asked him. He stood silently for a few minutes, with his eyes cast down. Then he put his hands on my shoulders, and looking into my eyes, he said, "You should do it. I can't say anything, but you can. You have to tell people about the greatness and goodness of our Lord." That's how I began my travels. I've gone to various countries in Europe and in America. Everywhere I go, people ask me to talk about Padre Pio when they hear what happened to me, and they don't grow tired of listening to me.

Whenever I would return from those trips, I would go to San Giovanni Rotondo. I always had the names of many people who wanted Padre Pio to pray for them: sick people, people in hopeless situations, and people in very difficult situations. He would listen patiently, ask for more details, and participate in their suffering.

It's true that at times Padre Pio would raise his voice with people in confession and scold them. But he did it with a precise purpose in mind. He did it for their conversion. Padre Pio was a very sensitive soul. When he would speak about the sick and their suffering, his eyes would well up with tears. Sometimes he was so moved that he couldn't speak. Often he would hide his feelings by keeping them to himself to the point that he would appear rather sullen. But this was only a defense mechanism.

Padre Pio also knew how to joke. He had a good sense for the right moment to crack a joke. Once I took advantage of some vacation time I had to go to San Giovanni Rotondo, and I stayed at the monastery the whole time I was there. After seeing me over and over again, Padre Pio said, "Ah, Canapone, Canapone, I made a mistake in choosing my career." I must have looked rather perplexed since I didn't know what he meant. Smiling, he explained: "Instead of being a monk, I should have been a railway worker. That way I would have always been on vacation like you."

In the winter of 1954, I arrived one cold evening in San

Giovanni Rotondo in the middle of a storm. I was cold and probably even had a fever by then. My throat was particularly sore, and I couldn't even talk. I went up to Padre Pio's cell, and I found him there with the superior of the monastery, Fr. Carmelo Durante. I greeted him in a whisper. Padre Pio looked at me worriedly. "What happened to you?" he asked. Then, feeling my clothing, he said, "You're soaking wet, you poor thing." He turned to the superior and said, "See if there's something we can put on him so that he can warm up." The superior didn't know what to do. He raised his arms as if to say, "What should I give him?"

Then Padre Pio began to look around his room. Behind the door he found a big brown scarf. He took it and said to me with a smile: "You're lucky. It's almost new. I've worn it only a few times." Then he put it around my neck. It was a huge scarf. It covered my shoulders and fell down to my knees. While he was putting the scarf over me, I felt a pleasant warmth overcome me. "I already feel better," I said, and I realized my voice was perfectly well. My hoarseness was gone. "Did you see how much the warmth helped you?" Padre Pio asked.

That evening I went back to the hotel with Padre Pio's scarf on me, and I continued to use it during the following days. Before returning home, I went to give it back but Padre Pio told me to keep it. It was a wonderful gift.

On another occasion, Padre Pio gave me a rosary. Like everything else he touched with his hands, even the rosary had a wonderful fragrance to it, and it still does some twenty years later. Then he gave me a crucifix, some holy cards with some words that he himself wrote on them, and a few other small items.

One day I was kneeling in front of the altar at the church and Padre Pio stopped in to pray. I was in front of him on the opposite side. I noticed that he was searching through his pockets. I got up, walked up to him, and asked, "Do you need something?"

"Ah, Canapone, I lost everything," he said. "I lost my snuff-box and my handkerchief. Maybe I left them in my room."

"I'll go get them," I said. "You stay here. In the meantime, if you'd like, I can lend you my handkerchief. It's new."

I knew that he often used a handkerchief to wipe up the blood that would flow out of the wound on his side. Padre Pio took my handkerchief, and I noticed that he put it under his habit where his heart was. Later, he returned it to me washed and ironed. But the blood stains were still there.

I tried to be useful when I was in San Giovanni Rotondo. Since I was an electrician, I would walk around the monastery repairing sockets, plugs, and switches. Padre Pio liked this. I would spend some time with him in the evening in the garden or on the porch. It was his time for relaxing. He would sit for the most part, but at times he would get up and walk around. Few people had permission to be with him. From time to time those who did have permission included the actor Carlo Campanini, the singer Beniamino Gigli, the scientist Enrico Medi, Professor Pietro Valdoni, the mayor of San Giovanni Rotondo, the head of the police, and a few others. Father would talk, tell jokes, and recall stories about his life.

Once he told how upset he was with those who took advantage of him. "At least they appreciate me for something," he said with a smile. "They sell me for nothing. Once, back in 1922 or 1923, I heard someone shout under my window: 'Padre Pio for twenty cents!' I looked out and saw a boy waving my picture in the air. I was mad, so I shouted: 'You little rascal, I heard you selling me for only twenty cents!' The boy was scared and ran off."

Padre Pio would talk about science and the beauty of creation with the scientist Enrico Medi. When he was with Gigli the singer, he would always say to him, "Listen, Beniamino. Sing the song *Mamma* for me," before going to bed up in his room. The famous tenor would stand up and begin to sing, but he could never finish it. At a certain point Padre Pio would be overcome with emotion, begin to cry, and get up and go to his cell.

Once, on a summer afternoon, I sat down at the entrance of the monastery, waiting for it to reopen. I knew that the door-keeper took a break at about three o'clock. At a certain moment I heard footsteps. "It's the doorkeeper," I thought, so I got up to go in. The door opened and it was Padre Pio. "What are you doing here?" he asked. "I was waiting for someone to open the door so I could go up and see you," I answered. "Oh, so you haven't seen any of us old black bags yet?" he said. I laughed at this little joke and he laughed too. Then I said, "Father, there are a lot of people waiting outside for your blessing. Can I go and open the church?" He answered, "Why not? By all means go and open it."

The people went into the church and gathered around Padre Pio. Everyone was trying to get close to him so that they could kiss his hand and say something to him. There was a woman in the group who was dressed rather gaudily and who would repeatedly say in a loud voice, "Father, pray for me because my husband has left me." She kept saying this in a rather boring yet hysterical voice, which grated on everyone's nerves. She didn't have the least respect for other people or for the sacred place she was in. At a certain point, Padre Pio stared at her with one of his withering looks and said, "If you had been a decent person, your husband wouldn't have left you." The woman was dumb-founded and left the church immediately.

When he was gruff, Padre Pio always had some reason for being like that. He knew the psychology and the mentality of every person who came to him. He was able to read people's hearts and minds, and he knew how to relate to each person for their own spiritual well-being.

One time Carlo Campanini convinced one of his friends who was an actress to go and see Padre Pio. This actress, who was rather famous, was very curious about the things that were happening around Padre Pio, but hadn't given a thought about her own soul. When she arrived in San Giovanni Rotondo, she booked a room at the hotel and let Campanini know she was there, thinking that he would be able to introduce her to Padre Pio. But Campanini told her that there was no such thing as influence in San Giovanni Rotondo. If she wanted to meet Padre Pio, she had to go to church and to confession. The actress tried to dress inconspicuously. She put on some big dark glasses, went into the church, and got in line to go to confession. When it was her turn, she knelt down in the confessional. But she was only there for a couple of minutes.

No one knows what Padre Pio said to her. But people saw her get up rather distraught and leave the church in a hurry. Campanini caught up with her at the hotel and found that she was furious. She was so angry that she was crying and railing against Padre Pio. "He's anything but holy. He's rude and ill-mannered. He sent me away without any kind of instruction," she protested. Campanini tried to console her, but the actress didn't want to have anything to do with him. "You can go away, too," she said. "I never want to hear again about that monk, and I never want to see you again."

I left for Rome. A week later, while Campanini and I were in San Giovanni Rotondo again, the actress called. She was desperate. "I can't fall asleep," she told Campanini. "Padre Pio is pursuing me. I see him everywhere. I feel like I'll never be peaceful again if I don't talk with him." She returned to San Giovanni Rotondo, and this time her visit with Padre Pio was very different. Padre Pio had achieved his goal. The woman was no longer just curious. Now she was thinking about her own spiritual well-being. She went to confession, received Communion, and returned time and time again to see Padre Pio.

Besides me, Padre Pio also loved my entire family. Whenever I would go to see him, he always wanted the latest news about my wife and my children. He was the one who gave them their first Holy Communion, first to Augusto and then to Maria Pia. My daughter was a very vivacious girl. When she was little, she never wanted to go to church to pray. But she trusted Padre Pio, and when we would go to San Giovanni Rotondo, she would run up to him like he was her uncle. He would take her into his arms and play with her. "You should scold her," I would say. "She doesn't want to go to church to pray, and she's very naughty." But he would answer with a smile, "No, she's a good girl." Then he would ask her some catechism questions and would have her repeat some little prayers after him.

In 1963 I suddenly felt a deep desire to pray for Padre Pio's parents. I don't know why, but it seemed to me that Padre Pio would welcome some prayers for his beloved parents who were already deceased, so I prayed especially for this intention for several weeks. Then I stopped.

Later, when I returned to San Giovanni Rotondo, I went to confession with Padre Pio. By that time I had completely forgotten about his parents. Yet before I began my confession, Padre Pio said to me: "Canapone, thank you very much."

"For what?" I asked.

"For the prayers you said for my parents."

I was with Padre Pio in some of the worst moments of his life, when he was kept in seclusion and not allowed to meet with his followers. I would go and visit him, and I always found him very sad. One Sunday, when he was looking out the window at the little square in front of the church, which was completely empty, he said: "Once that square was full of cars. You could see license plates from every province in Italy. Now there's not even one car there, not even one with a license plate from Foggia." He continued to look at the square in silence, then said: "Thank God that I always have work to do. Before I would listen to confessions. Now I pray. May God's will always be done."

TWENTY-TWO

The Second Persecution

Padre Pio was sixty-five years old in 1952. He had had the stigmata on his hands, his feet, and his sides for more than thirty-four years. According to Professor Valdoni, he would lose a cup of blood from his wounds each day. At the same time he was prone to heart ailments and high fevers. Physically he was very weak, and it was only the strength of his iron will that kept him on his feet.

His greatest desire was to be able to rest, but he knew that this was impossible. When he felt down, he would speak about death as freedom. Ever since he had been sent to San Giovanni Rotondo in 1917, he had lived as a cloistered monk. He had not enjoyed one day of vacation. The only time he left the monastery was to vote. His days were divided between his confessional, where he would hear confessions, and his kneeler, where he would pray and meditate.

Normally, everyone would have loved and respected a man of such deep spiritual knowledge. Instead, for reasons that no one will probably ever be able to explain, he was hurt, humiliated, slandered, tried, and condemned in especially harsh ways, especially during the last fifteen years of his life. His most basic human rights were violated. Many people forgot about his long life of sacrifice, suffering, bearing the stigmata, conversions, and miracles. At the same time, some people continued to accuse him of having demonic powers.

Such an incredible and absurd accusation can probably be attributed to greed. The work that Padre Pio was able to do with the help of his spiritual sons and daughters and his followers now constituted a huge financial empire. Hundreds of thousands of dollars were spent on the House for the Relief of Suffering alone, which was still being built. Every day donations came into San Giovanni Rotondo for Padre Pio's work. These accounts were overseen by several different people, and the sums that were being deposited were staggering. As a member of a religious order, Padre Pio had taken a vow of poverty. He could not have even one cent to his name. As we have already seen, Pope Pius XII gave him a limited dispensation from this vow so that he might personally oversee the donations that were received for the House for the Relief of Suffering.

Unfortunately, around this time the Capuchin Order fell prey to a bizarre financial scheme, which was masterminded by a man named Giambattista Giuffre. Giuffre began his career as a bank clerk at the Credito Romagnolo in Imola, where he was born. Within a few years he had become famous throughout Italy for his financial prowess, especially in Church circles, where he was called "God's Banker." Giuffre would pay interest in advance on money that people would lend him, at rates that often exceeded 30 percent.

The Capuchin friars, who were not accustomed to handling money, must have felt that such a person was providentially sent by God to them. Their monasteries had been damaged during the war, and they would never be able to repair them if they had to depend on the normal offerings of their donors. At a certain point, they decided to see if Giuffre could help them resolve their financial problems. The superiors of several monasteries asked their most enterprising monks to seek donations and loans from friends and relatives, and to take them to "God's Banker" so that they might immediately draw on the high interest rates he was offering.

Since several monasteries in the province of Foggia were also facing serious financial difficulties, some monks decided to resolve them by taking Giuffre's method one step further. "Why don't we take some of the money that comes in for Padre Pio's work to the banker that God has provided?" they asked. Fortunately, Padre Pio did not think highly of Giuffre. On several occasions he expressed his reservations about the man and his unconventional methods of doing business. Quarrels broke out among the monks regarding Giuffre.

Along with the discontent, accusations were also being made about Padre Pio's lifestyle, his contacts with people, and his alleged charismatic qualities. The monks began to doubt everyone and suspect everyone. The religious community was divided. Peace disappeared from the monastery.

These disagreements spilled over the walls of the monastery and even spread among Padre Pio's lay collaborators, especially those who were working for the House for the Relief of Suffering. Soon, reports about these problems appeared in the newspapers. The news reports were often exaggerated and written with a certain zeal that bordered on fanaticism. It was totally predictable, therefore, that at one point Padre Pio's superiors and Church authorities would have to intervene in the whole affair.

Two officials from the Holy Office arrived in San Giovanni Rotondo in 1951 to look into the situation: Msgr. Giovanni Pepe and Abbot Emanuele Caronti. They left on December 31. On January 16, 1952, the Holy Office informed the head of the Capuchin Order that they had found "a few problems" in San Giovanni Rotondo. Following some inquiries from the ecclesiastical tribunal, the monks of San Giovanni Rotondo were asked "not to encourage pilgrimages and not to distribute Padre Pio's picture and writings."

On July 30, a decree from the Holy Office was published in *L'Osservatore Romano* that put eight publications about Padre Pio on the index of forbidden books. On August 6, 1953, a new superior was sent to Foggia, Padre Pio's religious province. Normally this task is entrusted to a friar who comes from the religious province where the monastery is located. However, this time, as punishment, an outsider, Fr. Teofilo from the province of Tuscany, was chosen for the task.

In August of 1958, Giambattista Giuffre declared bankruptcy. Everyone who had lent money to "God's Banker" was left empty-handed. The friars were especially affected. It is hard to determine how much money they lost in this disaster, but it is estimated to be hundreds of thousands of dollars. The superior general of the order wrote a highly confidential report on the situation: "We were forced to pay an enormous sum that left us in ruins and on the edge of economic disaster." The Holy See ordered that restitution be made to every person who was cheated. The Pope created a commission of cardinals to oversee the matter and to try and mitigate the effects of the scandal.

In order to pay back their creditors, the heads of the various monasteries tried to gather funds from every source possible. Once again, they started to show interest in the income that Padre Pio's work generated. This time Padre Pio's superiors asked him to give them the donations, but he told them he was unable to do so since the money did not belong to him.

By refusing to do so a second time, more disagreements and hostility broke out. New accusations were made against Padre Pio, and new criticisms were invented. In an effort to destroy him, some of his more fanatical opponents ended up committing one of the most serious sins against Catholic morality: violating the seal of confession. Both the confessor and the person who is confessing have a strict obligation not to break the seal of confession, and no one has the power to abrogate this obligation. Nonetheless, some of Padre Pio's fellow monks installed tape recorders in his cell and in his confessional in an attempt to gather proof against him and his followers. Afterward, some of these recordings were sent to Rome.

In the spring of 1960, some visitors to Padre Pio's confessional noticed that something strange was going on. Before Padre Pio would arrive to hear confessions, two friars would mysteriously bustle about and plug something in the wall. Afterward, a rustling sound could be heard. Nobody suspected a tape recorder. When Padre Pio would leave after hearing confessions, the mysterious friars would reappear and take out the plug.

Padre Pio himself was the first to discover the tape recorders and report what was happening. He asked the archbishop of Manfredonia, the Most Reverend Andrea Cesarano, to come to San

Giovanni Rotondo. In tears, he told him about the whole affair and showed him the microphones that were hidden in his cell. "See what my fellow monks are doing to me?" he asked.

Padre Pio also reported the matter to several of his collaborators and followers. He turned over the pocketknife that he used to cut the wires of the microphones to Giovangualberto Alessandri, a judge in the Court of Appeals in Florence. The blade of the knife still had traces of an electrical discharge.

The press garishly reported the whole incident of the hidden microphones. *L'Osservatore Romano* intervened and issued a denial, describing the news reports as "scandalous, false, and slanderous." But Padre Pio's friends responded to the zealous denial by publishing some overwhelmingly conclusive evidence, including copies of the letters that the main protagonists in the whole affair had written each other, outlining all the details for carrying out their criminal plan.

Material from these recordings was used to prepare a lengthy dossier of accusations against Padre Pio and his collaborators, which, in turn, was presented to Pope John XXIII.

In the summer of 1960, the Most Reverend Andrea Cesarano, the archbishop of Manfredonia, suddenly received a telegram summoning him to the Vatican. At nine o'clock in the evening Pope John XXIII received him in an audience. The report on Padre Pio was on his desk. The pope began to page through it while making comments on it. Archbishop Cesarano was Padre Pio's superior as well as an old friend. The accusations in the report were very serious. Padre Pio was accused of being an inept administrator of the House for the Relief of Suffering, of being at the mercy of a group of fanatics, and, above all, of being an immoral person. This latter accusation was the most despicable. Padre Pio, who was seventy-three years old at the time, was accused of having sexual relations with some of the women who came to him for confession.

Tears welled up in Archbishop Cesarano's eyes as he listened to the accusations. He explained to the pope that whenever Padre Pio went down to meet with guests, he would go into a small room, where he would communicate with his visitors in the guest room through a little window that was twenty inches wide and two feet high. Otherwise they were separated by a big wall.

In an interview I did with Cardinal Giuseppe Siri, he confirmed that the accusations in the dossier were indeed very serious: "For months I defended Padre Pio to Pope John XXIII. We spoke about him at every meeting we had. I had many responsibilities at the time, and I would often meet with the pope. Each time we met we ended up talking about Padre Pio. The pope was a very good man, a true saint. But he was worried and confused by what was reported to him. In the end, he was convinced that the poor monk had nothing to do with the accusations against him, but the larger matter still needed to be clarified."

Padre Pio's Capuchin superiors shared this desire. On April 10, 1960, the superior general of the order, Fr. Clement of Milwaukee, sent a letter to Pope John XXIII, "imploring him that an apostolic visitation be made to Padre Pio." On April 30, in an audience with the superior general and his collaborators, Pope John XXIII assented to their request. On July 22, 1960, the Holy Office entrusted this delicate task to Msgr. Carlo Maccari, the secretary for the Vicariate of Rome. He found himself facing the most intricate matter that he ever had to resolve. Before leaving for San Giovanni Rotondo, Monsignor Maccari took part in a four-hour summit meeting at the Capuchin headquarters in Rome.

Monsignor Maccari's visitation started on July 29, 1960, and ended on October 10, 1960. Although he was cold and severe in his meetings with Padre Pio, it is very likely that he was convinced that the accusations were unfounded. The visitation took place when Padre Pio was celebrating his fiftieth anniversary as a priest. His friends were planning some rather festive celebrations, but Monsignor Maccari ordered that the plans for the celebrations be suspended. Work on a special issue of the newsletter, *Casa Sollievo della Sofferenza,* to honor Padre Pio on this occasion, was also suspended. No special speeches were to be made observing the anniversary.

At the end of his visitation, Monsignor Maccari ordered that some measures be taken that were approved by the Holy Office. Padre Pio was prohibited from celebrating weddings and baptisms, having free contact with his followers, and hearing the confessions of certain people. He was told he could not spend more than a half hour saying Mass and that he could not spend more than three minutes with anyone in the confessional.

The apostolic visitor's measures also affected the monastery in San Giovanni Rotondo. It was placed directly under the jurisdiction of the Holy Office. As punishment, some monks who were friends of Padre Pio were transferred to monasteries outside of the province of Foggia.

Padre Pio was also forced to relinquish control over the House for the Relief of Suffering. He was obliged under obedience to sign over the title for the clinic, which was then deposited in the Vatican's bank.

The letter from the Holy Office outlining these measures closed with some rather harsh words: "Padre Pio is invited to comply with these rules by virtue of his vow of obedience as a religious. In the deplorable event that he should fail to do so, the use of canonical penalties will not be excluded." Such threats are not the norm in Church bureaucracy. Generally they are used only to confront rebels who have been habitually offensive in their attacks. By using such threats with Padre Pio, the Holy Office led many people to give credence to the accusations that were being made against him.

TWENTY-THREE

Defending Padre Pio

Besides the disciplinary measures that the Holy Office imposed on Padre Pio after Monsignor Maccari's visit, a new superior suddenly imposed some additional measures. This new superior was sent to San Giovanni Rotondo with the expressed assignment of "keeping strict discipline, squelching any kind of fanaticism, and making sure that Padre Pio observes the rules just like his fellow monks."

The new superior, a Sicilian, set about his assignment with the utmost zeal. The result was a climate of discontent and tension, not only among the monks but also among Padre Pio's faithful followers. He immediately put up signs in the church, the monastery, and the sacristy warning people not to approach Padre Pio outside of the confessional.

He dismissed the friar who had been assigned to help Padre Pio for the past two years as he grew older and sicker. He forbade the friars to show any kind of special respect to Padre Pio, such as kissing his wounds, helping him up the stairs, and taking some glasses of beer up to his room as was the custom on days when it was sweltering. He even forbade Padre Pio to weep when he was celebrating Mass, and prohibited him from visiting the sick at the hospital.

Padre Pio always celebrated Mass on Christmas, the Epiphany, Easter, and Pentecost at the monastery in San Giovanni Rotondo. On those days pilgrims from around the world traveled to the monastery to celebrate these solemn feast days with Padre Pio. The new superior ended this forty-year-old tradition.

The new superior also made it a habit to follow Padre Pio as he passed through the crowds. If Padre Pio would stop to greet someone, he would abruptly intervene by saying, "Move quickly, Padre

Pio. How many times do I have to tell you that you shouldn't stop to talk with people?"

Within a few months, the new superior had made himself the enemy of Padre Pio's faithful followers. Letters of protest began to pour into the monastery, while others were sent to the Holy Office in Rome. There were also public controversies and disputes, some of which ended up in court.

On May 5, 1963, the new superior had a stormy encounter with the mayor of San Giovanni Rotondo, Francesco Morcaldi, regarding Padre Pio's feast day. It was the custom to celebrate that day in a very special way. On May 4 the mayor called the monastery to ask the superior what he had organized for Padre Pio's feast day. The superior told him that, just like any other day, Padre Pio would celebrate Mass at five o'clock in the morning, as well as another Mass in the afternoon. The mayor suggested that the afternoon Mass take place at seven o'clock so that more people could attend. "I don't think it's wise to do so," the superior replied. They agreed that the mayor and the town council members would come to the monastery at nine o'clock so that they could convey to Padre Pio their best wishes on his feast day.

The next day the mayor and the town council members arrived at the monastery promptly at nine. There was a large crowd waiting at the door. The superior complained about all the commotion and wanted to send everyone away. Padre Pio, who had not been told about the mayor's arrival, appeared in the background, shuffling along with great effort. People ran to greet him, and the mayor made his way to the front of the crowd to kiss Padre Pio's hand. Suddenly, the superior jumped in front of Padre Pio, pushed him into a cell, and locked him in.

"You cannot imagine how mad I was," Francesco Morcaldi recalled. "Suddenly, I had an idea. I left the monastery and immediately sent a telegram to the secretary of state, Cardinal Cicognani. I wrote: 'The people of San Giovanni Rotondo, mortified that they were unable to express their best wishes to Padre Pio of

Pietrelcina on his feast day, implore Your Eminence to intervene with His Holiness to eliminate the restrictions on his priestly ministry.'"

That afternoon the people of San Giovanni Rotondo organized a spontaneous demonstration. Men and women gathered in the streets of the town, shouting threats to the superior of the monastery. They held up signs calling for Padre Pio's freedom and punishment for his jailers.

The next day the superior sent a letter to the mayor deploring what had happened. The mayor wrote back, blaming the superior's behavior toward Padre Pio for provoking the demonstration. "Your deliberate attempts," Morcaldi wrote, "to deprive the people of the joy of showing Padre Pio their affection and gratitude confirmed their conviction that Padre Pio is under relentless surveillance and that you wish to limit his contact with people. By doing so, you are also limiting his ministry. And you can well understand that his ministry is not limited to his priestly ministry."

Reports of this controversy appeared in the newspapers, causing further confusion and misunderstanding. The serious tensions that existed in San Giovanni Rotondo during Padre Pio's first persecution returned to the town. There is only one person, someone thought, who might be able to resolve the situation: Emanuele Brunatto, Padre Pio's eccentric spiritual son who, in the twenties, was able to trap and overthrow Padre Pio's enemies and critics.

Brunatto had been living in France for several years when Padre Pio called for him. There is no doubt that it was Padre Pio himself who summoned him, although the reasons why he wanted to see Brunatto are not all that clear. According to some people, Brunatto was the author of the reports that were published in the newspapers. Under the pretext of defending Padre Pio, Brunatto ended up slandering the Capuchins and the Holy Office. Padre Pio wanted to see Brunatto so that he might reprimand him and force him to desist from his disparaging press campaign. According to other people, Padre Pio wanted to enlist the support of this eccentric but devoted spiritual son, not for himself but in an attempt to clarify the whole mess which threatened to destroy his work. It will be the role of history to ultimately decide which theory is right. Here is the chronicle of events as I learned from those involved.

"Toward the end of 1961, I was in San Giovanni Rotondo," Giuseppe Pagnossin recalled. Pagnossin is an industrialist from Venice who was one of Padre Pio's spiritual sons and who was one of his most active defenders in the sixties.

After Mass, I and some other people managed to get close enough to Padre Pio to kiss his hand. Suddenly, he turned to me and said with a sorrowful look, "Go get Brunatto and bring him to Italy." Since I didn't know a person by that name at the time, I asked Padre Pio, "Who's Brunatto?" He answered me: "Find out."

That same evening, I spoke with various people in San Giovanni Rotondo and learned about Brunatto and the role he played during the persecution in the twenties. I considered Padre Pio's request to be an order, so I immediately began to look for Brunatto. After a few weeks I was able to trace him to Paris. I made an appointment and went to meet him. "I'm under orders from Padre Pio to bring you to Italy," I said. "I'm ready to go," he answered. "How much time will you give me to finish up my business here in Paris?" he asked. "Are four weeks enough?" I asked. "Fine," he replied, and we made plans to meet on January 14, 1962, at noon in front of the train station in Nice.

Emanuele Brunatto arrived right on time for our meeting. I went by car to pick him up, accompanied by Dr. Giuseppe Gusso, a doctor from the House for the Relief of Suffering, and by Giovangualberto Alessandri, a judge. Brunatto had a passport that was more than thirty years old. It had been issued by the former Kingdom of Italy. It was absurd to try and cross the border with it, but we didn't have any choice. We called upon Padre Pio and made an attempt to cross. The customs official looked at the passport and didn't say anything.

Brunatto set up headquarters in the Hotel Michelangelo in Rome. He asked for an audience with Cardinal Ottaviani. He was granted an audience immediately and had a long discussion with him. Since Cardinal Ottaviani was head of the Holy Office and one of the men who signed the disciplinary measures imposed on Padre Pio, he seemed prepared to make some changes if the serious accusations against Padre Pio were dropped. He told Brunatto that the situation was very complex and asked him to be patient. Upon returning to his hotel, Brunatto immediately wrote a report on his conversation with Cardinal Ottaviani. Since it is a one-sided report, we cannot be sure that he faithfully described the conversation he had, but I quote it because it is extremely important. In fact, it is apparent from the conversation that the crux of the whole "Padre Pio question" was the House for the Relief of Suffering. The hospital was now a huge enterprise, and many people had an interest in taking it over. In their attempts to appropriate it, people talked about it, argued about it, and made deals about it—almost always in secret. Here is Brunatto's account of his conversation with Cardinal Ottaviani, handwritten on stationery from the Hotel Michelangelo:

Ottaviani: "I have given direct orders that Padre Pio's freedom be respected."

Brunatto: "It's not certain that the present superior will respect Your Eminence's orders."

Ottaviani: "I can assure you that the present superior is one of Padre Pio's supporters."

Brunatto: "And what would you do if he were not a supporter?"

Ottaviani: "I have given special instructions pertaining to you. You can go to San Giovanni Rotondo and speak with Padre Pio whenever you want to and for as long as you want to."

Brunatto: "I thank you immensely. But I can't accept your offer, even though it breaks my heart. I can't go to San Giovanni Rotondo if the whole crisis is not resolved. People might say that I'm receiving orders from Padre Pio. I don't think that Padre Pio's freedom can be assured unless the priests who were always supportive of him are able to return, such as Fr. Carmelo of Sessano."

Ottaviani: "Fr. Carmelo? No, Mr. Brunatto, let's let the present superior finish his three-year term of office."

Then we went on to discuss the House for the Relief of Suffering.

Ottaviani: "You must be a faithful son of the Church and accept the Church's decisions."

Brunatto: "I'm sorry. The founder of the hospital, as well as the founding committee and the donors I represent, cannot accept a *fait accompli* that was totally against our will as expressed in our letter of October 1960 to the Secretary of State. It seems to me that everyone involved in this matter has been betrayed, including Your Eminence. Monsignor Testa came to Paris under orders from the Holy Office to discuss with me the future of the clinic. At that very moment, Padre Pio was forced, in the name of holy obedience, to accept solutions that were exactly the opposite of what Monsignor Testa and I agreed upon for the basis of our discussions. Some serious moral force was used there."

Ottaviani: "No force was used there. Padre Pio himself asked that he be allowed to read the letters and documents before signing them."

Brunatto: "Allow me to question what the superior general of the Capuchins told Your Eminence. I do not believe that Padre Pio read the Cardinal's letter, nor that he was able to closely examine the title transfer."

Ottaviani: "Padre Pio himself asked that he be allowed to return the signed documents the following day so that he could have time to think about it."

Brunatto: "The superior general is protecting Giuffre's accomplices who are under his orders. We cannot trust him. In any case, we were never consulted. Moreover, what was done was the opposite of what we asked for."

Ottaviani: "Don't be so insistent, Mr. Brunatto. At this point I am powerless because the whole matter is now in the hands of the Committee of Cardinals."

Brunatto: "The Committee of Cardinals does not have the right to change the mandate given by the donors and the founding committee."

Ottaviani: "Show me the text in the charter of the foundation regarding this, and then we can talk about it."

Brunatto: "I'll gladly do so. But I can assure you even now that our position is and will remain as follows: we will accept any investigation the Holy See wants to do. The more that is done, the happier we will be. But we do not intend to see that, directly or indirectly, today or in the near future, Padre Pio is deprived of his right to do what he wants to do with what has been given to him."

Ottaviani: "Be fair, Mr. Brunatto. We acted in Padre Pio's best interest so that the Capuchin Order could not touch Padre Pio's work."

Cardinal Ottaviani's words did not deter Brunatto. Brunatto realized that the cardinal was privy to everything that was going on and that Padre Pio was all alone, at the mercy of his enemies. Brunatto called together a meeting of Padre Pio's closest friends. At the meeting the decision was made to establish an organization for defending Padre Pio. On May 30, 1962, the "International Association for the Defense of Padre Pio" was formed in Geneva, Switzerland. Emanuele Brunatto was named president of the association, and a committee of six well-known jurists who were experts in international law acted under his authority. They included two Frenchmen, two Italians, a Swiss, and a Belgian. The coordinator of the committee was Jean Flavien Lalive, a lawyer from Geneva who was already First Secretary of the International Court of Justice, a juridical and political advisor on the Middle East, and Secretary General of the International Commission of Jurists.

The six members of this association began to make plans for appeals and petitions. They also prepared exposés and reports for civil and religious authorities. They charged that those persecuting

Padre Pio were violating his basic human rights.

The Italian courts refused to consider the reports, citing Italy's Concordat with the Vatican. Church authorities, on the other hand, ignored the reports. At this point, Padre Pio's friends decided to turn to the United Nations. They began to prepare a "White Paper" on Padre Pio, gathering together documents to demonstrate that Padre Pio's dignity and human rights had been violated.

On March 9, 1963, Lalive wrote to Fr. Piedmatten, a Dominican priest who was the ecclesiastical advisor for the Center of International Catholic Organizations in Geneva, asking him to act as an intermediary in a last effort to resolve the whole matter with the Vatican without too much publicity. But his letter was in vain.

In June of 1963, the "White Paper" defending Padre Pio was ready. Before it was officially presented to the United Nations, Padre Pio's friends sent a copy of it to Pope Paul VI, to U Thant, the Secretary General of the United Nations, and to Antonio Segni, the President of Italy.

The Vatican did not respond. Fr. Piedmatten, who was responsible for contacts between the Holy See and Lalive in Geneva, said: "The Secretary of State for His Holiness, with whom I have had a few conversations in this regard, is not concerned about the presentation of this 'White Paper' to various governments, nor with the reaction of the international press,... and is convinced that the steps that the International Association for the Defense of Padre Pio is taking at the United Nations can be stopped in due time. Brunatto and his friends are proud people who are entertaining false hopes. Vatican authorities are not afraid of them."

Fr. Clemente of Santa Maria in Punta, who had been elected special administrator a few months before for the Capuchin province of Foggia, was very worried. He tried to resolve the whole matter with Padre Pio without causing an uproar. He sent Luigi Ghisleri, an engineer, to Geneva in an effort to convince Emanuele Brunatto to come to terms with the Vatican. On January 10, 1964, Ghisleri wrote Fr. Clemente: "Following your invitation, I was able to contact Mr. Brunatto, and I met with him today in Geneva. The situation truly is serious, and I am under the impression that Mr. Brunatto himself is no longer in a position to stop the extreme measures which the committee that he oversees has decided to take in order to obtain a settlement with San Giovanni Rotondo. The committee will meet on the 17th of this month to decide the date on which they will present the "White Paper" to the member states of the United Nations. In my opinion, Mr. Brunatto might be in a position to delay the matter if there is some attempt to immediately negotiate an overall solution to the problem. But some concrete step needs to be taken, such as replacing the present superior of San Giovanni Rotondo with a person whom Padre Pio trusts, such as Fr. Carmelo of Sessano.... I've done everything I can. You need to make a decision based on your authority."

By then it was too late. The decision was made to present the "White Paper" on March 25. Brunatto's organization had already sent out fifty invitations to representatives of many countries, as well as to newspaper reporters and Church authorities. The conference was scheduled to be held in the Grand Salon of the Hotel Richmond in Geneva. Copies of the "White Paper" were also sent to all the bishops attending the Second Vatican Council, which was taking place at that time.

But at the last minute a *coup de théâtre* changed everything. "Upon returning to Italy on March 15," Giuseppe Pagnossin told me, "I found a special delivery letter from Judge Alessandri in which he told me that Padre Pio had ordered that the conference in Geneva be called off. I immediately called Brunatto, telling him about the letter. I said to him, 'Do you remember when I came to you in Paris in 1961 with orders from Padre Pio to bring you back to Italy? Well, now I'm coming to you with another message from Padre Pio: stop everything. I'm not asking any questions, and I'm sure that you won't either.'

"Brunatto did not ask for an explanation, but found himself in deep trouble. It would be an immense task to stop the international machinery that he had already set in motion. Clenching his teeth and hiding his wounded pride, he set himself to the task. First he postponed the conference to April 2, then he called it off altogether. 'In my role as a shield, I'll act like I'm just a puppet, which I deserve,' he wrote me. 'But I don't want to complain, and I don't want to regret it, even if I'm boiling inside. I know how to be a useful and humble instrument. I only have to obey and keep silent.'

"What happened? We only learned what happened after Padre Pio's death. In 1969 we read the memorandum that Fr. Clemente of Santa Maria in Punta wrote: 'On January 30, 1964, Cardinal Ottaviani called me to the Holy Office to tell me that it was the pope's desire that Padre Pio be able to carry out his ministry in complete freedom.' Returning to San Giovanni Rotondo, Fr. Clemente lifted the restrictions placed on Padre Pio after Monsignor Macari's visitation. At that point the presentation of the 'White Paper' in Geneva no longer served any purpose."

TWENTY-FOUR

Heroic Obedience

The failure of Padre Pio's group of friends to present their "White Paper" at the United Nations appeared to be a victory for the Capuchins and the Holy Office, at least from the point of view of public relations. In reality, though, the press campaign on Padre Pio's behalf had indirectly damaged the image of the Capuchin Order and the Holy Office. Even though the whole matter was now over, the Capuchin Order and the Holy Office were still concerned about the criticism that the story had generated. From their point of view, they had always acted for Padre Pio's well-being, and they wanted to document this. They decided to ask Padre Pio for a written statement to this effect, certain that no one would criticize their actions when confronted with such a document.

On December 14, 1964, Padre Pio issued the following statement: "For some time the press has been publishing some rather outrageous reports about me, implying that I was being constrained and persecuted by Church authorities. I feel that I have the need and the duty before God to deplore these false reports and declare that I enjoy full freedom in my ministry. I am not aware of having enemies or persecutors. Moreover, I am pleased to publicly affirm that I find understanding, comfort, and protection from the superiors of my religious order and from Church authorities, and that I do not need any other defenders outside of God and his legitimate representatives.

"I am writing at length for the sake of truth and justice, and I am tired of the errors that are damaging souls and the Church. They sadden me since I only desire good for everyone and the glorification of our Lord."

Padre Pio's written statement was immediately sent to the newspapers, which prominently published it. This statement, which has been passed down in history as Padre Pio's "denial" of any so-called persecution, has little value. The fact is that Padre Pio simply copied down what someone else had prepared for him. Fr. Clemente of Santa Maria in Punta wrote a report to this effect immediately after Padre Pio's death.

In August of 1963, Fr. Clemente was named the Apostolic Administrator of the Capuchin province of Foggia. He was responsible to the Holy See for overseeing the conduct of the friars, especially those at San Giovanni Rotondo. He was also responsible for seeing that the sanctions that were issued after Msgr. Carlo Macari's visitation in 1960 were applied in the monastery of Santa Maria delle Grazie and respected by all the friars.

Padre Pio did not welcome the arrival of this fellow monk. Fr. Clemente himself admitted this in his memo: "On orders from the Holy Office, I had to dismiss Fr. Eusebio of Castelpetroso, who had been helping Padre Pio for many years. Padre Pio did not appreciate this, for reasons that are easily understood. Sick, almost powerless to move, he continually needed help, even for his most intimate needs. Padre Pio accepted Fr. Eusebio and trusted him. It would be hard for him to get used to another monk. It is probably for this reason that he had some rather harsh words for me one day. After asking me why I was sent to San Giovanni Rotondo, he said that he would have had a lot of things to say to me but he held back from doing so because of the presence of his fellow monks. Then he added that every time I came to San Giovanni Rotondo, it made him sad."

The idea of obtaining a written statement from Padre Pio denying his so-called persecution dates back to January of 1964. In his memo of 1969, Fr. Clemente wrote: "On January 3, 1964, I asked Padre Pio, on behalf of the minister general, to take some effective action to defend the Capuchin Order, which was being negatively attacked in the press. He told me he would gladly do so if he were free. 'I only wish to be like any other Capuchin monk,' he said. Consequently, I asked him for an authoritative document that I could present to those who were attacking us."

Padre Pio's response only confirms that persecution did exist. Padre Pio, who felt that he was being discriminated against, wanted to be treated like his fellow friars. The request was made for an "authoritative document" to present to those who were attacking the order. But a statement from Padre Pio would serve little purpose, insofar as it would be a stark contrast with the facts that everyone knew.

Fr. Clemente did not insist. For a whole year he did not bring up the topic. Then in December, at the request of the Holy Office, he agreed to try once again to obtain such a statement. He wrote about this request in his report: "On the evening of December 11, after a rather arrogant call from Emanuele Brunatto expressing his intention to continue his defamatory campaign in his newsletter, *Franciscus,* a meeting took place at the Holy Office in Cardinal Ottaviani's apartment. Cardinal Ottaviani, Monsignor Pietro Parente, and I thought that it would be very useful to obtain a condemnation from Padre Pio of the defamatory press campaign. The statement should be requested from Padre Pio as a favor and not as an obligation."

During the night the secretary of the Holy Office prepared the text of the statement and gave it to Fr. Clemente. In his memoirs, Fr. Clemente wrote:

"On December 12 Monsignor Parente read me a text that was prepared from Cardinal Ottaviani's suggestions, that I was to give to Padre Pio in case he agreed to write such a statement. Monsignor Parente also told me that they had decided against the idea of sending someone from the Holy Office to San Giovanni Rotondo to make the request to Padre Pio, and that the task had been assigned to me."

Fr. Clemente left Rome and went straight to San Giovanni Rotondo. On December 14 he approached Padre Pio: "I informed

Padre Pio while he was in the sacristy of the old church about the slander that was being published in the press and in particular in Brunatto's newsletter. I asked him, on behalf of Cardinal Ottaviani, if he could do something to benefit the Capuchin Order and the Church. Padre Pio immediately agreed. 'Give me a text and I will gladly sign it,' he said. I then read him the text prepared by Monsignor Parente and he approved it."

If the request was made "on behalf of Cardinal Ottaviani to benefit the Capuchin Order and the Church," how could Padre Pio not readily agree to it? Later, however, he told several of his spiritual sons and daughters that he was forced to make the statement.

The Holy Office adopted the same posture concerning Padre Pio's will. On October 4, 1960, two months after Monsignor Maccari's visit, Padre Pio drew up the following document: "I, the undersigned Padre Pio from Pietrelcina, known in my secular life as Francesco Forgione, son of the late Grazio, hereby name in this handwritten will, as sole heirs of the shares of the Society for the House for the Relief of Suffering and the funds and property connected with the House for the Relief of Suffering in San Giovanni Rotondo, which were registered in my name under a sovereign concession of the late Pontiff, Pius XII, as well as any other possessions that might belong to me at the time of my death through this concession, to a legal entity that the Holy See will establish in San Giovanni Rotondo, in order to assure the continuation of the above-named House for the Relief of Suffering."

Clearly he is referring to a legal entity that will be established in San Giovanni Rotondo sometime in the future. Padre Pio entrusted this will to Angelo Battisti, one of his spiritual sons and the administrator of the House for the Relief of Suffering for eleven years. The Holy Office was aware of the existence of this document and wanted to see it. Fr. Clemente wrote in his diary: "February 19, 1964. I asked Padre Pio where his will is, and added that the Secretary of State did not have it in its possession. He said he would have to ask Angelo Battisti for it. He said that he is prepared to write another one in case it is nowhere to be found, copying from a text that will be given to him."

Three months went by before the will was found. Fr. Clemente wrote: "May 6, 1964. Angelo Battisti had the will locked up in a safe at the House for the Relief of Suffering. Through my intervention, he entrusted it to the Secretary of State. However, it was not considered to be complete enough, so Padre Pio was asked to rewrite his will, and two texts were prepared by the Institute for the Works of Religion and given to Padre Pio on May 6. He took them and asked me if he could copy them when his hand was better and he was able to write. I told him that there was no hurry, and I asked him not to tell anyone about it and to give everything to me personally.

"May 8, 1964. Padre Pio asked me to read what he had copied to know if he was doing it right.

"May 11, 1964. Padre Pio gave me everything he had written. He did not copy just one text but both of them."

By copying both texts and presenting them to the Holy See, Padre Pio was making a very eloquent statement. He had already drawn up "his" will and did not intend to change it. If other people were not satisfied with his will, he was ready to write what they wanted, but without getting involved himself or imposing his desires on them. This is the reason why he copied both of the texts that were given to him without choosing one or the other, and signed both of them while giving them the same date. Here are the two wills:

Will A: "I name the Holy See and the Supreme Pontiff *pro tempore,* as the sole heir of all my tangible and intangible assets, both those that belong to me or that are given to me, as well as all assets that belong to me under various names, for example, the 'Work of Padre Pio of Pietrelcina, House for the Relief of Suffering, San Giovanni Rotondo.' This will revokes all preceding wills that I have made. May 11, 1964. San Giovanni Rotondo. Padre Pio from Pietrelcina, Forgione, Francesco."

Will B: "I name the Holy See and the Supreme Pontiff *pro tem-pore,* the legatee of all my possessions (deeds, accounts, trusts, etc.) and property, both those that belong to me or that are given to me, that are in my name at the bank of the Vatican Institute for the Works of Religion, or that are in accounts in the name of 'Work of Padre Pio of Pietrelcina, House for the Relief of Suffering, San Giovanni Rotondo.' This will revokes all preceding wills concerning the possessions in question. May 11, 1964. San Giovanni Rotondo. Padre Pio of Pietrelcina, Forgione, Francesco."

While all this was taking place, Padre Pio's health was steadily declining. Even though he had never experienced a day in his life without some physical suffering, ailments that are typical of old age were gradually added to the strange and mysterious illnesses from which he was already suffering.

His body was already destroyed, and only his steel will kept him going. He suffered from frequent and serious attacks of bronchial asthma that threatened to suffocate him. He was often overcome by dizzy spells that made him lose his balance and fall down. At times his health forced him to stay in bed without celebrating Mass, but this was seldom the case because he had such a strong sense of duty. One day when he was forced to stay in bed because it was impossible for him to stand up, he summoned two of his fellow monks and said, "Come and pull this lazy guy from bed." He then had them walk him to his confessional.

In 1959, he fell seriously ill. On April 25, he was confined to bed. His doctors were summoned. They were anxious and frightened. On June 2, his condition worsened and Drs. Pontoni and Gasbarrini both examined him. On June 30, there was another examination with Drs. Gasbarrini, Pontoni, Valdoni, and Toniolo. Their diagnosis was unanimous: a malignant tumor in the lung. Padre Pio had only a few months to live. Afterward, his condition steadily grew worse.

Then, in August, an amazing incident occurred that cannot be explained except through supernatural intervention.

"At that time," Fr. Mario Mason, a Jesuit priest who is the founder of the Marian Eucharistic Movement, told me,

I was traveling in Italy carrying a statue of Our Lady of Fatima from town to town, after the statue had already traveled around the world. I arrived in Italy with the statue on April 25, the day that Padre Pio fell ill. I went to Foggia with the statue on August 5. From there I was to go to Benevento for two days. However, the bishop of the town, who was old and sick, was upset. He said that everyone was out of town because of the holidays, and that very few people would attend the religious ceremonies that were planned. So we decided to postpone the ceremonies in Benevento. I would spend another day in San Giovanni Rotondo.

I knew that August 10 was the anniversary of Padre Pio's ordination to the priesthood, and that many pilgrims were already arriving in San Giovanni Rotondo. There would be a huge crowd there to welcome us, and so it was.

I arrived with the statue in Padre Pio's town on the fifth. Throughout the night people flocked to pray before the statue of Our Lady, asking for Padre Pio's healing. At about ten o'clock in the morning of the following day, the helicopter pilot who transported the statue of Our Lady, my driver, some missionaries, and I went to visit Padre Pio in his cell. The monks who were caring for him had been told to make sure that we did not tire him out. We found him lying in bed, sweating and gasping for breath. We said to him: "Father, give us your blessing and give me a word to say to the pilgrims who are interceding with Our Lady for you." With great effort and in a whisper, Padre Pio answered, "God bless you for all the good you're doing for the Church and for Italy. Tell the people to practice all the good things that Our Lady is inspiring them to do.

At about noon, when there were only a few people in church, Padre Pio was carried on a stretcher and placed in front of the statue of Our Lady of Fatima, which he wanted to see. He prayed for a few minutes, and then he was taken back to his cell.

At two o'clock, we left San Giovanni Rotondo. When the helicopter took off, I told the pilot to make two passes over the building complex where Padre Pio's work was located, and then we went straight to Foggia. When we were already some distance away, I felt a strange and strong attraction to go to Padre Pio, as though he were calling me. I said to the pilot, "Turn back, head toward the shrine, and fly over the monastery." The captain did as I said. When we were over the exact place where I knew Padre Pio's cell was located, we remained there in the air for a few moments. Later I was told that Padre Pio, hearing the noise from the helicopter, prayed the following prayer: "Holy Mary, when you came to Italy you confined me to my bed with these illnesses. Now that you are going, are you going to leave me like this?"

After having just said these words, his entire body shook violently. The monks that were caring for him were frightened and thought he was dying. But the phenomenon lasted only a few seconds. Suddenly Padre Pio felt better. Color returned to his face, and he was breathing normally and regularly. He said that he didn't feel any pain, that he felt strong again, and that he wanted to get out of bed. The doctors were immediately summoned. He was carefully examined. There was no trace of his terrible illness. Two days later, Padre Pio was able to celebrate Mass again, to hear confessions, and to meet with people.

In a letter that he wrote to one of his spiritual sons on August 13 of that year, Padre Pio confirmed his sudden and miraculous healing, obtained through the intercession of Our Lady of Fatima: "Thank the Virgin Mary for me," he wrote. "On the day she left, I felt better again."

But this miraculous healing did not improve Padre Pio's health to any great degree. Although he was able to continue his ministry, his afflictions and sufferings continued.

In 1962, he began to have difficulty seeing, so much so that he was dispensed from having to recite the Divine Office. Almost a year later, he began to have serious problems with his legs, which were unable to support him. He complained that he was not able to feel them. In 1966, he was permitted to celebrate Mass sitting down. The following year, he began to use a wheelchair to get from one place to another in the monastery. His asthma attacks caused pain in his chest, rapid heartbeats, cold sweats, and a lack of breath. He also suffered from arthritis in his knees and in his back.

At the end of his life, he was tormented by spiritual suffering as well. He had visions of the devil that were caused by the evil one. On the night of July 5–6, 1964, a roar was heard coming from his cell. When his fellow monks ran to his aid, they found him sprawled out on the floor with a wound on his forehead. One day he was having a discussion on demonic spirits with the friar who was caring for him. Padre Pio told him, "They don't leave me in peace for a second." On another occasion, frightened by terrifying visions, he told Fr. Alessio: "If you saw what I saw, you'd be dead."

TWENTY-FIVE

September 23, 1968

Padre Pio was perfectly aware of the day when he would die. When Padre Pio received the stigmata, Jesus told him something that he never recorded in his letters but which he confided to some of his spiritual children. Realizing that his hands, feet, and side were bleeding, he turned to Jesus and begged him to take away the physical signs: "Let me suffer and let me die from suffering," he prayed. "But take away these signs that cause me so much embarrassment." Jesus told him: "You will bear them for fifty years, and then you will see me." Exactly fifty years later, the wounds disappeared and Padre Pio died.

There are numerous testimonies that prove Padre Pio knew the exact day of his death. In 1967 his niece, Pia Forgione, visited him to ask his prayers for some sensitive family matters. "Within two years I will no longer be here," he said. "I'll be dead and a lot of things will change." The conviction and certainty with which he repeated these words made a deep impression on his niece. She wrote them down and left them on file with Domenico Giuliani, a notary in San Giovanni Rotondo.

A young photographer from San Giovanni Rotondo, Modesto Vinelli, managed to take some photographs of Padre Pio a few months after he had received the stigmata in 1918. The wounds are clearly visible in the photographs, and the photographer was selling copies of these pictures to the faithful. One day something happened when he was in Rodi Garganico. Upon seeing these photos, a man began to swear and blaspheme. He took one of them, tore it up, and trampled on it. Vinelli's reaction was to kick him and slap him. A violent fight ensued. The blasphemer was hurt, and Vinelli was thrown in jail for forty days. When he was set free, Vinelli went to Padre Pio and told him, "I was sent to jail for defending you." Then he told him everything that had happened. Padre Pio listened to him and said, "Modesto, we have fifty years ahead of us."

Vinelli did not understand what he meant. Every year on the twentieth of September, the anniversary of the apparition of the stigmata, Modesto Vinelli would visit Padre Pio to wish him well, and Padre Pio would answer him with the same Sybillic words concerning a certain period of time. On the twenty-fifth anniversary of the stigmata, Padre Pio told him: "Modesto, remember that we still have twenty-five years."

Vinelli was worried. He began to think that Padre Pio's words referred to the amount of time he had left to live. In 1968, the fiftieth anniversary of the stigmata, Vinelli was extremely anxious. On the morning of September 20, he went as always to see Padre Pio. In a very sad but loving way, Padre Pio said: "Modesto, the fifty years are over." Vinelli was flabbergasted. A couple of monks had to hold him up because he was shaking so much. Three days later, Padre Pio died. Modesto, however, lived until 1983.

"On September 19, 1968," Fr. Alberto D'Appolito told me, "I was on the porch of the monastery with Padre Pio and some other monks. A man from Naples arrived with a bouquet of beautiful red roses that he offered to Padre Pio for the fiftieth anniversary of his stigmata, which was going to take place two days later. Padre Pio looked at the roses, took one of them, and gave it to the man. He asked him to take it to the shrine of Our Lady of Pompei. The next day the man went to Pompei and gave the rose to a nun at the shrine, explaining that Padre Pio had sent it for Our Lady. The nun put it in a vase with some other flowers on the altar. On September 23, when that nun heard that Padre Pio had died, she went to the church to pray. Seeing that the flowers in front of Our Lady had died, she was going to throw them out. She was amazed to discover that Padre Pio's rose was still fresh and fragrant. A year later, when I accompanied another pilgrim to Pompei, I personally saw that rose. It was still fresh in a glass case. Only the stem was a little yellow."

The Capuchin fathers decided to organize a big celebration in San Giovanni Rotondo to observe the fiftieth anniversary of the appearance of the stigmata, along with a meeting of the "prayer groups" that Padre Pio founded. To make it easier for pilgrims to come, the festivities were postponed from September 20, which fell on a Friday, to September 22, which was a Sunday.

When the pilgrims began to arrive in San Giovanni Rotondo on the evening of September 19, the hotels and pensions were already full. Many people had to spend the night in their cars. On September 20, Padre Pio spent the day as usual. He celebrated Mass at five o'clock in the morning, then heard confessions and prayed. There was a spectacular procession that evening. A huge crowd, led by the mayor and members of the city council, processed to the monastery with flaming torches. When the crowd arrived in the small square in front of the church, they prayed together and then stood outside the walls of the monastery under the window of Padre Pio's cell, hoping that he would look out.

Padre Pio did not take part in this celebration. Probably he was not pleased that there was such a huge celebration for a mystical experience that he always tried to hide. Moreover, he did not feel well physically. That evening he went to bed earlier than usual, but he was unable to fall asleep.

After a restless night, at the time that he was supposed to get up for Mass, he had a severe asthma attack. A doctor had to be called. The attack was very serious, and doctors feared the worst. For this reason, the superior of the monastery and several of Padre Pio's fellow friars kept vigil in his room. They all tried to encourage the old monk, but he said over and over, "It's the end. It's the end."

He was not in any condition to celebrate Mass that day. He wanted to get up in the afternoon and was able to make it with help to the gallery of the church, where he attended Mass and blessed the crowd that was there.

September 22 was a Sunday. Delegates of "prayer groups" from around the world were gathered together. Padre Pio was feeling better. At half past four in the morning, he went to the sacristy to celebrate Mass as usual at five o'clock. Since it was the day of the major celebration, the superior of the monastery ordered the Mass to be a Solemn Mass with singing. Consequently it would be more tiring for the celebrant. Padre Pio was in no shape to celebrate such a Mass. He complained, but, for some reason, no one listened to him. Fr. Raffaele of Sant'Elia á Pianisi later mentioned that Padre Pio was upset when he learned that the Mass would have to be chanted, and said, "And if I don't?" He was told, "Those are the orders." And he obeyed.

That Mass was the last Mass that Padre Pio celebrated, and it took superhuman strength to do so. A recording was made of that Mass, and numerous photographs were taken. Padre Pio's tired and trembling voice can be heard on the recording. His face appears troubled in the photographs. When it came time for the Preface, Padre Pio was so exhausted that he was unable to sing it so he recited it. Shortly thereafter, he became totally confused. Instead of the Our Father, he sang the Preface. At the end of Mass, he collapsed on the altar. He was so worn out that he had to be taken to the sacristy in a wheelchair.

His vestments were removed, and he was taken to his cell, where he rested in bed for a couple of hours. Then he wanted to get up. At half past ten, he went to the window of the church choir to bless the crowd. At six in the evening, he went down to the church and attended evening Mass from the gallery in the church. At the end of Mass, he tried to get up to bless the people, but he was unable to do so. He was completely bent over and unable to move. His fellow friars lifted him up, set him in his wheelchair, and wheeled him to his cell.

Even in those moments of terrible suffering that preceded his death, Padre Pio continued to think about others and do what he could for them. That morning, while he was resting in his cell trying to regain the strength that he had spent saying his last Mass, he performed yet another miracle. Fr. Alberto D'Apolito, one of his most beloved disciples, was the one who was able to obtain it from him.

"Among the many pilgrims who came to San Giovanni Rotondo for the festivities," the monk told me,

there was one named Gino Pin from Biella, one of Padre Pio's spiritual sons, along with his family. I was Gino's good friend, and I thought about doing something that he would appreciate —giving him a holy card with a note handwritten by Padre Pio. On the morning of September 21, I went to Padre Pio and, without telling him whom the holy card was for, asked him to write something on it. Padre Pio blessed it and wrote, "May Jesus and Mary always relieve your suffering."

I was upset when I read those words because I knew my friend's family was going through some hard times. I even thought about not giving him the holy card, but I changed my mind. Even Gino was upset when I gave it to him. He asked me with tears in his eyes, "Did you read what Padre Pio wrote?"

"Don't let it upset you," I replied. "You know that Padre Pio is with you."

In the evening Gino came to me very upset. He said, "Fr. Alberto, Padre Pio's words have come true. My daughter, Maria Pia, has been admitted to the hospital with a high fever and abdominal pains. The doctors think it's acute appendicitis or peritonitis and they will need to operate."

My friend spent the night at the hospital with his daughter, and her condition grew progressively worse. In the morning he said to me, "Maria Pia is very sick. I want to take her back to Biella so that we're home if the worst happens. I'd like a word of advice from Padre Pio so I know what to do."

I didn't know what to do. Padre Pio was sick. I didn't want to disturb him, but my friend Gino was asking me for a big favor, so I got up the courage and went up to his cell. Padre Pio was sitting in an armchair, totally absorbed in prayer. I called out to him, but he didn't hear me. Then I touched him on his knee. "What do you want?" he asked, raising his eyes. I told him what had happened to my friend and said, "My friend wants to know whether he can take the girl to Biella or if it's better to stay here with her." With hesitation, Padre Pio replied: "Stay in the hospital. If the operation is needed, she will be operated on here and not in Biella. I'll pray."

Since I was alone with him, I got up the nerve to insist. I said to him, "Father, my friend is poor. He doesn't have enough money to stay with his family in San Giovanni Rotondo. Why not ask Our Lady to heal the girl without an operation?" I said this with my eyes looking down. I didn't want to look up because I knew that I was asking for an enormous favor. Padre Pio didn't answer. I didn't have the courage to look him in the eyes. But after a couple of minutes of complete silence, I had to do so. Timidly I looked up, and I saw that Padre Pio's eyes were fixed on me. "All right," he said. "I'll ask Our Lady." I ran to tell Gino what Padre Pio had said. A few hours later, the doctors found the girl sitting up in bed. They examined her closely. She was healed, and they discharged her that same day.

For several years, the monks at San Giovanni Rotondo had not let Padre Pio spend the night alone. He was old, had a lot of ailments, and was especially prone to asthma attacks. For these reasons they decided it would be good to have someone close by who could help if needed. Fr. Pellegrino of Sant'Elia á Pianisi was entrusted with this responsibility. He was the one who cared for Padre Pio in the last hours of his life.

That evening I went as usual to Padre Pio's room at about nine o'clock," Fr. Pellegrino told me.

This had been my job for about three years. Padre Pio slept very little, one or two hours at the most. He spent the rest of the time in prayer. Between one and two, he would get up so he could start getting ready for Mass.

I was in a room that was connected to Padre Pio's room by a door, and that had an intercom so that I could hear every little noise. When I went on duty that evening, Padre Pio was already in bed. There were two people in the room who left when I came.

From nine o'clock to midnight, Padre Pio called me five or six times. He asked me what time it was. He looked pale and had some tears on his eyelashes, but he seemed more at peace than on other nights.

At midnight he asked me rather sheepishly, almost afraid that I would say no, "Can you stay with me, my son?" I told him I could. Generally I would sit in the armchair, but that night Padre Pio wanted me to sit in a chair next to his bed. He grabbed my hands with his hands and squeezed me hard. He was trembling like a feverish child.

From midnight to one, he would ask me what time it was every two or three minutes. It seemed like he had an appointment, and that he was impatiently waiting for the time to come. Tears flowed peacefully from his eyes, and I would wipe them away. Toward one o'clock he asked me, "Have you said Mass?"

"Father, it's time for Mass," I answered. He added, "This morning, you'll say it for me."

A little later he wanted to go to confession. I wasn't his usual confessor, but I had heard his confession at various times before during the night. At the end of his confession, he asked me to renew his act of profession as a religious monk. His request made me shudder because it's our custom as monks to do so on our deathbed. I did as he asked, and when he was finished he said: "My son, if the Lord calls me tonight, ask all my brothers to forgive me for the trouble I've caused them. Ask them also to pray for my soul." I had a rather sharp reaction to his words, and he was upset. After a little while I asked him for forgiveness and said to him: "Father, I'm sure the Lord is still going to give you a long life, but if you're right, I ask you for a last blessing for our fellow monks, for your spiritual children, and for the sick."

"Yes," he said, "I bless them all. But ask the superior to give them all this blessing from me."

Padre Pio remained silent for a few minutes. Then he said, "I don't breathe well in bed. Help me get up." I insisted that he stay in bed, but finally I gave in. I helped him get dressed. I took him to the sink, and he put some cold water on his face, combed his beard, and sat down in the armchair. He said, "See if there are stars in the sky." I told him there were. "Then let's go out," he said.

He got up from the armchair alone. He stood up completely straight, which he hadn't done for years. I went to help him, but I was amazed when I realized that he didn't need any help. He moved very vigorously, as if he were twenty years younger. He walked out of the room and down the corridor. When he got to the veranda, he turned the light on with his hands, which he never did anymore. When we were outside under the stars, he looked around in awe, and his face seemed to light up. We stood there in silent contemplation for a few minutes, then he sat down. When he would go out on the veranda at other times, he went there to pray. That night he looked at a precise place on the veranda, the place where his body would be brought after his death.

After about ten minutes, he began to grow pale. "Let's go back to the room," he said. I helped him get up, and I realized he was heavier now. He wasn't able to stand up straight, and I was unable to support him. I ran to get the wheelchair. When we got back to the room, it took a lot of effort to put him in his armchair.

Until then, I didn't think Padre Pio might be coming to the end of his days. But then I saw him grow paler and paler while he was sitting in the armchair, and his lips were turning purple.

I got scared. He kept repeating, "Jesus, Mary," in a voice that grew steadily weaker.

At a certain moment, he looked straight at the wall and asked me, "Who's that there?"

"Those are pictures of your loved ones, your mother, your father, and some of the sick," I answered. He said: "I see two mothers." I thought his vision had grown weaker. Going up to the wall and pointing at the picture, I said, "This one is of your mother." Padre Pio looked at me and said, "Don't worry, I can see you very well. But there's two mothers there." Then I realized that perhaps the "other mother" was Our Lady.

Everyone knew that Padre Pio often saw Our Lady. I myself witnessed these strange experiences. Sometimes I would spy on him when he was praying. Often I sensed he was having a conversation with someone. A marvelous light emanated from Padre Pio's face whenever that happened. That night, he didn't start talking with the "two mothers" in front of me, but I understood from the entranced look on his face that he was seeing someone.

When this form of ecstasy was over, his physical condition quickly went downhill. It was hard for him to breathe. I was worried, and I went to the door to call somebody, but he said: "No, don't disturb anybody." I stayed with him for a few more minutes, but then I decided to go out and find somebody. I called Brother Gugliemo, who made a phone call to Dr. Sala, the doctor who was caring for Padre Pio. I also called our father superior and some of my fellow monks.

The doctor came right away and tried to give Padre Pio some oxygen to keep him alive. He also gave him some shots. He called Dr. Giuseppe Gusso, the director of health services at the House for the Relief of Suffering, who came right away with another colleague. But it was too late. At half past two, Padre Pio died, without a tremor.

We were all deeply affected. We prayed. Some people were crying. After a while we carried his body to the veranda that was adjacent to his cell. Dr. Sala and I began to dress him and prepare him for burial. Fr. Raffaele, the superior of the monastery, and Fr. Mariano were with us. As soon as we undressed Padre Pio's body, we realized that the stigmata had disappeared. I had often seen the wounds that Padre Pio had on his hands. They were deep wounds in the middle of his palms, covered with bloody scabs. I saw the wound on his side only once, in 1958. Padre Pio had lost a button on the shirt he was wearing, and when he asked me to sew it back on he had to take his shirt off. The wound on his side was about two or two and a half inches long and an inch wide. It seemed quite deep to me, but it wasn't bleeding.

During the last years of his life, though, the stigmata on his hands and feet were progressively fading, almost to the point where they disappeared. At first there were some bruises on his feet, which I remember seeing when he would soak his feet. Later, though, when I got a closer look, I realized that there weren't any more marks. His hands and legs still hurt him. You only needed to touch his back with your finger and he would wince with pain. In those final years he needed to use a wheelchair because he couldn't stand up anymore.

People who got a closer look at his hands during those last few months of his life realized that he no longer had any bloody scabs on them. Checking the handkerchief that he used to cover the wound on his side, I noticed the same thing.

On September 22, when Padre Pio was celebrating his last Mass, scales that were almost perfectly white fell from his hands. When Dr. Sala and I were preparing his body after he died, a last scale fell from his left hand. We checked his feet, his hands, and his side very carefully. The skin looked as new as a baby's skin. You couldn't see anything where the wounds had been, not even the slightest trace of a scar. Fr. Giacomo took some photographs, and Dr. Sala himself did a scientific report.

The disappearance of the stigmata left us rather perplexed.

Dr. Sala immediately said that it was a miracle even greater than the stigmata since he was able to verify that dead tissue had been regenerated. We didn't know, though, what to do. We referred the whole matter to our superiors. They told us not to say anything and to put the half gloves and slippers on Padre Pio's body so that the people could see him like he was when he was alive.

TWENTY-SIX

The Cause for Padre Pio's Beatification

News about Padre Pio's death quickly spread around the world. Pilgrims and followers began to arrive in San Giovanni Rotondo. His body was placed in a walnut coffin and put on view in the monastery church on a catafalque under the balustrade of the main altar. There was no end to the people who came to pay their last respects. Two days later his body was put in a metal coffin covered with glass.

The funeral took place on Thursday, September 26, at half past three in the afternoon. More than a hundred thousand people were present. The funeral cortege traveled through the main streets of town, a distance of almost five miles, and both sides of the streets were filled with people. Police helicopters circled overhead and threw flowers on the crowd. Dr. Enrico Medi, the famous scientist, recited the rosary over a loudspeaker, commenting on the various mysteries and referring to episodes in Padre Pio's life.

Twenty-four priests concelebrated the funeral Mass at seven o'clock in the evening. Afterward, Padre Pio's body was carried in procession past the House for the Relief of Suffering as a final tribute to the sick. Then his coffin was carried by hand down into the crypt of the church, where it was buried in a niche during a private ceremony.

On September 27, at half past four in the afternoon, the crypt was opened to the public. It was the beginning of pilgrimages that thousands of people would make.

On November 23, 1969, one year and two months after Padre Pio's death, the Most Reverend Antonio Cunial, the apostolic

administrator of the diocese of Manfredonia, ordered that preliminary steps be taken for Padre Pio's beatification and canonization.
On October 15, 1970, he named two special delegates to follow
the cause. On February 28, 1971, he ordered the clergy and the
faithful to turn over to the Curia all writings by Padre Pio. On
January 16, 1973, Monsignor Vailati submitted the required documentation to the Sacred Congregation for the Cause of Saints to
begin the process for his canonization.

These steps were carried out very quickly in the diocese of
Manfredonia. Theoretically, the cause for Padre Pio's canonization
could begin in 1973. Then, nothing happened for ten years. His
cause remained blocked in the Holy Office—the supreme, ecclesiastical tribunal that had persecuted Padre Pio for fifty years and had
issued numerous decrees and disciplinary measures against him,
without ever having revoked them. Even though Padre Pio was
dead, he still was "condemned" by the Holy Office. Given these
conditions, the cause for his beatification was never initiated.

It was the pope who intervened to remove the obstacles. Pope
John Paul II has always been a supporter of Padre Pio, whom he
met in 1947. At that time, Karol Wojtyla was a young priest who
was studying theology at the Angelicum in Rome. During one of
his vacations, he went to San Giovanni Rotondo for the express
purpose of meeting Padre Pio. We know that he had a long talk
with Padre Pio at that time and that Padre Pio heard his confession.

It has been reported that Padre Pio prophesied at that time that
the young Polish priest would become the pope, and it appears that
such a prophecy was indeed given. This story has been circulating
for many years, and the Vatican has never denied it.

Direct contact between Padre Pio and Karol Wojtyla was not
limited to that one encounter. Contact continued afterward,
though no documentation exists to indicate how. One episode
dates back to 1962. At that time, Karol Wojtyla was the vicar of
Krakow, and was present in Rome for the Second Vatican Council.

He received an urgent message notifying him that a family friend back home, Wanda Poltawska, a forty-year-old professor of psychiatry who was also the mother of four children and a survivor of a German concentration camp during the war, was dying from a tumor in her throat. Doctors said that the growth of the tumor could not be stopped and that surgery would be useless.

Karol Wojtyla decided to turn to his highly esteemed friend. He wrote a letter to Padre Pio. It was delivered immediately to Angelo Battisti, the administrator for the House for the Relief of Suffering, so that he could take it with him to San Giovanni Rotondo. "I left immediately," Angelo Battisti told me. "As soon as I arrived at the monastery, Padre Pio told me to read the letter to him. He listened in silence to the brief message in Latin and said, 'I can't say no to that.' Then he added, 'Angelino, keep that letter on file because one day it will be important.'

"The next week I was given another letter to take to Padre Pio. This time Karol Wojtyla was informing him that Professor Poltawska had been completely healed. This miraculous event took place the day before they were going to attempt surgery on her."

A few years after Padre Pio's death, the Polish bishops sent a letter to Pope Paul VI asking him to open up the process for the monk's beatification. From everything we know, Karol Wojtyla suggested that this letter be sent. These facts demonstrate the high regard that Pope John Paul II always had for Padre Pio, and why he was interested in using his authority to remove any obstacles to his canonization.

The process for Padre Pio's beatification formally began on March 20, 1983. During the past few years, the procedure for beatification has been simplified. It now consists of only one step, which takes place in the diocese where the candidate died.

The process begins with a preliminary phase of preparation that precedes the process *per se*. The writings of the candidate are carefully examined, and a biography is compiled from these documents.

If the results of this initial phase are positive, Church authorities will then issue a decree opening up the process.

The second phase is the investigation phase, during which testimonies are heard. Everything is then sent to Rome. There the material is put into order, updated, and sent to press. The dossier is then presented to a committee of theologians. Each theologian examines the material individually, and writes up a personal report expressing his opinions. Then they meet together, discuss the material, and vote. If they vote to proceed with the process, the documents from the investigation and the material from the theological committee are passed on to a committee of cardinals, who repeat the work of the theological committee. If the cardinals are in favor of proceeding, the Cardinal Prefect of the committee refers the matter to the pope. The pope has the final word. If the pope decides that it is right to do so, he issues a decree saying that the candidate has heroically exercised Christian virtues during his or her lifetime.

This is the part of the process that involves the judgment of men. But the Church wishes to know God's opinion, and requires divine confirmation of their judgment by a direct "sign" from him: a miracle. The miracle has to be a miracle that occurred through the intercession of the candidate for beatification, and it has to be a miracle that occurred after the candidate had died. Miracles that occurred while the candidate was living have no value in these final stages of the process for beatification.

A whole process of investigation has been instituted to examine the alleged miracle. First of all, two doctors carefully examine the miracle. Each one votes individually on the validity of the miracle. If they both agree, the miracle is then referred to a committee of five renowned doctors, who can be either believers or nonbelievers. Their task is to determine whether the miracle in question can be explained by medical science. If they establish that there is no logical explanation for the healing from a human or a scientific point of view, the whole matter is referred to a commission of cardinals.

Their job is to determine whether the healing took place through divine intervention and through the intercession of the candidate. If they rule that it did, the case is sent to the pope, who makes the final judgment. It is at this point that the person can be beatified.

Has Padre Pio performed miracles after his death?

"Here in San Giovanni Rotondo we receive reports of miraculous graces," says Fr. Gerardo Di Flumeri, vice-postulator for the cause of Padre Pio's beatification. "We don't keep all of them on file. We request medical documentation and testimonies for the more significant ones. I personally keep tabs on this process. The quantity of material that has been gathered is overwhelming."

Fr. Gerardo randomly pulls some letters from a drawer full of correspondence. "From Cuneo," he says, "a mother writes: 'My son, Mauro, developed a tumor a couple of years ago, and the outlook was not very good. Mauro was admitted to several hospitals, and all the specialists said the same thing. You can imagine how desperate we were. I prayed to Padre Pio and made a vow to go on a pilgrimage with Mauro to San Giovanni Rotondo if he was healed. My prayers were heard. Mauro is fine. Every sign of the tumor has disappeared.'

"From Boscoreale, in the province of Naples, Antonio Carotenuto writes: 'On May 17 I came down with a form of paralysis that left me immobile for five months. It was the result of a hernia to a disk in my back. I was admitted several times to the hospital, and finally Dr. Giuseppe Giuda told me that I needed to have surgery right away. Before the operation, I prayed to Padre Pio. The night before the operation, I had a dream. I saw Padre Pio smiling at me. He reached out to me with his hand and said, "Don't be afraid. Nothing's wrong with you. You're fine." I woke up crying with joy. Nurses from the hospital came running to my room. I told them what had happened. In the morning, the doctor examined me before operating and discovered I was healed. The hernia to my disk had disappeared.'

"Mrs. Giuseppina Sireci Chimento writes from Turin: 'One morning in October of 1980, after having suffered from indescribable pain in my right hand because of a form of arthritis, I turned to Padre Pio and asked him to take away the pain. Nothing happened. That night I went to bed and forgot about my prayer. Contrary to how I usually slept, that night I slept fine. In the morning, I didn't have any pain. The fingers on my hand have become normal, and I can move them perfectly.'

"I can continue reading for hours," Fr. Gerardo said. "All the letters are like this, full of mysterious events and healings that cannot be explained. As I have said, we follow up on some of these cases in a special way. The letter is kept on file, and we begin to gather more complete documentation. We already have many cases like these, and they're all very interesting.

"On October 23, 1968, Giuseppe Scatigna from Palermo underwent surgery to remove a lymphoglandular tumor in his abdomen. The pathology report was not very hopeful. The patient prayed to Padre Pio. On November 8 he was admitted to the House for the Relief of Suffering for a checkup, and there was no sign of the disease. He was discharged.

"Antonio Paladino was confined to bed for thirty-three years, completely paralyzed after an accident at work. On the night of December 12, 1968, he felt someone touch him on the left shoulder. He saw Padre Pio, who said to him, 'Get up and walk.' He got out of bed and began to walk.

"An interesting case took place in Houston, Texas, in 1973. Tony John Collette, twenty years old, came down with an incurable disease. He was diagnosed in 1969 with a disease that eats away at the muscular nervous system. The young man immediately had several surgeries and was the subject of all kinds of examinations, studies, and research projects. His case was so rare that it was written up in the *Medical Journal*. He suffered pain throughout his body and had metal supports for his back and braces on his lower limbs. He was able to walk only with great difficulty on crutches.

"After a long stay in St. Joseph's Hospital in Houston, the doctors told Tony they couldn't do anything more for him and sent him home. That night he suffered from terrible pain. At about three o'clock in the morning, he saw a man come into the room, who said to him smiling, 'I want to help you. Don't be afraid.' Tony recognized the man as Padre Pio, to whom he had prayed many times. While the mysterious visitor looked on, he felt his whole body shudder. This was followed by a sensation of indescribable peace. Within seconds he felt completely relaxed and peaceful. He didn't feel any more pain. A few minutes later Padre Pio disappeared and Tony dozed off. In the morning Tony's doctors, relatives, and friends were shocked. They realized that, suddenly and inexplicably, he had been healed. Tony could walk quickly and easily without braces and crutches."

Fr. Gerardo also told me about another extraordinary case that occurred in England. It happened to a Protestant woman, Alice Jones, who had never heard about Padre Pio.

With the help of a friend, Franco De Giorgi, a journalist based in Great Britain for many years, I have reconstructed this marvelous story as told by Alice herself. She lives in St. Helens, near Lancashire, an industrial town about twelve miles from Liverpool. Alice Jones is forty-eight years old. She lives in a small house with her husband, Frank, who is three years older than she, and her Scotch terrier named Whisky. Their two daughters, Alison and Leslie, are now married and have families.

"In 1973 I was working as an elementary teacher," Alice said. "On March 27, during the morning classes, I was lifting a heavy table when a student accidently bumped me and made me fall. I tried to get up but my legs felt like cotton. Several colleagues came to my rescue and took me home, since I felt a piercing pain throughout my body. The doctor prescribed some sedatives and complete rest for a few weeks. Gradually my condition grew worse in the following months.

"In March of 1974, I was admitted to Broadgreen Hospital in Liverpool, where I had a long operation. The surgeons discovered that my spine was constricted and distorted. They also discovered that I had a tumor that was causing paralysis in my left leg. A couple of years later, I was admitted to St. Helens Hospital, where some steel supports were inserted in my spinal column. As a result, I was unable to bend my body. I was in bed for twelve months with a cast on my arms and my chest. Every four hours a small lift was used to lift my body so that the nurses could change my position. The operation was a failure.

"I went home even more depressed than before. I was able to get around only by using a brace and an orthopedic shoe on one leg that had a spring to move my foot back to its normal position, a steel brace on my chest, and two crutches.

"The pain was indescribable, and I huddled on the floor all day long, afraid to breathe lest it cause spasms in my back. A period of deep depression followed, during which I often considered suicide. I took about twenty tranquilizers a day and drank about half a bottle of whisky. I was no longer a human being. I was such a wreck that I couldn't even go to the bathroom alone.

"Then I lost my faith and was no longer able to pray. My husband suggested that we go on a pilgrimage to Lourdes, but I refused because I didn't have faith in anyone or anything, even in God. I had lost my job, we had spent all our savings, and then my mother, whom I adored, died. Since I was completely bedridden, I couldn't even go to her funeral.

"In 1980 the Church of St. James the Great, to which I belonged, celebrated the centennial of the Anglican Diocese of Liverpool by inviting two priests from other dioceses to conduct a mission. One of them was an Anglican priest that I had heard of, Rev. Eric Fisher. He had given a course on "spiritual healing" in our church, but I had refused to participate in it because, at that point,

I no longer believed. Also, I couldn't move, and I didn't want to be carried around. I had never met Rev. Fisher, yet he was the one who insisted on visiting me at my home when he heard about my situation.

"He came to visit on Tuesday, May 27, 1980. He was a young and friendly man, very different from what I had imagined. I told him that I had been paralyzed for seven years, and expressed my doubts about his gifts as a 'spiritual healer.' I also asked him not to talk to me about God. 'OK, let's talk about you,' he replied. I began to pour out all the bitterness that I had repressed within me for seven long and painful years, confiding in him my decision to commit suicide. I vented all my anger. Then he touched my back with his hands and I felt, for the first time in many years, a tingling warmth that remained with me all night long.

"Rev. Fisher left and my younger daughter, Leslie, who was twenty-one at the time, noticed a strong fragrance of roses and violets in the room. 'That priest sure uses a strong after-shave,' I commented. However, I didn't smell any perfume.

"Rev. Fisher returned the next day, Wednesday, May 28, at eleven o'clock in the morning. I was sprawled on the floor, which was the most comfortable position for me. My daughter, Leslie, was in the living room with her husband, Steven. Rev. Fisher told me that he had prayed at length for me and had a revelation. My deformities and my pains would disappear.

"He said: 'Take off the brace on your leg and throw it away.' I felt my paralyzed leg, and I felt a piercing pain that I had never experienced before. It was overwhelming, as if my leg was pierced by a hot iron. With much difficulty, I got up off the floor and sat in an armchair. Rev. Fisher insisted, 'Try to walk.'

"Suddenly, superimposed on his face, I saw the image of an old man with a beard, dressed like a monk. He had a scar on his face and his hands were closed, like they were stiff. He moved closer to me. I noticed that the old man was talking to me. It was a language that was different from mine, but strangely I understood what he was saying. He said, 'Jesus, Jesus.' Then he lifted up his hand and added in a whisper, 'Your foot is strong now and your leg is healed. Get up and walk.' I hesitated. For seven years I hadn't taken a step without any help. The old monk insisted, this time with a commanding tone to his voice: 'In the name of Jesus, walk!' I followed his orders, and without any help I walked across the room.

"The monk suddenly disappeared, and Rev. Fisher remained in his place. At the same time all my pain disappeared. I didn't know if I was dead or alive. I didn't know who had appeared to me. He was too old to be Jesus. Without knowing why, I thought it was Moses. Rev. Fisher gave me his blessing and left saying, 'Now you no longer need me.'

"After the initial amazement, I ran to my bedroom, took out an old pair of high-heel shoes that I hadn't worn for seven years, put them on, took my grandson in my arms, and began to dance around the house in a fit of joy.

"I called my husband right away, who had been an orthopedic nurse for more than thirty years at the hospital. 'Frank, Frank, I can walk. I can move. I don't have any more pain,' I shouted through tears. He thought I had taken an overdose of painkillers and that I was hallucinating. 'Hold on. Don't do anything. I'll be right home,' he reassured me."

Frank Jones confirmed his wife's story: "When I saw her for the first time twirling around in those high-heel shoes, I thought I was dreaming. All night long we were unable to sleep. At five o'clock in the morning I checked her back, and I couldn't find anything wrong. For years it had been as cold as an ice cube, now it was warm and flexible. Blood was flowing normally. There was no trace of the tumor."

While Frank was lighting up his pipe, Alice Jones continued her story. "My daughter and my son-in-law, who were present at the time, never saw the monk. But they noticed the strong fragrance that he had left in the air, which I myself couldn't smell. The next day we all went to church. Rev. Fisher gave me a holy card. On one side there was a picture of a monk with a beard. 'That's him,' I exclaimed in surprise. 'It's the old man that appeared to me. Who is it?' I asked. 'That's Padre Pio, an Italian monk, a friend of those who suffer,' Rev. Fisher said, adding that he had met him and that he had become one of his followers several years before when he had made a trip to San Giovanni Rotondo.

"Until then, I had never heard his name, nor had I seen his picture. I was even more surprised when I learned that he had died in 1968.

"Ever since the day that he appeared to me, I've never needed crutches, painkillers, or even an aspirin. I was so convinced of my healing that I even turned in the certification I had that I was a semi-invalid.

"But the surprises weren't over. On August 9, 1980, I had some X rays taken on the advice of Dr. Francis Mooney, a fervent Catholic and a famous pathologist. Strangely, they showed that my backbone was still badly deformed. From a medical point of view, I shouldn't be able to move normally, yet I am able to dance, walk, and bend enough to touch the floor with the palms of my hands, move and bend my torso without any pain or difficulty. Nobody has been able to explain the disparity between the X rays and reality.

"I'm still an Anglican," Alice Jones concluded, "but my life has changed completely. I've become more religious. I've learned to pray to Our Lady and to pray the rosary. I often think about Padre Pio. I haven't seen him since that apparition in 1980, but I always feel his presence near me."

Editor's Note

On Sunday, May 2, 1999, an estimated 200,000 people gathered in St. Peter's Square for a solemn Mass at which Pope John Paul II beatified Padre Pio of Pietrelcina, the humble Capuchin priest who said that his only desire was "to be a poor friar who prays."

"When I was a student here in Rome," the pope reminisced in his homily, "I myself had the chance to meet him personally, and I thank God for allowing me today to enter Padre Pio's name in the book of the blessed."

Those who went to San Giovanni Rotondo to attend his Mass, seek his counsel, or confess to him, the Holy Father stated, "saw in him a living image of Christ suffering and risen. The face of Padre Pio reflected the light of the Resurrection." The pope also noted that Padre Pio "shared in the Passion with a special intensity: the unique gifts which were given to him, and the interior and mystical sufferings which accompanied them, allowed him constantly to participate in the Lord's agonies, never wavering in his sense that 'Calvary is the hill of the saints.'"

The pope also alluded to the many trials that Padre Pio had to endure during his lifetime: "No less painful, and perhaps even more distressing from a human point of view, were the trials which he had to endure as a result, it might be said, of his incomparable charisms. It happens at times in the history of holiness that, by God's special permission, the one chosen is misunderstood. In that case, obedience becomes for him a crucible of purification, a path of gradual assimilation to Christ, a strengthening of true holiness.

"At the same time," the pope said, "his charity was poured out like a balm on the weaknesses and sufferings of his brothers and sisters.... With the House for the Relief of Suffering, he wished to show that God's 'ordinary miracles' take place in and through our charity. We need to be open to compassion and to the generous service of our brothers and sisters, using every resource of medical science and technology at our disposal."

After the process for Padre Pio's beatification formally began on March 20, 1983, the tribunal heard testimonies from sixty-nine people attesting to Padre Pio's virtuous life. These hearings took three years. The historical committee's research required even more time. Finally, on January 21, 1990, the diocesan investigation was officially closed. The oral testimonies and written documentation were gathered into 104 volumes and sent to the Vatican's Sacred Congregation for the Causes of Saints.

Seven years later, on October 21, 1997, a group of cardinals and bishops investigating the cause for his beatification recognized that Padre Pio had exercised the theological and other virtues "in a heroic manner." Pope John Paul II published their verdict in a degree on December 18 of that same year.

In the meantime, the Sacred Congregation for the Causes of Saints continued its investigation into a particular miraculous healing that could be attributed to the intercession of Padre Pio—a necessary component of the process for beatification. The Congregation accepted a miracle involving Consiglia De Martino, a married woman with three children who lives in Salerno, Italy.

On October 31, 1995, Mrs. De Martino began to feel a heavy pain in her chest and stomach, as though her insides were being torn away. In spite of persistent pain, she did her usual housework the next day and accompanied her daughter to school. She was on her way to Mass when she felt increasingly ill and stopped at her sister's home, only to discover a painful swelling in her neck that already formed a lump the size of a grapefruit. Frightened, the two women went immediately to the hospital where, after two CAT scans, the doctors diagnosed a diffuse lymphatic spilling of approximately two liters caused by a rupture of the lymphatic canals. Even though surgery was advised, Mrs. De Martino decided to wait.

Mrs. De Martino was a member of one of Padre Pio's prayer groups, and made monthly pilgrimages to pray at his tomb. So she immediately called a monk at San Giovanni Rotondo, Brother Modestino Fucci, who had known Padre Pio personally, to solicit his prayers. Brother Modestino went immediately to Padre Pio's tomb to pray. He was sure his request would be heard because Padre Pio had promised him as much during their time together at the monastery.

On November 2, there was a reduction in the fluid deposit in Mrs. De Martino's neck, as well as a marked reduction in the pain. By the next day, the swelling had almost completely disappeared. An abdominal X ray and examination showed no more evidence of unusual liquid in her system. Finally a CAT scan on November 6 confirmed the complete disappearance of the liquid deposits. She was dismissed with a clean bill of health soon after, and successive exams revealed no aftereffects of her illness. On April 30, 1998, a committee of medical experts announced the "extraordinary and scientifically inexplicable nature" of Mrs. De Martino's cure. On December 21, 1998, in the presence of Pope John Paul II, the decree of the miracle was promulgated, thereby opening up the way for Padre Pio's beatification.

TWENTY-SEVEN

Padre Pio's Prayer Groups

Almost all of the great priests in Church history have founded religious congregations or associations to which they entrusted the task of carrying on their teachings and their spirituality. Padre Pio is one of the few great priests who did not establish any congregation.

At one point in his life, he thought about setting up something along the lines of a Third Order to take over the House for the Relief of Suffering. In fact, he gathered together about seventy people, including some of his most devoted spiritual sons and daughters, and held some preliminary meetings to legally establish such an organization. But everything came to a halt when the various accusations, controversies, and investigations erupted. Padre Pio himself went into hiding and devoted himself to prayer. This spirit of humility was the impetus for a new and original movement known as Padre Pio's "prayer groups."

These groups were formed spontaneously. They had no rules or regulations. From the beginning this spontaneous movement enjoyed extraordinary vitality. The origins of these prayer groups can be found in the distant past. They are intimately connected with the essence of Padre Pio's personality. Once, when speaking about himself, Padre Pio said, "I'm only a monk who prays." People who have known Padre Pio affirm that they always saw him praying. As he went from place to place in the monastery, he was always praying the rosary. Even when he was still very young, he confided in his spiritual director: "I pray constantly."

He did not consider this life of prayer only for himself. He always recommended it to those around him. From the very beginning of his ministry in San Giovanni Rotondo, he would spend hours in prayer each week with the youth. This custom of praying together has been observed ever since by Padre Pio's followers. In the fifties, it was formalized in a spontaneous organization, in response to Pope Pius XII's exhortation to the faithful around the world.

The pope's words found an immediate response in Padre Pio's heart. He told some of his collaborators, "Children, let's roll up our sleeves and be the first ones to respond to the pope's call." Thus, the "prayer groups" were born.

Without any one person's intervention, and without any explicit instructions from Padre Pio, these groups have been growing at an incredible rate. Some dioceses were hostile at first to these prayer groups, but eventually they were accepted and even encouraged. There are now more than two thousand of them around the world. Recent popes have acknowledged them and praised them. They are Padre Pio's spiritual heritage that lives on.